Pregnant Men

Pregnant Men

Practice, Theory, and the Law

Ruth Colker

Indiana University Press

Bloomington and Indianapolis

© 1994 by Ruth Colker

The paper used in this publication meets the minimum requirements of American
National Standard for Information Sciences—Permanence of Paper for Printed
Library Materials, ANSI Z39.48-1984.

Manufactured in the United States of America

Library of Congress Cataloging-in-Publication Data

Colker, Ruth.
Pregnant men : practice, theory, and the law / Ruth Colker.
p.   cm.
Includes index.
ISBN 0-253-31371-6 (cloth : acid-free paper).—ISBN 0-253-20898-X (paper : acid-free paper)
1. Feminist theory.   2. Equality.   3. Equality before the law.   I. Title.
HQ1190.C655   1994
305.42'01—dc20   94-3922

1 2 3 4 5 00 99 98 97 96 95 94

Ruth Colker, professor of law at the University of Pittsburgh, is the author of
Abortion and Dialogue: Pro-Choice, Pro-Life, and American Law, which has been
named an Outstanding Academic Book of 1993 by the Association of College
and Research Libraries. She has written on feminist theory and abortion in such
journals as the *Harvard Law Review*, *Yale Law Journal*, *Columbia Law Review*, *Yale
Journal on Law and Feminism*, *Harvard Women's Law Journal*, and *Columbia Journal
on Gender and Law*. In addition to her scholarship, she has served as a legal advocate on behalf of women working with the NOW Legal Defense and Education Fund as well as the ACLU.

for my clients who have taught me my theory

and

for my family who has lived with my practice

Contents

Part Three. The Practice of Theory

Acknowledgments

MANY PEOPLE CONTRIBUTED to the making of this book. With a young child at home, this book would not have been possible without the support of my husband, Edward Eybel, who rarely complained when I asked him to baby-sit in the evenings while I pounded away at the computer (or squeezed in a nap during the middle of the afternoon).

Tulane Law School, where I worked while I wrote the first draft of this manuscript, was very supportive of this project. Dean Kramer gave me the gift that I needed most—time. The librarians, especially Kevin Hourihan, Kim Koko, Katie Nachod, and Ray Lytle, were always extremely helpful, enabling me to write this book at home while they responded to my many research requests. My colleague Adeno Addis read many chapters in their early stages and was always available so that I could discuss my latest ideas for a chapter with him. My students were frequently my laboratory for sharing new ideas; their responses to my often outrageous lectures are found on these pages. My research assistant, Rebecca Sember, provided me with invaluable assistance. And I thank my secretary, Toni Mochetta, for helping me in every way possible.

In addition, I thank my new home—the University of Pittsburgh School of Law—for supporting the final stages of this project. My colleague Jules Lobel provided me with insightful suggestions on our many runs through the park. My research assistant, Sharon Noble, helped me track down difficult sources and assisted with the final citation check. Librarians Mark Silverman and Nicki Singleton also helped me with some difficult last-minute requests. And my secretary, Nadine Hamlett, performed numerous tasks, which saved me a great deal of time. Finally, I thank Debra Sherman (Pitt Law School '96) for preparing the index with her careful eye for detail.

Faculty and students at other law schools also helped make this project possible. I was able to present earlier versions of chapters of this book at Southern Methodist University Law School, Northwestern Law School, University of North Carolina Law School, University of Pittsburgh Law School, University of Texas Law School, and the Lavender Law III Conference in Chicago, Illinois. The students at the Hastings Law School were also very supportive by inviting me to participate in a conference and symposium on the practice/theory dilemma that, in many ways, inspired this book. In addition, Professor Patricia Peppin, whom I met at the Texas symposium, sent me useful material from the

Canadian courts. The feedback that I received at each of these workshops and conferences was invaluable.

Carole Chervin, senior staff attorney at Planned Parenthood, helped me with many of the arguments that I develop in chapter 4, and Deborah Ellis, legal director of the National Organization for Women Legal Defense and Education Fund, helped me with many of the arguments that I develop in chapter 5. I thank them both for their time, energy, and enthusiasm.

Most of all, however, I would like to thank my clients—the poor women of Mississippi and Louisiana—who taught me what it would mean to have the state take away their reproductive freedom. It is their lives that have inspired this book.

Introduction

It is common to say that something is good in theory but not in practice.
I always want to say, then it is not such a good theory, is it? To be good in
theory but not in practice posits a relation between theory and practice that
places theory prior to practice, both methodologically and normatively,
as if theory is a terrain unto itself.

—Catharine A. MacKinnon[1]

I BEGAN WRITING this book in May 1992, shortly after completing my first book, *Abortion and Dialogue: Pro-Choice, Pro-Life, and American Law*, which was a theoretical account of my religious-feminist perspective with some practical applications. The book was highly aspirational, suggesting that we should practice law in a way that promoted good-faith dialogue on the divisive issue of abortion. Organizationally, it moved from theory to practice. As I was completing the book, I was engaged in litigation to overturn the Louisiana abortion statute that criminalized nearly all abortions. This experience, among others, caused me to modify my highly aspirational feminist-theological perspective to deal with the harsh realities of the broken society in which we live. As I said in the Afterword to that book, "When women are attacked by hostile state legislatures, they unfortunately must respond in self-defense even when that self-defense is not as dialogic as we may ultimately desire."[2] When I wrote those words, I knew I had a lot more to learn about combining theory and practice and therefore promised myself (and the reader) that "I shall try to answer this question as I continue to practice law."[3]

This book represents an attempt to further answer the question of how to combine theory and practice. I have chosen to tackle two issues that are central to many versions of modern feminist theory—the anti-essentialism critique and equality theory. The anti-essentialist critique suggests that feminists often refer to "women" in a way that is not inclusive of the most disadvantaged women in society. I decided to ask whether my efforts on behalf of women truly benefited all women in society. Equality theory suggests that similarly situated people should be treated alike. Because there are no "pregnant men" to whom we can compare pregnant women, I decided to ask whether equality theory could be used to redress women's subordination in the reproductive health context. Finally, I decided to explore these questions by moving from practice to theory rather than the reverse.

The questions that I raise in this book are not new to me. Ever since I decided to go to law school, I have wondered whether one can be a feminist and a lawyer, or whether the term *feminist lawyer* is an oxymoron. Until I began to write this book, however, I always assumed that my practice needed to be modified in light of my theory rather than the reverse. Inspired by Catharine MacKinnon's suggestion that a theory is not very good that does not work in practice,[4] I decided to see what I could learn theoretically from my practice. As I argue in this book, my practice of law has shown me that we do need to use equality doctrine within a litigation context to further women's rights in society, particularly in the reproductive health context, and that anti-essentialism need not stand in our way. In fact, anti-essentialism can give us the tools to focus on the needs of the most disadvantaged women in society, thereby making our use of equality doctrine as inclusive as possible. Nevertheless, we need to be pragmatic in our use of anti-essentialism and equality theory so that these tools can be as powerful as possible on a practical level.

Many of the examples that I discuss in this book involve trying to overturn modern restrictions on abortion, such as waiting period rules. My choice of examples is itself a highly practical decision, which is worthy of explanation. Many books, such as Ronald Dworkin's *Life's Dominion*,[5] have recently been written on the topic of reproductive freedom with the central purpose of defending the Supreme Court's decision in *Roe v. Wade*.[6] These books are not very practical because the future legal battles are not likely to be about the validity of *Roe*, since the Supreme Court reaffirmed its central holding in *Planned Parenthood of Southeastern Pennsylvania v. Casey*[7]—that privacy doctrine prevents a state from banning abortion altogether. In the future, we should expect the courts to focus their attention on more subtle restrictions, such as a twenty-four-hour waiting period. My practice has shown me that these kinds of restrictions have a devastating impact on the most disadvantaged women in society but are likely to be upheld under existing privacy doctrine. In addition, polls suggest that many members of the public consider such restrictions to be "reasonable."[8] Practically, then, it is crucial that the public be made more aware of the devastating impact that these restrictions have on the lives of the most disadvantaged women in society and that we develop successful legal strategies to challenge these kinds of restrictions. By focusing on modern restrictions on abortions, I therefore hope to modify my theory in light of an important area of practice and to educate the public about the importance of developing successful legal strategies in this area. The potential for working effectively in this area was recently strengthened by the appointment of Ruth Bader Ginsburg to the United States Supreme Court. As I discuss in chapter 7, her application of equality theory to reproductive rights represents some of the most insightful and practical work on this subject. I therefore hope that we will soon have a more receptive legal forum for those arguments. This book is therefore practical on many levels—in its inquiry about how theory should be modified in light of practice and in its choice of examples for discussion.

Although it is typical to begin books with theory and then move to practice, the organization of this book is exactly the opposite to emphasize its practice-based orientation. In part 1 of this book, I offer experiential accounts of how I have tried to move from practice to theory in my own work as a lawyer, teacher, and writer. In chapter 1, I share my recollections from several legal and political projects, discussing how I found it necessary to modify my theoretical perspective to conform to my experiences as an activist and as a lawyer. In chapter 2, I discuss the practice of teaching law and how I have had to reject some well-accepted feminist tenets to be an effective teacher. In chapter 3, I discuss my essay for the *Harvard Law Review* entitled "The Example of Lesbians," in which I used an invitation to write for the *Harvard Law Review* as an opportunity to educate the public from an anti-essentialist perspective about the lives of lesbians. I try to show how practical considerations should guide even our choice of theoretical topics for publication.

In part 2, this book moves to slightly more theoretical terrain as I expose the essentialism of some recent court decisions. I show how the courts' essentialism causes real harm to women in society; I argue that theory matters to women's lives. In chapter 4, I discuss the Supreme Court's recent decision in *Planned Parenthood of Southeastern Pennsylvania v. Casey*[9] and the Fifth Circuit's recent decision in *Barnes v. Moore*[10] to show how the Supreme Court's newly articulated "undue burden" standard purports to protect disadvantaged women in society, while in fact, it only protects middle-class married women from domestic violence. In chapter 5, I discuss the Supreme Court's recent decision in *Bray v. Alexandria Women's Health Clinic*,[11] which held that the Ku Klux Klan Act was not available to protect women from violence at abortion clinics. I argue that the Court's essentialism made it unable to see the need to protect the most disadvantaged women in society from public violence when they seek abortion services and are faced with the violence and harassment of groups like Operation Rescue.

In chapter 6, I move my focus from anti-essentialism to equality theory to consider the troubling theoretical problem of using equality doctrine to protect women's reproductive freedom. The source of this problem is that there are no "pregnant men" to compare to pregnant women. I argue that a practical examination of the courts' treatment of men who are similarly situated to women in the reproductive health context can help us out of this theoretical dilemma. Looking at cases involving the new reproductive technology, I argue that men in similar situations are systematically treated better than women. Thus, I argue that we can meaningfully use equality doctrine to discuss women's inequality in society due to rules relating to reproduction, because "pregnant men" are, in fact, treated much better than pregnant women.

In part 3, I revisit anti-essentialism and equality theory to ask how they need to be modified in light of my practice. I argue that some proponents of the anti-essentialist critique have overstated the usefulness of that critique by making it too difficult for us to discuss women's treatment "as women" in society under equality doctrine. I argue that we can be sensitive to anti-essentialist concerns while also talking about women's treatment as women in society. Finally, in the Appendix, I provide the reader with a copy of the brief that I filed in the Mississippi abortion case so that the reader can see how I have used both equality doctrine and an anti-essentialism perspective to benefit the most disadvantaged women in society.

Because I refer to the "anti-essentialism" critique throughout this book, I need to provide the reader with a working definition (which I will try to expand in light of my practice). Anti-essentialism is an emerging perspective within the feminist and critical theory movements. It questions the "essentialist" assumptions underlying many discussions of law and policy. Essentialists have a unitary view of women that is based entirely on consideration of the lives of white women in a way that is not inclusive of various subgroups of women. Thus, as bell hooks points out in her pathbreaking *Feminist Theory: from margin to center*, Betty Friedan's *Feminine Mystique* was essentialist in its treatment of women.[12] Friedan discussed the special problems of middle-class housewives with husbands and children who did not have a career outside the home. Her words meant little to poor women who had always worked outside the home and who often raised children without the assistance of a husband. Similarly, Susan Faludi's recent book *Backlash*[13] focuses on the problems of middle-class career women. In a sense, she updates Friedan's observations by following how society has treated these middle-class women once they entered careers outside the home. Lesbians, poor women, African-American women, women with disabilities, as well as other groups of disadvantaged women are as invisible in Faludi's presentation as in Friedan's.

Anti-essentialism provides two basic insights. First, it challenges us to see the diverse ways that a policy or practice touches on women's lives. Second, it challenges us to see when biological arguments are being used to exaggerate, distort, or ignore the differences between men and women. Biological essentialism can, in fact, be thought of as a subcategory of essentialism. Biological essentialism tends to see the differences between women and men as natural rather than socialized and is therefore often insensitive to the differing ways that socialization can act upon biology.

Although I have learned about all aspects of my theoretical perspective through the practice of law, I may have learned the most about anti-essentialism. When I speak about my anti-essentialist perspective at conferences, I am often told that such a perspective will not work in practice, because it forces us to look at people in a too highly individualistic way to make useful group-based arguments. Further, I am often told that anti-essentialism is too indeterminate to guide us in making legal arguments.

Critics of anti-essentialism are certainly correct to note that courts can use anti-essentialism as an excuse not to recognize group-based problems of inequality. For example, in *City of Cleburne v. Cleburne Living Center*,[14] the Supreme Court refused to conclude that people with mental retardation are a "quasi-suspect class," because such people are a "large and amorphous class." One must wonder why the Court considered people with mental retardation to be any more "large and amorphous" than African-Americans or women, whom the Court had earlier granted suspect- and quasi-suspect-class treatment. *City of Cleburne* is an excellent example of the fact that the courts can use anti-essentialism as an excuse to fail to accord equality rights to subjugated groups in society when it is not convinced that those subjugated groups, in fact, need suspect-class status.

The fact that anti-essentialism can be manipulated to undermine equality rights does not mean that anti-essentialism must be rejected entirely. By trying to incorporate an anti-essentialist perspective into the practice of law, I believe we can learn how to use anti-essentialism in a moderate or pragmatic way, thereby achieving its benefits without undercutting equality arguments or becoming mired in indeterminacy.

Similarly, I frequently refer to "equality theory" in this book. Equality theory is probably familiar to the reader; nevertheless, it requires some explanation. Basically, equality theory requires that like things be treated alike. Equality theory, however, is not so simple when applied to the reproductive health context. In its simplest form, equality theory would require that pregnant women be treated like pregnant men. But, of course, there are no pregnant men. Does that therefore mean that equality theory is not applicable to reproductive health issues?

In my previous writings (including *Abortion and Dialogue*), I have always been committed to using equality theory in the reproductive health context, because I, like many feminists, strongly believe that restrictions on women's reproductive capacity are central to their subordination in society. Until I began litigating in the area of reproductive rights, I had not tried to implement those theoretical ideas into practice. In this book, therefore, I have decided to tackle the "pregnant men" problem to see if we can develop practical insights into how society would treat men if they could get pregnant. I have tried to learn whether equality theory has a practical place in our lives.

I am a lawyer, a feminist, a teacher, and a theoretician. I write about ideas as I try to implement them in real court cases. I try to choose practical strategies that comport with my theoretical agenda, and I try to modify my theoretical agenda continually to fit my practice. This book is therefore an attempt for me to think out loud with the reader about how we, as feminists, can try to alleviate women's subordination in society while working on behalf of *all* women. It is not an easy task nor a completed task for me. I have tried to make this book work in both theory and in practice.

Some readers may be surprised by the tentative tone of this book. I have many more questions than I have answers. I take the postmodern definition of the self seriously in that I see myself as an evolving rather than as a static self. This book is part of this evolution. Therefore, it is filled with evolving ideas rather than answers. I hope that the reader will join me in this conversation so that we can develop effective strategies to work on behalf of all women, not simply the women who have the time and money to read this book.

Notes

1. Catharine A. MacKinnon, *From Practice to Theory, or What Is a White Woman Anyway?*, 4 Yale J.L. & Feminism 13 (1991).
2. Ruth Colker, Abortion and Dialogue: Pro-Choice, Pro-Life, and American Law 159 (1992).
3. *Id.*
4. MacKinnon, *supra* note 1, at 13.
5. Ronald Dworkin, Life's Dominion: An Argument about Abortion, Euthanasia, and Individual Freedom (1993).
6. 410 U.S. 113 (1973).
7. 112 S. Ct. 2791 (1992).
8. *See, e.g.*, USA Today at 10A (December 18, 1992) (reporting that a January 1992 Gallup poll found that 75 percent of Americans support a 24-hour waiting period rule).
9. 112 S. Ct. 2791 (1992).
10. 970 F.2d 12 (5th Cir. 1992).
11. 113 S. Ct. 753 (1993).
12. bell hooks, Feminist Theory: from margin to center 2 (1984).
13. Susan Faludi, Backlash: The Undeclared War against American Women (1992).
14. 473 U.S. 432 (1985).

PART 1

From Practice to Theory

1

The Practice of Lawyering

Pervading [the] new literature of practice is the conviction that justice occurs
meaningfully when it occurs locally, in the setting of individuals' concrete
circumstances. Only through critical self-reflection situated in active practice
contexts can lawyers, who must be both thinkers and actors, sensitize themselves
to the differences of experience and viewpoint between themselves and their
clients, and among their clients. Only then may they effectively re-create the legal
system as one resonant with the voices of the nondominant.[1]

I. Introduction

MOST FEMINIST SCHOLARSHIP is premised on the assumption that we should
move from theory to practice. This is particularly true of the field of
"feminist jurisprudence," which applies feminist principles to the practice of
law. A typical example of this approach is Catharine MacKinnon's *Feminism Unmodified*,[2] which begins with a description of her anti-subordination approach
to law and then applies that approach to rape, sexual harassment, and pornography. Although MacKinnon's practice of law has been extensive, the reader
gets the impression that her practice of law has never forced her to modify her
theoretical perspective. I, too, used this approach in my previous book *Abortion
and Dialogue* by first describing my feminist-theological perspective and then
applying it to the area of reproductive freedom. I, too, never suggested how my
practice of law caused me to modify my theoretical perspective.

Ironically, MacKinnon has recognized that a theory is only as good as it is
in practice,[3] thereby suggesting that we should be open to modifying our theory
in light of our practice. Similarly, there is now a "theoretics of practice" movement within the field of legal education in which clinical professors and pro
bono lawyers (like myself) have begun to ask what their practice of law can tell
them about their theory of law.[4] This book is a part of that emerging jurisprudence.

In considering how my theory should be modified in light of my practice,
however, I am not going to limit myself to the practice of law. The observation
that our theory should work in practice should extend to *all* aspects of our lives.

Thus, I will examine three aspects of my professional life—the practice of law, teaching, and writing—and see what my practical experiences in each of these areas can teach me about my theory. I will consider the three general aspects of my theory as described in the introduction—my aspiration for good-faith dialogue, my preference for equality theory, and my anti-essentialist perspective. Although my practice has not forced me to abandon any one of these perspectives entirely, it has forced me to be more flexible and pragmatic in understanding the application of these perspectives.

In this chapter, I examine how my experience with the practice of law in the area of reproductive freedom and gay rights has required me to modify my theoretical perspective. The major arena in which I learned the limitations of my theoretical perspective was my litigation in the area of reproductive freedom. During the 1991–92 academic year, I wrote four briefs in abortion-related cases, which I will be discussing in this chapter. Each of these briefs was written to protect a woman's right to choose whether to carry a pregnancy to term.

The first case attempted to challenge the Louisiana abortion statute that banned nearly all abortions. My brief was an amicus brief on behalf of disadvantaged women in the state of Louisiana and was filed in the court of appeals. The second case involved a challenge to the Mississippi abortion statute that imposed a twenty-four-hour waiting period and an onerous "informed consent" provision, among other features, on women seeking abortions. In this case, I also filed an amicus brief in the court of appeals. The third case attempted to prevent a Louisiana state judge from appointing a lawyer to represent the fetus and from permitting direct examination of the purported father of the fetus in a case involving an adolescent seeking judicial permission to have an abortion. In this case, I helped file the chief brief in the Louisiana Supreme Court. The final case represented an attempt to prevent Operation Rescue from blockading abortion clinics in Baton Rouge and New Orleans. I assisted in the preparation of the chief brief in Baton Rouge for a state court action and the chief brief in New Orleans for a federal court action. Aside from the Mississippi case, the plaintiffs were largely successful in each of these cases.

Another context in which I have learned more about my theory of law is in my work to protect the rights of gay, lesbian, and bisexual people. Although I have done some litigation in this area, much of my work has involved drafting legislation rather than litigation. Because enacting legislation can be an important area for furthering rights, I decided to include a brief discussion in this chapter of my efforts to help enact a gay rights ordinance for the city of New Orleans, which were ultimately successful.

Ironically, I was pregnant while I worked on the first three of the reproductive freedom cases and the final stages of passing the gay rights ordinance, and

I had a young infant at home while I worked on the final reproductive freedom case. My pregnancy and motherhood added enormous practical difficulties that, in turn, affected my theoretical perspective. My pregnancy made me so tired that I often found it difficult to continue with my practice of law. Despite my feminism, I felt guilty in putting my own physical needs above my professional practice. I confided in a colleague that I was frustrated that people had expected me to work so hard during my pregnancy. She said in response, "Did you ever try telling them that you are tired? You always walk around telling people how good you feel and then you are surprised when they don't empathize with your exhaustion!" I also felt somewhat selfish in deciding to have a child, since that choice would take time away from my political work. A friend confided in me that she felt embarrassed to tell co-workers she was pregnant with her third child, because they would consider her to be insufficiently committed to her work. (Of course, many men at her workplace have had several children with no one thinking that they were less committed to their work.) Her comments helped me to understand the subtle pressures to be a superwoman and to say "yes" to additional assignments. So long as women are a minority within the legal profession, I think it will be difficult to escape the work pressures that I experienced during my pregnancy. And I did not understand the extent of those pressures until I was pregnant myself. Being pregnant therefore affected my theoretical perspective, because it made me more committed than ever to the importance of helping other women not be coerced into becoming pregnant or continuing with their pregnancy. Thus, while I was writing briefs and reexamining my general theoretical premises, I was also learning in a very practical way why reproductive freedom is so important in women's lives.

One specific way that my pregnancy affected my theoretical perspective is worthy of mention. Until I was pregnant, I believe that I accepted the most extreme version of anti-essentialism—that biological arguments have no place in feminist theory.[5] Being pregnant, however, made me see that there are some genuine, distinctive biological experiences for women. Certainly, society often exaggerates, distorts, or ignores those experiences, as I discuss in chapter 6, but society's mistreatment of women's pregnancies does not mean that we, as feminists, should ignore the biological reality of women's reproductive capacity. Being pregnant, therefore, made me feel more flexible about my willingness to make references to women's distinctive biological capacity in my work while also being attentive to the ways that capacity can be distorted by society.

My thoughts on how feminist theory should be modified in light of my practice of law is inherently limited by my own experience. Most of my practical experience has been in the context of writing amicus briefs rather than chief briefs. Unlike a chief brief for a plaintiff or defendant, an appellate amicus brief provides the author with an opportunity to be both creative and political. A chief brief often has many mandatory elements such as the statement of facts, framing of the issues, and technical statutory arguments. A lawyer who writes the chief brief has enormous responsibilities to the client; irrespective of politics or dislike of a particular legal argument, the lawyer is obligated to make whatever argument will provide the best chance of winning. An amicus brief, particularly an appellate amicus brief, has few of those constraints. The amicus brief can be a creative opportunity to develop alternative arguments that do not fit neatly into the chief brief, although they are compatible with that brief. For example, it has become a routine practice for the American Civil Liberties Union to raise the equality issue in its complaint in an abortion case but not to develop that theory in any of its briefs in the case because of the stronger possibility of winning under privacy doctrine. By writing amicus briefs in the Louisiana and Mississippi abortion cases that raised the equality issue, I hoped to alert the court to the fact that the plaintiff does not necessarily lose if the right to choose abortion no longer gets heightened protection under privacy doctrine. Raising the issue in an amicus brief may slow down an appellate court that is willing to conclude that *Roe* has already been modified. Alternatively, it sets the stage for developing the equality issue on remand if *Roe* is overturned. Because an amicus brief is limited to twenty pages, it is not possible to develop the equality argument fully. At most, then, the amicus brief raises the issue so that it can be more fully developed at a later date if *Roe* is overturned. In writing amicus briefs on the abortion issue, I have benefited from reading equality briefs written by other practitioners; similarly, I hope that others will benefit from my briefs. I have therefore included my brief in the Mississippi case in the Appendix.

II. The Louisiana Abortion Case: *Sojourner T. v. Buddy Roemer*[6]

A. The Louisiana Statute

The focus of my practice has recently been on the abortion issue. That choice was compelled by the practical fact that I lived in Louisiana for eight years. Louisiana has consistently led the anti-abortion movement by enacting anti-abortion laws that criminalize nearly all abortions with virtually no exceptions and provide lengthy prison terms for an individual who violates the statute. Because this statute resulted in a direct attack on the ability of women to live a productive and healthy life, I felt that I had no choice but to get involved in the litigation. Given my preference for "dialogic" discussions, this was a difficult choice, because I knew that the potential for genuine dialogue was minimal in this context.

The Louisiana legislature's nearly absolute ban on abortion was a convincing example of a complete disregard for women's lives and well being in the purported name of protecting life. The statute contained several key elements that, in my view, made it the harshest in the country. First, the preamble expressly stated that the state's interest was to protect "the life of the unborn from the time of conception until birth . . . to the greatest extent possible." Second, the statute prohibited the termination of pregnancy with the following exceptions: (a) the woman who has the abortion is not subject to punishment; (b) the abortion is performed "to preserve the life or health of the unborn child or to remove a dead unborn child" from the pregnant woman; (c) the abortion is performed "for the express purpose of saving the life of the mother"; or (d) the abortion is performed upon a victim of rape or incest, where that victim has complied with numerous reporting requirements within one week of the alleged rape or incest. The statute contained no meaningful abortion exceptions—a woman had to be on the verge of death in order to procure an abortion. The sloppy language of the statute also suggested that many forms of birth control would be prohibited by the statute, since it purported to prohibit all devices that would terminate a pregnancy after conception (such as a low-dose birth control pill or an intrauterine device). The statute defined conception as the "contact of spermatozoan with the ovum" but did not define pregnancy,[7] thereby not making it clear whether devices that terminate pregnancy after conception but before implantation are lawful. No other state has passed a statute without a health exception and without explicit recognition that birth control would remain lawful.

When Louisiana passed its abortion statute during the summer of 1991, I immediately called the local ACLU affiliate, which had challenged the law, and offered my assistance at the trial court level. My services were not needed then; a federal judge quickly granted the plaintiff's request for an injunction,[8] and the case was headed to the Fifth Circuit. After the trial court decision was rendered, I called the ACLU and renewed my offer to assist; this time I made the specific suggestion that I would write an amicus brief for the Fifth Circuit focusing on the ways that this statute would impact disadvantaged women in the state. Moreover, I suggested that I would write the brief from an equality rather than a privacy perspective.

My suggestion that I write an equality brief focusing on the most disadvantaged women in the state arose from my theoretical commitment to an equality and anti-essentialist perspective. As I wrote in *Abortion and Dialogue*, abortion statutes impact disproportionately on the most disadvantaged women in our society, particularly adolescent females, poor women, minority women, and women with disabilities. It is my anti-essentialist lens that has enabled me to see the diversity of the impact. From an equality perspective, I believe that disadvantaged women cannot afford to be let alone in their reproductive lives—they need the state to make abortions available under Medicaid; they need public hospitals to provide abortion services along with other reproductive services; and they need the state not to impose financial barriers to abortions through waiting periods, hospitalization requirements, and physician-monitored informed consent. In my view, our abortion doctrine under *Roe* is too essentialist in that it is often premised on a white, adult, able-bodied middle-class woman who can afford to purchase reproductive services, including abortion. By focusing on equality arguments, I try to place the lives of disadvantaged women on the pages of briefs that are filed in court. That was my intention in *Sojourner T.*[9]

At the outset, I knew that I had many challenges to face in combining theory with practice in this situation. First, I knew that I would need to work with cocounsel who may have different theoretical or practical agendas. Specifically, I knew that the ACLU favored a privacy approach and might not be happy with my equality approach. As the author of a brief in support of the plaintiff-appellees, I felt that I had an obligation not to undercut their interests. However, I also believed that I was entitled to try to present alternative theories to the court. In fact, I have often questioned whether the ACLU's primary focus on the privacy approach has been to their clients' advantage, because it has meant a lack of development of alternative approaches such as equality. Thus, I knew that I wanted to be supportive of the ACLU while retaining my own political and theoretical integrity.

Second, I knew that I needed to be sensitive to the ways in which the facts of my case or my clients' needs may not fit my political or legal agenda. I understood that an amicus brief is on behalf of organizations, not myself as an individual. Although I fully believed that groups of disadvantaged women within my community would benefit from the articulation of an equality approach, I also realized that it was unlikely that they would understand the difference between an equality and a privacy approach. As lay people, they might understand that they were being represented in the appellate process; however, they might not share or care about my own theoretical choices. My dialogic side wanted to discuss these choices with potential clients; my practical side wondered if that were really possible. I did not choose to put much effort into these kinds of discussions. I did make sure that every group that signed the brief saw, at least, the summary of argument. However, I did not discuss with most of the groups the significance of the choice of doctrine.

I rationalized this decision by noting that representation in an amicus brief is not the same kind of representation as in a chief brief. The chief brief in this case already contained a privacy argument and purported to represent all of the women in the state. My brief simply supplemented the chief brief. In addition, my clients would not have been specially represented but for my volunteering to write an amicus brief. They had not identified themselves as needing legal representation. In a sense, they were doing me a favor by lending their name in support of my efforts rather than the reverse. Had they approached me with a specific agenda in mind and asked me to write a brief on their behalf, then I believe that my obligations might have been somewhat different. Most important, I truly believed that the arguments that I was making—which focused on the impact of the statute on the most disadvantaged women of the state—were beneficial to my clients. Had there been time to discuss my theoretical framework, I believe that we would have been in agreement on the central issues raised by the brief. Had I not had this belief, I would have not have pursued the task of writing the amicus brief. Nevertheless, I fell far short of my dialogical aspirations.

Third, I realized that I would be subject to the limitations of the judicial process through various technical conditions such as form and page requirements. I was only permitted to submit a twenty-page brief, which greatly limited my ability to include narrative material from my clients.

B. Finding Clients

I needed clients to represent. Consistent with my theoretical agenda, I wanted to find groups of disadvantaged women. At the outset, I extended an invitation to my colleague Wendy Brown to assist me on the brief. I asked her to assist me in finding clients, because Wendy had experience in that kind of work through her earlier work on an amicus brief in the *Webster* case.[10] In addition, Wendy is very active in the African-American community in New Orleans, so I thought she would be able to network effectively in our home community.

In late August, I began to call people at the ACLU and at Planned Parenthood to receive suggestions for contacts. Louisiana Planned Parenthood also initially indicated that they would be very interested in participating in the brief. They seemed like ideal clients, because they had an office in the St. Thomas housing project. After speaking with my contacts, I tentatively made up a list of community groups to contact. Nevertheless, I soon ran into problems getting groups to join the brief that fit my initial theoretical target.

The first group that posed problems was the Committee on Women of the Louisiana Psychiatric Association. This was the only group with which I attempted to work who came to me rather than my going to them. The chair of the committee heard about my work and asked if the committee could join the brief. I was a little reluctant, because the committee was comprised of doctors who obviously did not fit the profile of disadvantaged women that I had in mind.

On the other hand, these doctors served women who did fit my profile; more-over, the chair informed me that the committee would like to work with me to provide substantive medical guidance in the brief. At that point, I had no other organization interested in joining the brief and decided that the committee would be a good place to start. Thus, I modified my target group slightly before I even began my community outreach.

The committee soon posed additional difficulties for me. The committee was told by the Psychiatric Association that they could not join a brief as a commit-tee. Instead, the entire Psychiatric Association would have to join the brief. I had planned to describe all the participating groups as "women's groups." Obvi-ously, I could not do this if the entire association signed on. Nevertheless, I de-cided to make a modification to my description of organizations in order to ob-tain their participation. I thought that their participation would add credibility to my brief. In addition, I felt that they understood the purpose behind my brief so that their participation would be quite genuine. The Psychiatric Association was also the only group that came to me rather than my going to them. Since my first priority as a lawyer is to represent groups that desire my help rather than to seek clients, I felt a responsibility to try and represent them. Their par-ticipation, however, forced me to make a second compromise—not just to rep-resent women's groups. Nonetheless, their participation facilitated my discus-sion of women with disabilities, including women with mental illness.

One result of my including the association in my brief is that I helped foster dialogue in that organization about the Louisiana anti-abortion statute. In order to join the brief, the association had to discuss it at one of their meetings and obtain a favorable vote. Because the association was not ordinarily a political organization that took a position on controversial issues, this brief facilitated a discussion among the membership. I was happy to have helped facilitate that dialogue.

The next group that posed problems was Women for Women with AIDS. I approached their director directly about joining the brief, because I had previously worked with her on AIDS and gay rights issues. Although the director was en-thusiastic about her organization joining the brief, she informed me that she would need a consensus from all of her clients to participate. Not surprisingly, that proved to be impossible within the time constraints, leaving me with no AIDS-oriented group.

Nevertheless, approaching this organization did serve a dialogic function. After the brief was filed, their director informed me that they had decided to participate, but unfortunately, it was too late to include them. My request for them to participate served the useful purpose of getting this organization to discuss their position on the Louisiana abortion statute and achieve some consensus. I therefore learned that although litigation in the courtroom may not further dialogue, community activity surrounding litigation may. I began to realize that my prior thinking of the relationship between litigation and dialogue may have been too narrow in my focus on traditional litigation activity.

The lack of timely consensus on behalf of Women for Women with AIDS however left me in the difficult position of not having an AIDS organization participating in the brief. Because I had specific facts that I wanted to put in the brief about the Louisiana legislature's deliberate lack of concern for the health and well-being of pregnant women with AIDS, I needed the participation of an AIDS organization. I therefore decided to contact the NO/AIDS Task Force to seek their participation. Their board agreed to participate, but their lawyer drafted their statement of interest in such a way that I could not accept it. He insisted that they end their statement of interest with a paragraph making it clear that they were joining the brief *only* to the extent that it discussed the problems of women with AIDS. The paragraph read:

> As an agency that deals on a daily basis with the needs of HIV-infected individuals, many of whom are women, the NO/AIDS Task Force joins in this amicus curiae brief as it relates to the health of those women who are either HIV positive or have been diagnosed with AIDS which is addressed in Section I(B)(2) regarding women with handicaps. To that extent, the NO/AIDS Task Force supports this amicus curiae brief.[11]

I read that statement to Wendy Brown and another colleague; both agreed that it was unacceptable, because it undercut my other clients. The statement suggested that they joined the brief only insofar as it addressed the problems facing women with AIDS and not to the extent that it discussed other groups of disadvantaged women. This kind of problem can, of course, exist when you are attempting to represent multiple clients with somewhat divergent interests. My instinct and that of my colleagues was that anyone who joined the brief had to be able to join it in its entirety. This problem is not unique to brief writing. Anyone who has struggled to work in coalition politics has faced the problem of finding ways to bring groups together and not allow the larger community to pit one against the other. Writing a brief representing multiple parties can therefore be an aspect of coalition politics. I did not want my efforts to provide fuel for pitting one of my clients against the other. Either a group joined the entire brief or it was not a part of the coalition.

Interestingly, I had not really focused on the special needs of my clients until this point in the process. I was trying to find clients who could endorse my political agenda rather than considering how the actions of one group could undercut those of another group. The response to my efforts by the NO/AIDS

Task Force did remind me of my responsibility to look out for the needs of my clients. It awakened me to some of my ethical obligations.

Having clarified my own position through discussions with others, I then discussed the statement of interest with the then executive director of the task force and explained to him that I could not accept their participation unless that last paragraph was omitted. After brief negotiations, in which he offered to delete the last sentence but not the last paragraph, we agreed that it would be best for the task force not to participate.

I followed up my discussion with the director by writing a letter that was very critical of their actions. I criticized them for refusing to work with their lesbian and straight sisters who have been so central to the AIDS movement and for allowing fundraising considerations to make their organization narrow in focus.

The text of the letter follows:

Dear [Executive Director]:

I wanted to take a few minutes to communicate my disappointment to you and your Board over the resolution of your organization's participation in the *amicus* brief in *Sojourner T. v. Buddy Roemer* (the Louisiana abortion case).

When I initially sought your organization's participation, I understood that your Board might vote not to participate. Although I would have been disappointed, I would have respected that decision given the difficult nature of the abortion issue. The way the issue ended up being ultimately resolved, however, disappointed me much more. I would therefore like to share that disappointment.

I deliberately wrote the brief as a "moderate" abortion brief. It takes no position on the issue of what would be a constitutional abortion statute, except to argue that the absence of a "health" exception definitely makes the statute unconstitutional. I therefore focused on the health implications to various subgroups of women—adolescent females, women with physical and mental handicaps, and poor and minority women. Within the category of women with physical and mental handicaps, I focused, in particular, on women with HIV infection. The health implications that I discussed for each subgroup were quite dramatic—shortened life expectancy and serious infringement on health. Those effects were no more or less dramatic for women with HIV infection than for the other subgroups of women described in the brief. A shortened life is a shortened life.

When I circulated the brief to other community groups, they usually responded by giving me more examples of these health implications for their community, e.g., kidney and renal failure or complicating effects of drugs used to treat psychiatric illness. These comments were very helpful to me in revising the brief since, as a lawyer, it is hard for me to keep abreast of all medical issues relating to pregnancy.

The response by the NO/AIDS Task Force, however, is markedly different. Rather than suggesting how I could have better or more accurately discussed the implications of the abortion statute on women with HIV infection, the Task Force chose to limit its endorsement of the brief to the particular paragraphs referencing women with HIV infection. As I told you over the telephone, that limitation was not acceptable, because of the negative implications that it cast on my other clients—suggesting that their health problems were not obviously as dramatic and therefore deserving of the court's and legislature's attention.

The reason that I find the Task Force's response so unsettling is that it was actually being asked to do very little—simply agree that the health of women with HIV infection is implicated by compulsory pregnancy in a way that is comparable to that of other women. Nevertheless, it was not willing to stand beside its sisters in that way.

I have heard two comments recently which underscore the unacceptability of the Task Force's actions. First, on a T.V. show concerning gay and lesbian rights, a member of the audience had commented that "homosexuals" were immoral and that God had therefore responded to their immorality with the AIDS epidemic. A lesbian on the show responded that then God must much favor lesbians since (ignoring the CDC's [Center for Disease Control] absurd definition of lesbianism), lesbians had a very low incidence of AIDS. The member of the audience responded by saying that he had not intended to direct his comment against lesbians; it would be fine if we shipped only gay men off to concentration camps. The lesbian then responded that, no, if gay men were sent away, she would insist upon going with them. In the present context, this response does not seem to have been reciprocated. So long as women with HIV infection are not harmed by the state's abortion statute, the Task Force is seemingly willing to permit other women's health to be harmed by the statute.

Second, Sandy Lowe, staff attorney for the Lambda Legal Defense Fund, recently spoke at Tulane Law School. In a passing reference, she asked how the gay male community would have responded if it were lesbians, not gay men, who were first inflicted with the AIDS virus. The response of your organization to participating in this brief makes me shudder to consider what those consequences might have been.

As you know, even before women began to focus on the HIV implications on women, women have been very active in the AIDS movement. If it were not for women's early participation in the AIDS movement, we probably today would not have so much attention on the definition of AIDS and how that negatively impacts women. Nor would we have so much attention focused on the special problems of pregnant women with AIDS. Women were willing to make the connection from their civil rights concerns to that of AIDS in becoming involved in the movement at an early stage. It is extremely disappointing to see the AIDS movement (or a particular AIDS service organization) not willing, at all, to make a reciprocal gesture.

I understand that your organization is probably repeatedly requested to align itself with other organizations and that, on some occasions, those alignments may cause political and funding difficulties. However, I wonder what it means when an organization becomes so well-funded and acceptable politically that it turns its back on its sisters who helped it gain that stature in the community. I will be watching the NO/AIDS Task Force quite closely in the future to see whether I can support it financially and politically. Success, in the case of the NO/AIDS Task Force, seems to have had serious negative implications.

When the *Sojourner T.* case reaches the United States Supreme Court, I plan to repeat my efforts at getting community groups to collaborate on a similar brief. I will be back in touch with you at that time and hope that, by then, the Task Force has rediscussed this issue and modified its policy accordingly.

Sincerely yours,

Ruth Colker
Professor of Law

cc: Wendy Brown
Sandy Lowe

I have included the full text of my letter to the former executive director of the NO/AIDS Task Force so that the reader can see how I chose to deal with this problem within my own community. Because I see the project of writing an appellate amicus brief as a political task, I think it is important for groups to be asked to consider within their organization why they might or might not participate in the brief. The writing of the brief became an occasion for the NO/AIDS Task Force to discuss their position on abortion. In addition, it became an occasion for me to respond to their position as someone who is very active on both the AIDS and abortion issues. Although I was not pleased with their response, I believe that I did help create some important dialogue on this issue within their organization. The discussion within the NO/AIDS Task Force did not result in a strong pro-choice position; however, the discussion within Women for Women with AIDS did ultimately result in a strong pro-choice position. Thus, I feel pleased that I did create dialogue within the AIDS community irrespective of whether these groups participated in the brief itself.

Another community group with which I had difficulty was the National Council for Negro Women of Greater New Orleans. I had decided to contact them, because the national organization held a pro-choice position and had joined Wendy's brief in the *Webster* case. I had been warned that, to date, they had been reluctant to join local pro-choice efforts. But I also learned that their reluctance may have been because of time constraints rather than philosophical problems. When I sent the director of the organization a description of the brief, she informed me her board would be meeting soon and she would get back to me within a week or so. She suggested that I call her in ten days if I had not heard from her. I never did hear from her again; I left two telephone messages that were not returned. I asked Wendy to look into the situation; eventually she informed me that the council voted not to participate. We were never offered any explanation for their refusal. I do not know whether my request to this organization furthered dialogue on the abortion issue.

Planned Parenthood of Louisiana then developed problems joining the brief. Their attorney had decided to file a brief on the organization's behalf in the Fifth Circuit to argue an issue that related to their pending state court case—the abstention issue.[12] Although they were very much behind my efforts philosophically, they felt that they could not sign two briefs in the Fifth Circuit. A few months later, however, Planned Parenthood asked me to write an amicus brief in the Fifth Circuit representing disadvantaged women with regard to the Mississippi abortion statute. Thus, it is clear that Planned Parenthood's inability to participate in my Louisiana brief was for logistical rather than substantive reasons.

The final group that we tried to contact was an African-American sorority—Delta Sigma Theta. Wendy had contacts with that group and thought she could get them to participate. Unfortunately, her contact had graduated, and she was not able to get their permission.

As of about two weeks before the brief was due, only two community groups had agreed to participate—the Women of Color Reproductive Health Forum and the Louisiana Psychiatric Association. At that point, I frantically called the national ACLU and Wendy to say that we needed to obtain more clients. Eventually, I contacted Leslie Gerwin, a local attorney and former Tulane Law School professor, who heads pro-choice lobbying efforts in Baton Rouge. Leslie shared with Wendy and me a list of local pro-choice groups, along with telephone contacts. Leslie sent a mailing on our behalf, and Wendy and I followed it up with telephone calls. As it turned out, I do not believe that many of the groups actually received the mailing because of errors in the mailing addresses for many of the groups. Most groups had contact people rather than offices, and if the contact person became inactive, then the mail seemed to get lost. Thus, when Wendy and I made our telephone calls, we were usually talking with someone who knew little or nothing about our efforts.

Through Leslie's and Wendy's assistance, the groups that eventually joined the brief—Black Women for Choice; the Community Relations Committee, Jewish Federation of Greater New Orleans; Louisiana Choice, New Orleans Chapter; the Louisiana Psychiatric Association; Louisiana National Organization for Women; New Jersey Women Lawyers Association; and the Women of Color Reproductive Health Forum—represented a wide variety of organizations. Their reason for inclusion was more the result of happenstance than deliberate action on our part. The Jewish organization was part of the coalition because Leslie Gerwin had contacts with them, although they probably would have preferred a brief that focused on the religion issue. The New Jersey Women Lawyers Association was part of the brief because they were upset that their bar association had agreed to hold a meeting in New Orleans. Only about half of the groups were local groups that represented disadvantaged women and therefore fit my original profile for the brief.

In retrospect, I see that my difficulty in finding groups to fit my original profile was not an unusual problem, at least in the south. For example, I was also asked by Planned Parenthood to author a brief in the Fifth Circuit on the Mississippi abortion case *Barnes v. Moore*, which I discuss in the next section. Planned Parenthood wanted me to focus on the impact of the Mississippi statute on disadvantaged women. They assured me that they already had groups that wanted to be represented and simply needed me to write the brief. I was therefore able to focus my entire efforts on the Mississippi brief on the assumption that the selection of the groups to represent had already taken place. In fact, Planned Parenthood ended up facing many of the same problems that I faced in Louisiana in finding clients. They eventually developed a list of organizations for me to represent but were disappointed in how few of them were local organizations that directly represented disadvantaged women.

I had understood, to some extent, that it might be difficult to get women's organizations to support my brief. Thus, I chose to write a moderate or narrow brief that focused exclusively on the extreme harshness of the Louisiana statute without making assertions about other states' statutes. I made this choice clear to my potential clients, and in a couple of cases, it may have helped win their support. No matter how moderate my brief, however, I found that I could not persuade all the groups that I contacted to participate, since it was, at root, a pro-choice brief on the abortion issue.

In addition, I learned the not surprising fact that I could have gotten more organizations to join the brief if I had been able to give them more time to come to a decision. Had I been willing to wait until the last minute to file, I would have been able to get at least three more national African-American organizations to join the brief. Concerned about my increasing exhaustion, I stuck to my original deadline. I felt guilty about placing fears about my health over getting more organizations to join our efforts, particularly African-American organizations, but I asked Wendy to communicate to these groups that we would welcome their participation at the Supreme Court level.

In sum, the task of finding clients forced me to be quite pragmatic. I had to be willing to broaden my definition of whom I was representing and, in some cases, had to engage in quite active dialogue to persuade groups to participate. This process taught me that there are benefits to engaging in such dialogue even if a group does not ultimately participate in the brief, because I may help a group take the first step toward developing a pro-choice perspective.

C. Working with Students

Obtaining student assistance at Tulane Law School, where I was teaching at the time, seemed appropriate for two reasons. First, it would make the task of writing the brief easier, especially concerning research that might need to take place at the medical school library. Second, it would help to politicize the law school community with respect to the abortion issue. Although most students seemed to be pro-choice, there had not been a ground swell of activism on the abortion issue among the students. I hoped that my leadership on the issue would inspire them to become more politically involved.

Tulane Law School has a community service requirement for its students. They must complete twenty hours of community service in order to graduate. It also has a women's law association, which had never been particularly active politically. In the last couple of years, however, the women's law association had begun to sponsor public lectures on reproductive health issues. At the time, I was teaching an eighty-person family-law class, which directly focused on feminist as well as reproductive issues. I knew that I would need help with the brief, especially because of the constraints of my own pregnancy, and wanted to get that help in a way that would most likely mobilize my home community. Turning to the community service program for assistance, as well as publicizing my efforts to the women's law association and my family-law class, seemed to be the best direction to take.

Nevertheless, I was concerned about how useful the student assistance would really be. One logistical difficulty was organizing a large number of students and keeping them busy. In addition, I would not be selecting the students;

they would be selecting the project. I therefore had no way to insure the quality of their efforts—I realized that some students might agree to do an assignment but might not do it well. Delegation could therefore weaken the quality of the research, and supervisory help promised from the Dean never materialized. Thirty students quickly signed up to work on the brief, and I set ground rules immediately to limit and control student participation. First, I decided to take steps to limit the number of students who would be involved with the project. I required all students who wanted to participate to attend a meeting on September 13, and I refused to take any volunteers after that date. I also required the student work to be turned in on September 23 so that I would have a chance to review it before writing the final project (and could accept late submissions from the students). Second, I assigned two students to each assignment so that I could be reasonably assured of adequate work quality. Because I knew most of the students who volunteered, I was also able to assign some of the more difficult assignments to the best students. Finally, I told the students to provide me with a photocopy of any source upon which they relied so that I could double-check their research.

Not surprisingly, the student work varied enormously in its quality. I had students, for example, provide me with cases that they had not checked to see if they had been overturned. If I had not checked their research, I could have greatly embarrassed myself. Other students, however, went to the Medical School Library and did extensive medical research that I found very useful. My most pleasant surprise from the students was their timeliness. Accustomed as I am to students handing in assignments late, I was pleased to see them take this deadline seriously.

Politically, student involvement seemed to be successful. I kept running out of copies of the brief, and students often came by my office to tell me how much they enjoyed working on it. When I organized a moot court on the case for the ACLU attorney Janet Benshoof, most of the student volunteers attended the moot court exercise. Many of them also attended the oral argument in the Fifth Circuit. Thus, I did seem to arouse in them a keen interest in the case. When I later initiated a similar project on a Mississippi abortion case, many of them volunteered to assist again, even if they had already completed their mandatory community service requirement. Therefore, I was able to benefit personally from their logistical assistance, while they became more involved in their political community.

Nevertheless, my interactions with the students may not conform to what some feminists consider to be authentically "feminist." I interacted with the students in a hierarchical and relatively formal way, which, as I discuss in the next chapter, is often not considered to be feminist. For practical reasons, I felt a very strong need to maintain control, which influenced how I related to the students. As I have often found in the educational environment, the practical needs of the situation often make it impossible to utilize a traditionally feminist style of interaction.

D. Developing the Argument

The most obvious area in the brief in which to incorporate my theoretical perspective was in the substantive argument. This aspect of the brief-writing process taught me the most about the limits of my theoretical perspective. I had written a great deal about the abortion issue but, until this brief, had never practiced in this area of the law.

In my academic writings, I have insisted that we should be pursuing an equality perspective rather than a privacy perspective on abortion. My reasons for preferring equality over privacy are both theoretical and practical.[13] A group-based, equality approach is more consistent with how feminists consider the abortion issue; an equality approach, if successful, provides fuller protection for all women in society (by reversing the abortion-funding decisions); an equality approach can best enable us to indicate our valuation of fetal life while also valuing women's right to choose to terminate a pregnancy; and an equality approach is more communitarian than individualistic. I have never liked the privacy approach, because it is too individualistic in nature; moreover, I prefer an equality approach, because it best describes how pregnancy-related restrictions relate to women's overall equality in society. I believe that women should have the right to choose whether to terminate a pregnancy not because of women's right to control their bodies but because of women's right to insist that they be given the opportunity to achieve full and equal citizenship in society. Because we unfortunately live in a society that does virtually nothing to facilitate pregnancy, childbirth, and child care and, instead, imposes all of these burdens on women, I believe it is essential for women to be able to choose pregnancy rather than to be coerced into maintaining an unwanted pregnancy. The burdens placed on women's reproductive capacity by society are, in my view, fundamental to women's inequality in society. Thus, I have tried to develop an equality perspective in my academic writing to explain why abortion-related restrictions violate the equal protection clause of the Fourteenth Amendment.

Practically, it is very difficult to implement this theoretical perspective because of two major doctrinal stumbling blocks—the Supreme Court's decisions in *Geduldig v. Aiello*[14] and *Personnel Administrator v. Feeney*.[15] These stumbling blocks require some elaboration. Under the Constitution, explicit race- or gender-based classifications receive heightened scrutiny with race-based classifications receiving somewhat higher scrutiny than gender-based classifications. The state has the difficult burden of justifying the validity of these classifications. Classifications that are reviewed under heightened scrutiny are virtually always invalidated. In the gender area, a major question, however, is what is a gender-based classification? Are pregnancy-based classifications gender-based when all pregnant people are treated the same? In other words, can we consider a pregnancy-based classification to be gender-based when we do not know how pregnant men might be treated? In *Geduldig*, the Supreme Court answered that question in the negative by ruling that pregnancy-related restrictions are not per se gender-based restrictions. Plaintiffs who could demonstrate discrimination on the basis of a pregnancy-based classification could not automatically get the Court to exercise heightened scrutiny. Many feminists have challenged the *Geduldig* decision, arguing that it is absurd not to view pregnancy as a gender-based classification.[16]

The fact that a plaintiff cannot get the Court to agree that a pregnancy-based classification is automatically a gender-based classification does not mean that the plaintiff has no hope of prevailing legally. When a classification is not explicitly gender-based but causes a disproportionate *impact* on the basis of gender, it is still possible to prevail under the Constitution. Under that scenario, a plaintiff must demonstrate that the state *intended* to create the disproportionate impact. The question that arises under that scenario is, What satisfies evidence of intent? The Court answered that question in *Feeney* when it ruled that a petitioner can prove gender-based intent only if she can also demonstrate that the legislature passed the legislation *because of* rather than *despite* its impact on women. Virtually no cases have been successful under this stringent requirement. Both the *Geduldig* and *Feeney* rules therefore make it extremely difficult for a plaintiff to prevail in an equality-based reproductive freedom case. A major practical question I therefore had to consider was whether I wanted to challenge the *Geduldig* or *Feeney* rules. In order to prevail in an equality-based challenge, I needed to find a way to get around or overturn one of those rules.

Although I agree that *Geduldig* was wrongly decided and should not preclude a petitioner in an abortion case from receiving heightened scrutiny, I chose not to challenge *Geduldig* in the Louisiana case; instead, I chose to try to get around the *Feeney* test. Nevertheless, I did challenge the applicability of *Geduldig* to an abortion-related restriction in a brief that I filed in the Fifth Circuit on the Mississippi abortion statute.

Theoretical and practical reasons led to the decision of trying to meet the impact-intent standard that was set forth by the Court in *Feeney* in the Louisiana case. Theoretically, I believe that feminists have focused too exclusively on *Geduldig* without pursuing the possibilities under a *Feeney* approach. By using the *Feeney* standard, I hoped to turn its doctrinal problems into an advantage. The *Feeney* standard is problematic, because it requires the plaintiff to prove that the legislature intentionally created the disparate impact against women. Typically, that is a very difficult standard of proof. In the Louisiana case, however, strong evidence existed that the legislature knowingly harmed women's well-being through enactment of the anti-abortion statute. I wanted to put that evidence of intent into the record; the *Feeney* burden of proof would require me to do so. Thus, rather than try to avoid the *Feeney* standard by arguing that we had a case of per se gender-based discrimination, I decided to use the *Feeney* burden of proof directly. Although meeting the *Feeney* standard is seen as extremely difficult, I welcomed the opportunity to meet that standard of proof given the evidence that I had available.

Another way to consider the choice between a *Geduldig* approach and a *Feeney* approach is to think of the choice as one between a theoretical and a pragmatic approach. In order to proceed under a per se standard of discrimination, I would have had to devote a section of the brief to distinguishing *Geduldig* or arguing that *Geduldig* was wrongly decided. That discussion would have been theoretical and not tied to the special facts of Louisiana. By proceeding under the *Feeney* standard, I was forced to put facts about intent into the record. Because I wanted to put those facts into the brief, it was easy to choose the pragmatic approach over the theoretical approach. Nevertheless, I would not make that judgment in all abortion cases. Because such evidence of intent was not clearly present in the Mississippi case, I chose a somewhat more theoretical approach in that case to distinguish *Geduldig*.

Although I wanted to write an "equality brief," I was not sure how far that argument would reach in striking down abortion statutes elsewhere. Being a resident of Louisiana and personally committed to overturning our abortion statute, I chose not to focus on the broader implications of my argument on other pending cases. I felt comfortable with the idea that I was representing the disadvantaged women of Louisiana; other attorneys could represent women in other states. My focus, as I thought was ethically appropriate, was Louisiana.

I understand that other lawyers have used the amicus process to shape the law generally rather than to focus on the case directly before the court. That was an option I rejected, because I felt that it disserved the women of Louisiana. Louisiana has consistently had the most onerous anti-abortion law in the country. In my view, Louisiana's statute would literally cause the death of women to an extent not present in other states. I wrote this brief before the Supreme Court decided *Planned Parenthood of Southeastern Pennsylvania v. Casey*.[17] I was afraid that the Supreme Court would dramatically modify *Roe v. Wade* so that nearly all anti-abortion statutes would be upheld. But I thought that even a conservative court could see that the Louisiana statute was in a league of its own—that under any level of scrutiny it failed to pass muster, because it did not even provide an exception to protect the pregnant woman's health. Broad theoretical pro-choice arguments often, in my view, lose sight of the range of injustices that state legislatures have imposed on women's lives. I wanted to force Louisiana to be held accountable for its record of injustice against women. A broad theoretical argument would be less likely to achieve that result than a focused, pragmatic argument. Thus, I wanted to show how Louisiana stood out alone in the western world in its disrespect for women (and children). Some of my clients implicitly stated the same point of view when they asked me to write a "moderate" brief or, at least, that was how I chose to interpret their request. To be honest, I had decided to pursue this more moderate approach before some of my clients indicated that was what they wanted. I made no attempt to convince my clients to seek a broader and more theoretical approach.

As I had promised, I sent a draft of the brief to the national ACLU. I was not representing the ACLU, but I was writing a brief in support of their position in the case. They had assisted me by sending me equality briefs that had been filed elsewhere. Their briefs, however, proved not to be particularly useful in the Louisiana case, because they each took the route of arguing that anti-abortion statutes constitute per se gender-based discrimination, which was not the approach that I chose to take. Their briefs, however, did prove useful when I tried to distinguish *Geduldig* in the Mississippi case. Reading their briefs put me on notice that they would probably not be comfortable with my presentation of the equality position.

As I expected, the ACLU representative said that she was concerned about several aspects of my brief. First, she was concerned that it might undercut their arguments in similar cases involving Utah, Guam, and Pennsylvania statutes.[18] She did not think that there was a big difference between the Louisiana statute with a life exception and the Utah and Guam statutes with a health exception. Second, she did not like my conceding that the appropriate standard of review was intermediate rather than strict scrutiny. Intermediate scrutiny is the standard traditionally used in the gender-based equality cases; strict scrutiny is the standard traditionally used in the reproductive-privacy cases. She suggested that strict scrutiny could be obtained by arguing that reproductive issues are so basic to women's equality that they require strict scrutiny. (It was basically an additive argument—equality plus privacy equals strict scrutiny.) She said that she was going to argue strict scrutiny on remand if the court asked her to brief the equality issue, and she did not want to have to disagree with my brief on that issue.

In response to the first point, I said that my client was Louisiana, not Utah or Guam. She then pointed out that I might be undercutting my own clients if I gave the court a narrow avenue to overturn the Louisiana statute—leaving the legislature free to enact a statute with a health exception next year, which would be no better for my clients. As previously stated, I had decided to focus my efforts on the women of Louisiana rather than all the women of the United States. Thus, I was unconcerned about whether my argument would be applicable to Utah or Guam. However, I was troubled by the idea that I might be making an argument that would undercut the women of Louisiana. I therefore said that I would think further about this problem.

At this point, I had a serious dilemma. Was I undercutting my clients by making too narrow an argument and by not arguing for the highest possible level of scrutiny? I talked about this problem with many of my colleagues, some of whom had worked previously with the ACLU. They all agreed that a narrow brief was in my clients' best interest and that national organizations had a tendency not to consider the specifics of their clients' cases. But they did suggest that I could probably argue in the alternative about the level of scrutiny in case the court wanted an opportunity to apply strict scrutiny to a gender case. I therefore decided to argue in the alternative and drop clarifying footnotes so that I would not be appearing to endorse the Guam or Utah statutes. One problem with this approach was that it used up valuable paragraphs, and I had a strict twenty-page limit. So, for example, I deleted a discussion about Spain's regulation of abortion (as one of Louisiana's civil law ancestors) in order to argue in the alternative concerning *Geduldig* and the standard of scrutiny.

In response to the ACLU's second point, I said that I did not find the additive argument very convincing. The court would only reach the equality issue if it finds that *Roe* no longer requires strict scrutiny. In addition, the additive theory has never received much support from the Supreme Court. Nevertheless, I promised to think about the issue. I finally added one sentence making the additive argument, seeing no harm doctrinally in arguing for strict scrutiny. However, I did regret the loss of valuable space through that argument.

I sent the ACLU representative a final draft before filing the brief, and she only had one technical suggestion (about how I labeled the addendum). I assume that the ACLU was not totally pleased with the shape of my argument, but in the end, it was my brief not theirs. Because I value their work in the reproductive health area, I did my best to accommodate their views without undercutting my own and those of my clients. Since the brief was technically "in support" of the appellees (their clients), I did not feel it was appropriate to ignore the ACLU's views entirely. On the other hand, an amicus brief is not directly on behalf of the appellees, so I believe it was appropriate to differ with the ACLU's basic approach. In fact, one might argue that the importance of amicus briefs is to allow the development of positions that are not likely to be developed in the chief briefs. Thus, I hope that I supported the efforts of the ACLU while also presenting a novel theory to the court.

Trying to translate my equality argument into doctrinal terms made me aware of the practical limitations of my equality approach. It made me realize, as I also discuss in the adolescent abortion case, that it may not always be possible for me to translate my equality approach into practical legal doctrine (that is, assuming I want my client to have a chance of winning). I have to make the best arguments that I can within the constraints of existing precedent.

E. The Postbrief Political Work

Filing the brief was a political act. I wanted to get the equality arguments on the table and to describe in detail how the statute would impact on disadvantaged women in Louisiana. The public relations department at Tulane suggested that I write an op-ed essay on the brief, which was placed in the *Dallas Morning News*.[19] I spoke at Southern Methodist University Law School in Dallas on the Louisiana and Mississippi abortion cases in April 1992 where the op-ed piece had already generated some discussion of those issues. Also, the ACLU asked me to organize a moot court for Janet Benshoof who argued the Louisiana case in the Fifth Circuit. I conducted the moot court at Tulane and invited my student volunteers to attend. Many of the students also attended the oral argument. They reported to me how much they enjoyed being able to attend the moot court and to see the oral argument in progress.

Despite my misgivings about how I was using my clients for my own political ends, I take some consolation from the fact that the groups that ultimately participated seemed to be quite excited about their participation. Many of them called me after the Fifth Circuit oral argument to find out how the case was going. I can therefore hope that they attained some sense of empowerment through participating in the process, even if I was using them for purposes that they may not have entirely understood.

Although I had experienced some tension in working with the ACLU and developing an equality perspective, I later received substantial support from them for these efforts. Nadine Strossen, the president of the ACLU, indicated that she was very interested in the development of the equality theory. In addition, Janet Benshoof spoke about the equality perspective in a public broadcasting special on abortion. I, in turn, gained valuable insight on the equality theory through discussions with Benshoof. I was able to incorporate some of her ideas into my brief in the Mississippi case. Thus, I may have overestimated my differences with the ACLU during my work on the brief.

I have also scheduled numerous interviews and speaking engagements to publicize the situation in Louisiana. The law school's publication, *The Tulane Lawyer*, featured my pro-choice work in its March 1992 issue. I hope that article helps to inspire some Tulane graduates to become more involved in pro-choice efforts. I have also had some fun with my public speaking engagements on the subject, trying to get mileage out of the visibility of my pregnancy. For example, when a state legislator tried to describe my position as "pro-abortion," I stood up, displaying my eight months of pregnancy, and said that I would not be pregnant if I were pro-abortion rather than pro-choice. Such actions may be considered grandstanding, but they do make a point that many anti-abortion advocates want to deny—that I and others are pro-choice rather than pro-abortion.

In sum, I did not expect to be cited in the Fifth Circuit's opinion (and was not), but I did hope to inform others of the dramatic consequences that the Louisiana statute would have on women's lives. In that way, perhaps I could help avoid this result being repeated elsewhere.

F. Conclusion

Writing a tight, twenty-page argument that incorporates your theoretical perspective while representing clients is a challenging but enjoyable task. In the future, I would start earlier in trying to find clients, and I would develop more effective contacts in my own community. I might also try to stay more independent of national organizations so that I can be more careful to represent my local constituency (which I would hope to better identify). Despite my good intentions, however, I later ended up being even more dependent on national counsel in the Mississippi case, because I took no responsibility for finding clients to represent. In the Mississippi case, I also compromised in terms of what I said in the brief through consultation with both Planned Parenthood and the NAACP Legal Defense Fund. My pregnancy was a key factor in making this compromise. The brief was filed in the Fifth Circuit on February 19, and my baby was born on February 20—I was heading to the hospital, while my New York cocounsel was heading to the Federal Express office with the brief! If one wants to be part of a national pro-choice network, it may be that such compromises are a necessary part of the process.

Other compromises I made during the Louisiana litigation were stylistic. Despite my theoretical commitment to dialogue and providing space for women's voices, I did not try to do anything novel with respect to the form of the argument. My voice was probably a little less argumentative than is typical in a brief, because I disdain the rhetorical style of brief writing.[20] But I did not interweave women's voices or do anything else equally unusual, as has been done in some briefs. I felt so constrained by the page limitation that the only possible style of writing seemed to be a terse style. Thus, within the constraints that I identified at the outset, it was a satisfying project.

Ultimately, my clients prevailed in the Louisiana abortion case. In a brief opinion, the Fifth Circuit concluded that the Louisiana statute was unconstitutional in light of the *Casey* decision, which the Supreme Court decided after I wrote my brief. Although the brief that I wrote for the Louisiana case probably had little or no impact on the Fifth Circuit's decision, the ground that I broke in trying to describe the impact of the legislation on the most disadvantaged women in society may be helpful in other states under the *Casey* undue burden standard.

The lesson I learned about equality theory from working on this case was that I needed to be pragmatic in deciding how to implement an equality perspective. In this case, I had a good argument available under *Feeney*; in another case, such an argument might not exist, so *Geduldig* would have to be directly attacked. Further, I realized that the argument I developed would not be applicable to all jurisdictions; it had to be fine-tuned to best represent the women of Louisiana. In that way, it seemed to comport with anti-essentialism. I also learned how to utilize an anti-essentialist perspective while arguing under equality doctrine. By focusing on the burden on *subgroups* of women, I was able to make equality arguments while recognizing the diversity in women's lives. This effort was not perfect, since space limitations did not allow me to infinitely discuss all possible subgroups of women. Nonetheless, by being conscious of the anti-essentialist critique, I believe that we can avoid "essentialist" generalizations about women while making equality arguments.

III. The Mississippi Abortion Case: *Helen B. Barnes v. Mike Moore* [21]

In the Mississippi case, my involvement began at the appellate level. Planned Parenthood contacted me and asked me if I would write a brief, like my Louisiana brief, which represented disadvantaged women in Mississippi. The district court judge had enjoined the enforcement of the statute after a several-day hearing in which much of this impact was put into the record.[22] The case was now on appeal to the Fifth Circuit. An amicus brief would be due in the Fifth Circuit on February 19, and my baby was due on February 15, so I said that I would work on it as much as possible. My baby cooperated by not being born until February 20, so I was able to write the brief with some logistical help from Planned Parenthood and the NAACP Legal Defense Fund (LDF).

The Mississippi anti-abortion statute[23] is a somewhat more moderate statute than the Louisiana anti-abortion statute, although its impact on the women of Mississippi is dramatic. Like the statute affirmed in relevant part in the *Casey* decision, it imposes a twenty-four-hour waiting period and an informed consent requirement. Unlike the Pennsylvania statute, however, it contains a very limited medical emergency exception that requires a woman's pregnancy to pose a "grave peril of immediate and irreversible loss of major bodily function"[24] in order for a physician to waive the twenty-four-hour waiting period requirement. Moreover, Mississippi, unlike Pennsylvania, is the poorest state with a very inadequate health care system. I was therefore very concerned about the impact that the waiting period requirement would have on women in Mississippi. As I had learned through my work on the Louisiana brief, the way to begin to place disadvantaged women at the core of our abortion doctrine is to put their lives on the pages of briefs that are filed in court. That was my intention in the Mississippi case, as it had been in the Louisiana case.

In the Louisiana case I had decided not to challenge the *Geduldig* decision but instead chose to present evidence of intent under *Feeney*. Despite my broad theoretical statements in *Abortion and Dialogue* about the importance of using the *Feeney* approach and the undesirability of challenging *Geduldig*, I did not choose to use the *Feeney* standard in the Mississippi case. I wrote the first draft of the Mississippi brief under the *Feeney* standard, but as my co-workers at the NAACP LDF and Planned Parenthood suggested, it was not a very convincing argument. Mississippi does not keep very good records of its legislative history, which made it nearly impossible to establish intent. Because such evidence of intent was not clearly present in the Mississippi case, I chose to distinguish *Geduldig*. Nevertheless, even in the Mississippi case, I set up the doctrinal framework so that I also had the opportunity to discuss extensively the impact of the statute on disadvantaged women. Thus, what I learned from working on both the Louisiana and Mississippi cases was that I did not have to view the choice between the *Feeney* standard and the *Geduldig* standard as one dictating whether I could describe the impact of the statute on disadvantaged women. The impact could be described under either standard if I was committed to finding a way to do so. Again, my theoretical writings may have been too bipolar; practical considerations made me be more flexible and made me see the array of doctrinal options available to me.[25]

Another problem that I faced was how rhetorical to allow my writing style to be. I tried to make it somewhat less rhetorical by not challenging the legitimacy of the state valuing prenatal life. Instead, I tried to show how inauthentic was the state's recitation of this interest. Nevertheless, I may have underestimated the need to argue rhetorically. I like to think of my audience as acting in good faith, respecting the views of my clients even though they may disagree. In the Mississippi case, however, I received a good lesson in the naïveté of such a view. The appellants challenged our filing of the amicus brief in the Fifth Circuit in the Mississippi case. I did not take their challenge too seriously, never imagining that a court would not allow us to *file* our brief. I saw the challenge as being genuinely listened to but did not worry that we would not be permitted to speak at all. As it turned out, Edith Jones (an extremely conservative Reagan appointee) was the judge who decided whether our brief should be allowed in the record. She did admit it but said that it was open to reconsideration by the entire panel—a rather unprecedented step for her to take. As I understand the Fifth Circuit rules, we were entitled to a decision whether or not our brief was entered; a conditional order is not contemplated under the rules. Thus, I learned that I probably should have taken the defendants' opposition more seriously and not assumed that the court would consider it frivolous. In these conservative times, no opposition to our views, however absurd, seems to be frivolous.

Working on the Mississippi brief made me even more pragmatic in terms of the implementation of my equality perspective. I came to see that one needs to be very contextual in deciding whether to work around the *Geduldig* rule or the *Feeney* rule and whether to use equality doctrine at all.

Irrespective of what legal doctrine I chose to use in the Mississippi case, however, we were probably destined to lose. Within hours of the oral argument, the Fifth Circuit unanimously ruled that the state statute was constitutional in light of the Supreme Court's decision in *Casey*. We were given no opportunity, on remand, to demonstrate the disparate impact that the waiting period rule had on the disadvantaged women in the state.

IV. The Louisiana Adolescent Abortion Case: *In re Application of Jane Doe, A Minor*[26]

This case came to me through a former student, Vince Booth. Vince telephoned me to say that he had volunteered to work on an ACLU case, and the ACLU had recommended that he get in touch with me for assistance. He had an adolescent client who wanted an abortion. She had gone to a local judge for the bypass procedure, as required by state law. The judge had appointed a lawyer to represent the fetus and had allowed that lawyer to subpoena a witness, the purported father of the fetus. Fortunately, the judge also called the ACLU and asked them to find an attorney to represent the adolescent. The local ACLU office had no staff attorney; the director called people on her list of volunteers and came across Vince Booth. Vince had never done any abortion work; most of his knowledge on the subject came from my constitutional law class of several years before.

By the time Vince talked to me, the case was headed to the state court of appeals. The trial court judge had denied Vince's objections to the appointment of counsel and the subpoena of a witness. The court of appeals quickly denied Vince's request for a supervisory writ. By the end of the week Vince had filed a petition in the Louisiana Supreme Court. We spent the weekend writing a brief for the Louisiana Supreme Court. Because Louisiana state law tracks *Roe* and its progeny, we simply cited the federal case law and said that it was the law in Louisiana. As it turned out, there was no federal case law on the appointment of counsel to represent the fetus or the subpoena of a witness. But we emphasized that the United States Supreme Court had said that the proceeding must be confidential, and those two steps violated our client's confidentiality. It was a straightforward privacy argument and extremely individualistic. Vince actually asked me about making an equality argument (an age-based argument), and I told him that there was no point in doing so. We had a very strong case under privacy doctrine; our client needed an immediate ruling, which could be most readily obtained on settled law.

Four judges heard our case in the Louisiana Supreme Court. By Monday afternoon, we heard that we had won by a three to one vote. Even a conservative Catholic voted with us.

As much as I have written on the futility of privacy doctrine, I did not hesitate for a minute in using privacy doctrine in this case. Two key factors influenced my decision. First, there is a big difference between direct client representation and amicus representation. By writing amicus briefs, I can show the court alternative ways to reach a particular decision. I know that the more settled way will be discussed by the chief brief. In this case, I had the responsibility of writing the sole brief. Once I made the decision to accept the case, I made the decision ethically to use whatever arguments were necessary to win. Second, equality arguments are superior to privacy arguments when they both have an equivalent chance of succeeding. My key responsibility is to help my client, not to advocate a particular theory of law. My client wanted an abortion; she did not care what arguments were made to get it. When I have criticized others for not making equality arguments in abortion cases, I have done so in a context in which privacy arguments have little chance of working. Under Louisiana state constitutional law, that is not true. There is an imbedded privacy doctrine under state constitutional laws, providing a very solid foundation for such an argument.[27] I have not abandoned, however, the idea of making equality abortion arguments under Louisiana law. The Louisiana constitution contains a sex equality provision that has never been interpreted. In the appropriate context, I would enjoy developing that provision doctrinally.

The lesson for me in this case was that I should not be so quick to criticize others, especially when they are directly representing a client, if they make a strategic argument that has a good chance of prevailing. The kinds of arguments that I prefer to make are probably best made in an amicus setting. Many and varied voices should be a part of the litigation process; I should probably be more open to recognizing the utility of these many and different voices.

Schematically, it might be best to think of cases as ranging from emergency situations to broad class actions, in which the parties are somewhat contrived to create a lawsuit, to law-reform amicus briefs. Our responsibilities to our client may vary accordingly. Thus, in an emergency situation like the one that I faced in this case, a very pragmatic, utilitarian response may be appropriate. However, in an amicus setting, where I seek clients, it may be more appropriate to make the kinds of creative and theoretical arguments that I made in the Louisiana and Mississippi abortion cases. Rather than having one style of argumentation for all circumstances, we need to have many different styles available to us, depending upon the circumstances.

Nevertheless, I should note that this case and my participation in it was not as simple as it might appear. My client did not have to get permission from an Orleans Parish judge to obtain an abortion. She could have filed her bypass request in Jefferson Parish where the judges do not appoint counsel to represent the fetus. (I made sure that my client was informed of that fact.) The real benefit in going to the Louisiana Supreme Court on an emergency basis was to prevent this practice from happening to *other* female adolescents who were not eligible to file in Jefferson Parish. (A female adolescent could file for a bypass procedure in the parish in which she lived or the parish in which she sought to obtain an abortion. Thus, an adolescent who lived in Orleans Parish and sought an abortion in Orleans Parish would have had no choice but to file in Orleans Parish. Because of where my client lived and where she sought an abortion, she could have filed in Orleans or Jefferson Parish.) My case was not a pure emergency; in some ways, I was using my client to set up a case on behalf of other adolescents in Louisiana. But I chose to treat it like an emergency, because I did not know when we might again have a chance to challenge the practice of appointing counsel to represent the fetus in Louisiana state court. This practice had been occurring for nearly a decade and had never been challenged, because no one heard about the appointments of counsel until the cases were already complete. Thus, it is not even easy to figure out what is an emergency and what is a contrived class action lawsuit; a particular case may fit both of those categories. At bottom, our pragmatic judgment must prevail even though it may not be easily schematized into a nice theoretical framework.

V. Operation Rescue

The next abortion case that taught me the limitations of my theoretical perspective was my work in the summer of 1992 to keep abortion clinics in the New Orleans and Baton Rouge area open despite the efforts of Operation Rescue.[28] This case came to my attention when a New Orleans political activist called me to ask if she could talk to me about possible legal action against Operation Rescue in Baton Rouge and New Orleans. She explained that Operation Rescue had sent out a national mailing indicating that they would be coming to Baton Rouge in early July and had threatened to also come to New Orleans (or anywhere in the state where there were abortion clinics). Since New Orleans is about an hour's drive from Baton Rouge, that threat seemed real.

I agreed to meet with her and several of her political co-workers. The group that met with me was very politically astute. They said that they had heard an injunction might help their cause, but they were afraid of the legal process also getting in the way of their efforts. Specifically, they said that they did not want an injunction if it would thwart their efforts by making them unable to use bull horns to communicate with their people. They explained to me that they were primarily worried about maintaining physical access rather than speech. They brought with them sample material from other jurisdictions with some injunction language that they thought they might like. They underscored, however, that they were concerned about participating in the legal process and did not want to do so unless they could get my assurance that this process would not be used against them.

At the time, I knew very little about injunctive actions against Operation Rescue but said that I would try to make some phone calls to get assistance from national organizations. I also said that we needed some local attorneys, particularly attorneys in Baton Rouge, if any legal efforts were to be successful. Finally, I indicated that I had a three-month-old baby at home for whom I was doing most of the child care (as well as breast-feeding), so it would not be logistically possible for me to spend much time in Baton Rouge. That problem underscored the need to get assistance from local attorneys.

I started to make telephone calls that day and soon received a tentative promise of assistance from the NOW Legal Defense and Education Fund (LDEF). I also received assistance from national NOW in finding a Baton Rouge lawyer. To my great relief, the director of NOW LDEF decided to act quickly on the matter and offered invaluable legal assistance. I discuss the importance of having access to the federal courts to stop Operation Rescue in chapter 5; for now, I would like to focus on the difficult political and ethical issues that this action raised.

When this group of women came to me with a request for legal assistance and an assurance that the legal process would not be used against them, I did not know exactly what they meant. Unfortunately, I soon found out.

Politically, when I think about why we need injunctions against groups like Operation Rescue, my answer is that we need these injunctions to protect the lives and well-being of women. I do not think about these injunctions as serving the property interests of abortion clinics. In reality, however, it is not possible to bring an injunction action against Operation Rescue without the support of the clinics. The clinics *must* assert their property interests if we are to prevent Operation Rescue from "trespassing." The clinics' interests are often genuinely a property interest. In Louisiana, for example, there are no nonprofit abortion providers. (Planned Parenthood does not operate abortion clinics in Louisiana, at least not as of the summer of 1992.) The clinics are therefore interested in making a profit as well as serving women's health care needs.

I have no problem with donating my time to assist women in procuring abortions; however, it is a little more difficult to justify donating my time to keep for-profit abortion clinics open, because everyone else working for the clinic is being compensated for their time. In this case, each of the abortion clinics did have a lawyer whom they paid to handle their routine work. In one case, a clinic had also previously hired a lawyer to obtain a state court injunction for them.

This problem of donating my time to a for-profit organization was not particularly acute at the beginning of this case, because the clinic that we were primarily trying to defend was paying its own lawyer to assist us and covering many of the court costs. Friends of mine who have done similar work in other cities, however, have found the for-profit status quite problematic. For example, one lawyer friend was spending hundreds of hours to keep open a for-profit clinic. Finally, she went to the clinic and asked for minimal compensation for her hours. The clinic refused to provide her with any compensation and told her that she should feel free to drop the case. She genuinely had an antagonistic relationship with the clinic. Nevertheless, she decided to continue her work out of her desire to help the women of her city. I did not have such a strong dilemma, but I was aware that my primary political allegiance was to the women of my community rather than the for-profit clinics.

My ethical and political dilemma arose when my clients' interests started to conflict with the Baton Rouge clinic's interests. My clients were politically active women in the New Orleans area who believed firmly in the need to do extensive political work to protect the right to choose abortion services. Many of them had also worked at other clinic defense operations in other cities and believed that a show of physical force was necessary to deter Operation Rescue. Finally, many of my clients were active in the lesbian community and were committed to working with gay and lesbian people to defend abortion clinics. They saw pro-choice efforts as closely linked to the political rights of lesbian and gay people. I suspect that they understood that many of the pro-choice activists in Baton Rouge would have much more moderate politics.

I had assured my clients that I would try to make sure that the legal process was not used against them, by which I meant that I would work with them to devise acceptable injunctive language that would not limit anyone's free speech rights. Nevertheless, the legal process did eventually turn against my clients. My clients were obtaining considerable publicity by engaging in "media events" to publicize the lack of reproductive choice in Louisiana. For example, they held protest activities on the steps of the state capitol, and when Operation Rescue did start blockading one of the abortion clinics, they were quite visible in their attempts to defend the clinics. Many of their supporters wore nontraditional clothing, with many of the women wearing combat boots and many of the men wearing earrings and other "effeminate" items of clothing. For a conservative Baton Rouge community, these supporters certainly looked quite radical and, to many people, visibly lesbian or gay.

Although I never talked directly to the clinic director about the activities of the supporters, I repeatedly received phone calls from someone in Baton Rouge who was working on the case and was quite upset about the activities of the clinic defenders. She felt that their work was hurting the clinic politically; moreover, she feared that the clinic supporters would not be law abiding in their work. (The action on the capitol steps apparently was not legal, because there was a city ordinance against holding political rallies at that location.)

In the meantime, we were trying to prepare the case for trial. The clinic defenders were one of the plaintiffs in the Baton Rouge action that we filed in state court. In order to have "standing" in the case, a representative from the clinic defenders would need to testify in court. But tensions between the Baton Rouge supporters of the clinic and my clients continued to rise. The Baton Rouge people wanted my clients to promise that they would be entirely law abiding, but my clients did not have that kind of control over their followers. Moreover, they believed that their most vigorous supporters were the ones most likely to break the law, so they did not want to tell these people that they could not participate in clinic defense. Finally, they felt that many of the reactions from Baton Rouge people were not based on fear of someone breaking the law but instead on fear of visible gay and lesbian people working on the action. My clients felt like they had a much better idea of how to defend a clinic, due to their experience at other sites, than the Baton Rouge people. This problem got so heated that I was told that the clinic was insisting my clients not participate in the lawsuit. In particular, I was told that it would backfire if we allowed the clinic defenders to testify to establish standing, because on cross examination, they would be asked if they planned to abide by the law.

The clinic defenders also seemed increasingly uninterested in participating in the lawsuit. The judge had scheduled the hearing for the injunction during the first days of Operation Rescue's action. The clinic defenders wanted to be at the site of the action rather than in the courtroom. They also wanted to spend the crucial hours before the action in political work rather than meeting with lawyers. They therefore started missing meetings with lawyers in Baton Rouge.

I was quite upset about how the political/legal process was breaking down in Baton Rouge but had little time to deal with the problem. I had been asked by the attorney for the police department of the city of New Orleans to get a federal court injunction to prevent Operation Rescue from blockading abortion clinics there. We started our work on the New Orleans case two weeks after we started work on the Baton Rouge case, so I was working feverishly (while caring for my then four-month-old daughter) to prepare the New Orleans action for trial. I could not possibly drive to Baton Rouge to clear up the tension between the clinic defenders and the clinic.

Ultimately, I helped reach a compromise whereby the clinic defenders would not send anyone to court to testify about standing. The clinic defenders could therefore not waste time in court. After the clinic defenders failed to testify, we would not object to their being dismissed from the case. The clinic was then satisfied when they were dismissed.

We did not get an injunction in state court in Baton Rouge against Operation Rescue despite the fact that they were engaging in a nationally sponsored action to blockade the Baton Rouge clinic. Because we did not get an injunction, I did not find out if that injunction would, in fact, have been used against the clinic defenders. (As I discuss in chapter 5, we did get an injunction in federal court in New Orleans under the Ku Klux Klan Act—an option that the Supreme Court has since invalidated.)

I learned many lessons from this experience. First, I learned that multiparty representation can be quite difficult. What I think most irritated me was that the clinic never would have received volunteer assistance had the clinic defenders not initially contacted me. Nevertheless, there was tremendous distrust between the clinic defenders and the clinic. In the future, I believe that I should do more work initially to make sure that there are no conflicts between client groups before agreeing to represent many different clients. If I had had such discussions, I could have possibly agreed to serve only the clinic defenders and not serve the clinic as well. I could then have made arguments in court that only supported my client without also worrying about whether they furthered the interest of the clinic. Second, I learned that I should be more hesitant in assuming that a legal solution to a political problem is appropriate. All the signs indicated that a legal solution was not possible—we had to file in state court rather than federal court, and there were significant tensions among the plaintiffs. I should probably have advised the clinic defenders to be active politically but not to seek assistance from the legal process. As it turned out, there was nothing useful that I could get for them legally. And the time that they spent working with me probably detracted from the time that they had available to work politically.

The law has its limits; those limitations should be at the front of my mind when I am approached about a case rather than at the back of my mind. It is particularly disappointing to me that I did not see those limitations when my clients were clearly quite aware of them.

VI. The New Orleans Gay Rights Ordinance[29]

My last example involves lobbying for a gay rights ordinance rather than working on litigation. Legislative activity is obviously important political activity that deserves serious attention. My work on the ordinance began in 1986 when I worked with two other lawyers to draft an ordinance to be presented to the New Orleans City Council. I soon learned that our chief opposition would be the Catholic church and the religious fundamentalist communities. The other lawyers were not willing to try to work with those groups to achieve a compromise; I was. Several of us met with the archdiocese and discussed the value of their AIDS work. We stressed how important it was to the success of their AIDS work not to be perceived as being against the ordinance (as they had been two years previously). We reached an agreement in which they would not endorse the ordinance but they would not openly fight it. Unfortunately, they did not live up to their promise. A lobbyist was at the city council every day to argue against passage. The ordinance was defeated soundly.

Five years later, I was again asked to work with two other lawyers to draft an ordinance to be presented to the New Orleans City Council. Remembering the problems of the previous attempt, I did not assume that we could work with the church in good faith. I also did not believe that the content of the ordinance was very important; its passage was critical on a symbolic level. I therefore drafted language that would exempt all religiously based institutions from coverage by the ordinance. If they were not covered, I figured that they could not fight it. The language I suggested was broadened so that all nonprofit organizations were exempted.[30] (No one is exactly sure how that happened.) It passed by the same proportion that it had lost in the previous attempt despite the fact that little change had occurred in the composition of the council.[31] The reasons for passage go beyond the addition of the religious exemption. David Duke's candidacy for governor probably made some council members afraid to take the side of bigotry by opposing the ordinance. In addition, Magic Johnson's announcement that he was HIV positive influenced at least one council member to vote for the ordinance (despite the fact that Johnson claims to have acquired the virus through heterosexual transmission, and the ordinance was *not* about AIDS).

My theory said that the church could be trusted to act in good faith. My practice showed that the New Orleans archdiocese could not be trusted. I did not give them another chance to harm us; instead, I worked around them. The result is less than what we wanted (one of the other lawyers refused to work on the ordinance with the religious exemption). Is a weak ordinance better than no ordinance? In my opinion—yes; in the opinion of others—no.

When I presented an earlier version of this chapter at a symposium at Northwestern Law School in Chicago, one member of the audience came up to me and said that he disagreed with my decision to favor the religious exemption. He said that no one would expect a race anti-discrimination statute to contain a religious exemption; thus, we should not tolerate such an exemption for a sexual orientation nondiscrimination statute. I responded that his assumption was not so obvious in New Orleans and Louisiana where religion plays a dominant role in society. For example, Louisiana day-care regulations exempt religiously affiliated day-care centers from Class A requirements despite the fact that there is no reason to assume that a religious institution provides safer or more sanitary day care than others. His comments, however, made me realize that my decision to favor the religious exemption was extremely contextual, dependent on the unique circumstances of politics in New Orleans and Louisiana. In many other communities, I may have agreed with him that such an exemption was not tolerable.

Events following the passage of the gay rights ordinance support the view that the compromise statute was worthwhile. For example, New Orleans recently passed a Mardi Gras ordinance, which prohibited Mardi Gras krewes from discriminating in their membership practices if they wanted a Mardi Gras parade permit. Sexual orientation was included as one of the grounds of nondiscrimination. Although the Mardi Gras ordinance was controversial, the sexual orientation nondiscrimination provision received little public attention. (Interestingly, the gender nondiscrimination provision proved to be the most controversial.) Most recently, New Orleans passed a domestic partnership ordinance that provides gay and lesbian couples who register with the city some city benefits.

Thus, the passage of the gay rights ordinance may have acclimated the community to the acceptability of prohibiting discrimination on the basis of sexual orientation, thereby causing it not to be a major issue when it reemerged in the context of another ordinance.

The impact on my theory? Theoretically, I would have preferred to have been an optimist and given the church another chance to work with us. I would have liked to have believed any assurances that they would have provided. But in practice, I discovered there was a way around dialogue; avoidance was possible to some extent (although it required watering down the ordinance). In the past, I thought there were two major options—dialogue or rhetoric; and I made passing references to the possible role of silence.[32] But avoidance needs to be added to my repertoire. By working *around* an organization rather than confronting it, we may avoid some of the disadvantages of rhetoric without actually achieving dialogue. It turns out that my practice was less bipolar than my theory; my practice enabled me to discover alternative routes that my theory had not yet contemplated.

VII. Conclusion

I am pleased that I practice law while also writing feminist theory. It keeps me in touch with the limitations of my theoretical perspective as well as the limits of what benefits the courts can provide for women. My experience with the New Orleans gay rights ordinance opened my theory to considering more than the possibilities of dialogue and rhetoric. I learned the usefulness of avoidance as a technique for advancing a political agenda. I learned that my thinking about dialogue and rhetoric may have been too bipolar, thereby not enabling me to see the usefulness of other tools such as avoidance.

Working on the Louisiana and Mississippi anti-abortion cases also helped me see that I was being too bipolar in considering how to make equality arguments in abortion cases. I thought that one could only introduce evidence concerning the impact of statutes on disadvantaged women by proceeding under the *Feeney* standard rather than the *Geduldig* standard. My practice, however, taught me how to talk about disadvantaged women under the *Geduldig* test. Working on these cases also confirmed that one can try to be somewhat more dialogic in writing briefs than is traditional in abortion cases by acknowledging the legitimacy of the states' asserted valuation of life. On the other hand, I learned that the state is unlikely to be genuinely concerned with the valuation of life when it restricts abortions.

In addition, my experience in direct client representation in the Louisiana adolescent abortion case made me see the limited utility of my theoretical perspective when I participate in a case as the sole lawyer for a client rather than as an amicus. In the future, I will probably be more sympathetic to the difficult doctrinal choices that lawyers must make in representing clients and not expect theoretical consistency in those choices.

Finally, my experience with multiparty litigation in the Operation Rescue action led me to see how difficult it can be to represent parties with possibly conflicting political agendas. In addition, I learned about the limitations of the legal process when one is dealing with a client who wants to be active politically. In the future, I will be slower to assume that I can gain anything for my clients legally that they could not gain on their own politically.

My practice has forced me to emphasize my theoretical perspective that good-faith dialogue is not possible in our present society in the short term because it does not respect women. It is not possible to achieve my long-term goals of good-faith dialogue until respect for women is more prevalent in society; I cannot practice law under the false assumption that such dialogue does exist. Thus, my practice of law must often be argumentative rather than dialogic, because the preconditions for good-faith dialogue do not exist in our society. A major challenge for me is trying to figure out how to make my short-term and long-term goals more compatible with each other. Both my Mississippi and Louisiana federal cases represented attempts to move to my long-term goals by making arguments quite compatible with my theoretical perspective. The gay rights ordinance and the Louisiana state case represented attempts to achieve a concrete victory in the short-term but at a price that may be inconsistent with my long-term views. Although I have serious doubts about these short-term strategies, the challenge for me is to try to find more consistency between my short-term and long-term views; and it is my long-term rather than short-term views that may need to be modified. Modifying my long-term views would cause me truly to move from practice to theory.

Notes

1. *Foreword to Theoretics of Practice: The Integration of Progressive Thought and Action*, 43 Hastings L. J. xvii, xix (1992).

2. Catharine MacKinnon, Feminism Unmodified: Discourses on Life and Law (1987).

3. Catharine MacKinnon, *From Practice to Theory, or What Is a White Woman Anyway?*, 4 Yale J. L. & Feminism 13, 13 (1992).

4. *See generally Theoretics of Practice: The Integration of Progressive Thought and Action*, 43 Hastings L. J. 717 (1992).

5. For further discussion of that viewpoint, see chapter 7.

6. Brief for Black Women of Choice et al., Sojourner T. v. Buddy Roemer, No. 91-3677 (5th Cir. filed October 18, 1991) (*reprinted in* Ruth Colker, Abortion and Dialogue: Pro-Choice, Pro-Life, and American Law 163-75 (1992)).

7. Act No. 26 of the 1991 Louisiana session, codified at La. Rev. Stat. Ann. § 14:87.

8. Sojourner T. v. Buddy Roemer, 772 F. Supp. 930 (E. D. La. 1991).

9. That was also my intention in my book Abortion and Dialogue: Pro-Choice, Pro-Life, and American Law (1992).

10. *See* Brief Amici Curiae of the National Council of Negro Women, Inc.; National Urban League, Inc.; The American Indian Health Care Association; The Asian American Legal Defense Fund; Committee for Hispanic Children and Families; The Mexican American Legal Defense Fund and Education Fund: the National Black Women's Health Project; National Institute for Women of Color; National Women's Health Network; Organizacion Nacional de la Salud de la Mujer Latina; Organization of Asian Women; Puerto Rican Legal Defense and Education Fund; Women of Color Partnership Program of the Religious Coalition for Abortion Rights; Women of All Red Nations, North Dakota; YWCA of the U.S.A., and Other Organizations in Support of Appellees, Webster v. Reproductive Health Services, 109 S. Ct. 3040 (1989).

11. Sent to me by fax on October 17, 1991, from Executive Director of NO/AIDS Task Force.

12. The strategy with regard to the Louisiana statute was to have two parallel lawsuits pending—a state lawsuit arguing that the statute violated the state constitution and the federal lawsuit. Planned Parenthood had lead responsibility for the state lawsuit; the ACLU had lead responsibility for the federal lawsuit. A decision was first rendered in the federal lawsuit enjoining the enforcement of the statute, which put the federal suit on a faster track than the state lawsuit. *See* Sojourner T. v. Buddy Roemer, 772 F. Supp. 930 (E. D. La. 1991). The state court lawsuit was then stayed pending the outcome of the federal lawsuit. *See* Planned Parenthood v. Louisiana, No. 370917 (La. Dist. Ct. Aug. 14, 1991). The state court judge indicated, however, that he would enjoin enforcement of the Louisiana statute under state law if *Roe v. Wade* were overturned by the federal courts and the federal injunction were lifted.

13. For further discussion, see Ruth Colker, *Feminist Litigation: An Oxymoron?*, 13 Harv. Women's L. J. 137 (1990); Ruth Colker, *Reply to Sarah Burns*, 13 Harv. Women's L. J. 207, 207 n.3 (1990).

14. 417 U.S. 484 (1974).

15. 442 U.S. 256 (1979).

16. *See generally* Sylvia Law, *Rethinking Sex and the Constitution*, 132 U. Pa. L. Rev. 955, 983 (1984) (describing the numerous criticisms of *Geduldig* as a "cottage industry").

17. 112 S. Ct. 2791 (1992).

18. I am not comfortable in publicly reporting these conversations, because I believe the ACLU has done an extraordinary job in preserving our reproductive freedom on a small budget and with a very overworked staff. I fully understood why we had our differences on this brief. Out of respect for their work, I tried to accommodate their views as best as I could without sacrificing what I perceived to be the interests of my clients. Without their work, the Louisiana legislature would have gotten away with criminalizing abortion more than a decade ago.

19. Ruth Colker, *Louisiana Abortion Ban Is a Very Real Threat to Women*, The Dallas Morning News, Feb. 6, 1992, at 23A.

20. *See* Colker, *supra* note 13.

21. Brief of Amici Curiae National Black Women's Health Project et al., Helen B. Barnes v. Mike Moore, No. 91-1953 (5th Cir. filed February 19, 1992).

22. Barnes v. Moore, Civil Action No. J91–0245(W) (filed Aug. 30, 1991) (order granting preliminary injunction) (Judge Wingate).

23. House Bill 982 (Mississippi Regular Session 1991).

24. Miss. Code Ann. § 41–41–31 (Supp. 1992). By contrast, the Pennsylvania statute provided a medical emergency exception when a delay "will create serious risk of substantial and irreversible impairment of major bodily function." 18 Pa. Cons. Stat. Ann. § 3203 (Supp. 1991). The imminence and loss of major bodily function requirements in the Mississippi statute more substantially restrict a physician's judgment in treating a woman whose pregnancy poses health dangers than the Pennsylvania statute's requirements.

25. Although we ultimately lost the Mississippi case in the Fifth Circuit, Barnes v. Moore, No. 91–1953 (filed July 29, 1992), and won the Louisiana case, I do not think that those differences in results are attributable in any way to my decisions about how to describe the impact on women doctrinally. Instead, they can be explained by the Fifth Circuit's conclusion that the Mississippi statute is similar to the statute affirmed, in part, in Planned Parenthood of Southeastern Pennsylvania v. Casey, 112 S. Ct. 2791 (1992), and that the Louisiana statute is more stringent than the Pennsylvania statute.

26. 591 So.2d 698 (La. 1991) (December 16, 1991).

27. Since taking this case, I have questioned how I could have satisfied myself that this case contributed to my worldview while also making pragmatic arguments that furthered my client's legal interest. Arguably, as was suggested to me by one member of the SMU faculty, I could have interviewed the client and satisfied myself that she was not trying to further an individualistic, private sense of self that I might find objectionable before I decided to accept her case. In this case, I never met my client; Vince handled all of the daily contact with her. But even if I had met her, I am not sure that it would have been appropriate to interview her to satisfy my own set of values and aspirations. The interview itself may have become a part of her subordination in society. If I believe that the law should better respect women's ability to make both pro-choice and pro-life decisions, then I, as the pregnant woman's lawyer, should also respect her ability to make such decisions without subjecting her to needless interrogation.

28. My legal work resulted in a state court judge denying us an injunction against Operation Rescue blockading a Baton Rouge abortion clinic, see NOW v. Operation Rescue National, No. 382,750 (19th Judicial District La. July 8, 1992) (Judge Brown), and a federal judge granting us an injunction against Operation Rescue blockading abortion clinics in the New Orleans area, see NOW v. Operation Rescue National, No. 92–2289 (E. D. La. July 9, 1992) (Judge Livaudais).

29. No. 14976 Mayor Council Series, City of New Orleans (as amended November 26, 1991).

30. The ordinance does not apply to "any religious corporation, religious entity, religious association, or religious organization, or any non-profit corporation, or organization or groups, including charitable organizations, with respect to the employment of individuals, or with respect to the employment policies, practices, and procedures established by any such corporation, entity, association, or society." Section 40C-122(d).

31. The following council members voted for the ordinance in 1991: Boissiere, Giarusso, Jackson, Singleton, and Taylor. Wilson and Clarkson, the only two new members of the council, voted against it. In the previous attempt, only Jackson and Taylor had voted in favor; Boissiere, Giarusso, and Singleton had voted against it.

32. See Ruth Colker, Abortion and Dialogue: Pro-Choice, Pro-Life, and American Law 32 (1992) (reference to the value of ignoring hostile comments to preserve our personal safety).

2

The Practice of Teaching

The closest most legal academics come to practice is teaching—their students,
most of whom will practice, being regarded by many as an occupational hazard to
their theorizing.

—Catharine MacKinnon[1]

I. Introduction

IN THE OPENING quotation, Catharine MacKinnon derides the lack of legal practice in which many feminist academics are engaged. In addition, she mocks
the idea that teaching is itself a kind of practice. I agree with MacKinnon that
legal academics should practice law, but I also believe that our teaching is a type
of practice. Moreover, it is a type of practice that we should take seriously as
feminists. Several excellent articles, as well as a recently published book, on teaching law classes from a feminist perspective have made me ask myself whether
I have introduced feminist principles into my classroom teaching sufficiently and,
more fundamentally, what those principles should be.[2]

I want to begin by discussing two of the more recent writings on feminist
teaching methodology, particularly at the law school level, and respond to those
writings from my own personal experience. My overarching concern in review-
ing these writings is that there is a "party line" about what constitutes effective
feminist teaching that has gone largely unexamined. I am not entirely convinced
that each of these precepts is necessary or possible to achieve in the classroom.
I also think that these precepts do not consider different methods for most effectively teaching feminism in a variety of class sizes and subjects. I then examine my own teaching experience in a number of different contexts to offer the
lessons that can be drawn from them. I hope that this chapter will make the
reader, whether a teacher or a student, think more seriously about what constitutes a feminist teaching methodology.

II. Review of the Literature

There seems to be a "party line" in feminist theory about what is an appropriate teaching methodology. According to the party line, a feminist teacher is supposed to critique the law for reinforcing "objective" principles, adopt a nonauthoritarian role in the classroom, be nonlinear in orientation, and be very open in discussions with students. These principles flow from the feminist critique of the state as a domain of male domination. By trying to rid our classrooms of the dynamic of dominance and submission, teachers are supposed to promote feminist values. Two recent works by law professors Patricia Williams and Morrison Torrey that contribute importantly to the discussion of feminist teaching serve as good examples of this pedagogical approach. Nonetheless, I an uncertain about the value of these approaches, either as being necessary to feminist principles themselves or as being necessary components of a feminist approach to teaching at all.

A. *Patricia Williams,* The Alchemy of Race and Rights: Diary of a Law Professor[3]

Professor Patricia Williams's book has generated a great deal of dialogue about law teaching. As the name suggests, Williams uses entries from a diary kept throughout several years of her law teaching to share with the reader her distinctive methodology as well the students' reactions it provokes. Williams's book is truly a diary and thus is nonlinear in its form. She often uses parables to make her points. Therefore, it is difficult to list succinctly the key points that she tries to make. Instead, I will try to focus on a few of her observations to see how they comport with feminist theory and law teaching.

One of the first observations that Williams makes is that law students are taught to believe in what she calls "High Objectivity."[4] This principle of High Objectivity purportedly makes people uncritical of differences, authoritarian, and prone to universalize about things that are truly different. Williams teaches this critique to her students through the use of a story about a little boy who, when he told his parents that he was afraid of big dogs, was told by his mother that all dogs are really the same—size makes no difference. Williams reports that her students are confused by this and the other stories that she tells. In Williams's words: "They are confused enough by the idea of property alone, overwhelmed by the thought of dogs and women as academic subjects, and paralyzed by the idea that property might have a gender and that gender might be a matter of words."[5]

When I first read that example, I was in awe of Williams as well as aghast. I was in awe of her because she truly seemed to try to critique law at its most central core. By practicing law on an ongoing basis, I think that I have probably become too connected to the law to have the distance that would permit me to offer such a thorough critique.

But then I asked myself the question, Do I really agree with Williams's critique and do I think she has chosen an effective method of communicating it to her students? In fact, I think it is too easy to dismiss law as following the principle of High Objectivity for two reasons. First, the ability to distinguish cases is central to the practice of law. Frequently, you work on a case that looks quite similar to another case and you have to struggle to find arguments for why it is different from the other case. The ability to find differences is certainly as important as the ability to find similarities in legal practice. On what basis does Williams believe, I wonder, that law is centered around this principle of High Objectivity, which makes it unable to find differences?

It is possible that what Williams meant to say was that law purports to consider cases based on objective rather than emotional principles. Thus, if the dog scared the child and the child were run over by a car while he or she ran away from the dog, the law would teach us that the driver of the car should not be held more liable due to our sympathy for the child. Probably few law students graduate from law school, however, without realizing that a lawyer for the plaintiff in such a case will try to sway the jury's emotions, even if those emotional arguments have no valid foundation in the law. Thus, I could imagine a very useful class discussion on the role of emotions and empathy in the courtroom despite law's purported distance from those concepts. We could discuss why the law tries to pretend that emotional and political considerations are not present and how a lawyer might bring those feelings into the courtroom. Such a discussion might be considered feminist, because it tries to value emotionalism, which is often a devalued female trait.

Second, Williams's and other feminists' critique of the principle of objectivity do not convince me that objectivity has no proper role in a feminist jurisprudence. Williams herself proceeds from an objective principle—that law should *not* embrace objectivity. I suspect that her principle is even more than a negative. I suspect that she also embraces the principle that emotion has a place in the courtroom. I find it frustrating that feminists always critique the principle of objectivity in a way that suggests that they do not hold any objective principles themselves.[6] But if you do not hold objective principles then you have no way to judge what to accept and what to criticize. Rather than teach my students to disavow objective principles, I would want to help them grope with what principles they should adopt as basic to ordering their own lives.

Despite her critique of High Objectivity, I believe that Williams does make her students struggle with principles with which to order their lives. For example, she shares a story about talking with a young man in the dining car of a train. He explained that he does not give money to beggars but does talk with them to help him "remember that they're not just animals."[7] After describing more of this conversation, Williams observes that he "seems anxious to prove the benignity of his neglect."[8] She ends the story by noting that he did not tip the waitress at all. Williams does not comment further on the story. She leaves it for the reader to draw the lesson from the story. The lesson I draw from the story is how far we have come from our own humanity that we could look at another human and see him as less than human. Her story makes me desperately want not to be seen in her eyes as the man on the train, despite the fact that I rarely give money to beggars. Her story is loaded with ethical principles about humanity, compassion, guilt, and generosity. Its goal, I would suggest, is to move us toward a certain ethical vision that is held by Williams. Williams, I would suggest, has her own High Objectivity. It is just not consistent with the principles most commonly found in law.

Following her parable on the child and the dog, Williams comments that her students' confusion is reasonable in a confusing world and conjectures that "my students plot my disintegration, in the shadowy shelter of ivy-covered archways and in the margins of their notebooks."[9] In this and in the story of the man on the train, Williams's approach seems to illustrate a common precept among feminist teachers that the teacher should not hold the role of "expert" and try to explain "right answers" to her students. However, sometimes this methodology leads to students' frustrations. I was aghast at her story of the child and the dog, because as a teacher, I cannot imagine leaving my students so frustrated that they are plotting my disintegration. I believe that I have guidance to offer students through my experience as a lawyer and my study of feminist theory. I remember being quite confused in law school feeling that the professor was often "hiding the ball" in a way that confused rather than illuminated the discussion. I therefore have always tried to be a professor who was very clear in the classroom. I often begin class with a historical overview of the topic (if appropriate) and some basic statements about the particular rule we are studying. I then may move into a critique of the rule but only after I am convinced that my students understand the rule itself. One problem that I see with the style of teaching that Williams purports to use (I have never seen Williams teach) is that she moves to a critique before it is clear that the students understand the rule itself. I do not see why being clear, linear, and straightforward cannot be feminist. Yet many writers seem to assume that a feminist law teacher must teach in a completely nonhierarchical environment in which her own years of study cannot be given weight.

B. Morrison Torrey, Jackie Casey, and Karin Olson, "Teaching Law in a Feminist Manner"[10]

Professor Torrey and her students—Jackie Casey and Karin Olson—wrote one of the most interesting essays that I have read on the subject of teaching a feminist jurisprudence course. Unlike most articles on this subject, they coauthored a piece that shared the perspective of both teacher and student. Their article demonstrated that a teacher can try to incorporate feminist insights into teaching methodology by reducing a great deal of the classroom hierarchy. As such, it provides inspiration to those of us who teach in the area of feminist jurisprudence.

Professor Torrey used several distinctive steps to bring feminist methodology to the classroom. First, she wrote the students a letter before the semester began telling them what would be the assigned reading so that the students could get an early start if they desired. In addition, by communicating with the students, she showed them how much she respected their time. This effort appears to have been well appreciated by the students. Second, she made some personal disclosures about her own politics. She does not indicate whether she discussed anything about her personal life such as her marital status or sexual orientation—information that often seems to be relevant in my own feminist jurisprudence classes.

Third, Professor Torrey took a fairly passive role as group leader. In order to achieve shared leadership, anyone could speak without being called upon; if more than one person wanted to speak, the last speaker would designate the next. When problems arose in the class due to, for example, one student dominating the discussion, Professor Torrey would have the students rather than herself resolve the problem. From both her and the students' descriptions, it sounds like a fairly nonhierarchical classroom. (I wonder what name the students used to refer to her. I have found it difficult to get the students to be comfortable with calling me by my first name.) Finally, she used various techniques to insure that heated debate would remain productive, that the personal would be part of the discussions, and that students would be prepared and responsible. Professor Torrey did assign grades but detailed criteria with the students in advance so that they could understand the requirements for a particular grade.

Professor Torrey's methodology would probably work well in many small, elective feminist jurisprudence classes. Nevertheless, I have never managed to teach a feminist jurisprudence class where a student's unpreparedness did not force me to exert my authority. Her framework probably works best in a setting where students are genuinely interested in assuming responsibility. It is not clear to me, however, that her methodology would transfer well to other classroom settings.

III. My Own Teaching Experiences

A. *Introduction*

One limitation with the literature that I have discussed is that it does not adequately differentiate between teaching required mainstream courses like civil procedure, elective mainstream courses like family law, and theory courses like feminist jurisprudence (which may or may not be required). Moreover, it does not differentiate between teaching required and elective courses. In addition, the methodology that is appropriate for a course will depend upon its size. When I taught a feminist bridge to the entire first-year class at the University of Toronto, I could not use the same methodology as I would use in my much smaller feminist jurisprudence seminar. Nevertheless, authors rarely comment on how their teaching changes depending upon the size of the classroom.

B. *My First Teaching Experience*

My first formal teaching experience was as an adjunct professor in the Women's Studies Department at George Washington University.[11] I taught a course entitled Women and the Law. There were no more than ten students in the class. On the first day of class, I had the students introduce themselves by saying why they took the course. The women said how interested they were in women's studies and that they wanted some exposure to the law. The two men said that they chose the course because they figured it would be easy.

An experience occurred before the first class session was held that should have warned me of the difficulties that I would have with the men in that class. I was sitting by myself on the floor before the first class started when the two male students arrived. They looked around the corridor, saw me along with the other female students, and said somewhat loudly, "I guess the professor hasn't arrived yet." I corrected them by introducing myself, but their first look at me suggested that they had no intention of treating me with respect, since I apparently did not look like what they expected of a professor. I had short hair, wore pants, and did not wear makeup.

My general plan for teaching the course was that I would put together some exciting reading, lecture a little and open up the class for discussion. I had taught a feminist theory class at the Radcliffe Women's Center while in college, had been a teaching fellow in Harvard's government department in a class on women and politics, and had successfully used such a strategy in the past. In fact, I thought of teaching as a pretty easy exercise in a small class.

The two men in the class certainly proved me wrong. They would come to class unprepared, make bizarre comments that had no relation to the reading (mostly based on a television show they had seen the night before instead of doing the reading), took no notes, and engaged in private conversation with each other. I was hoping to be reinvited to teach this class and was very afraid of having one of these students complain about me. I was only a few years older than they were and certainly did not feel in control of the situation. Some of the women students would complain to me privately about these young men, and I would respond that the men were entitled to take the class, and I could not take sides in any class rivalry. Finally, after one of the men made one of his more stupid comments in class, one of the female students said, "I am paying a lot of money to take this class and I would appreciate it if the men in this class did not interfere with my learning. You come to class unprepared and interfere with my education. I resent that." The young men were floored, and I was practically speechless. I believe that I sheepishly made a comment that we should be careful not to generalize about all of the men in the classroom based on the comments of one of the men. I do not think anyone, particularly a woman, had ever confronted these men about their immaturity and sexism. The young men behaved after that.

I suspect that experience heavily shaped the kind of teacher that I eventually became. I learned that I needed to be in control, especially in a class in which the students were not necessarily feminists. I also learned that I could use the students as my allies if the class became unruly or difficult. Over the years, I have often been pleasantly surprised at how strongly my students will defend me. That has helped me enormously in maintaining control over a class.

When feminists write about law teaching, they often seem to assume that the only power dynamic is teacher-student. This is an essentialist assumption in that it fails to identify the other power dynamics that may be present. At the time that I taught the class at George Washington, I was a young, white woman with a female lover. My gender, age, and sexual orientation caused me to lose much of the power that I otherwise would have held as a teacher. It should not surprise us to learn that, as women in a male-dominated classroom, particularly in our early years as teachers, we may have to take steps to maintain our authority. By recognizing the range of environments in which we teach, I believe that we can be more pragmatic in developing effective teaching styles. Fifteen years later, as an older woman who is now married to a man and well established in my field, I am not exposed to those kinds of control problems in the classroom.

When I was a faculty member at Tulane Law School for eight years, I was dismayed to see how difficult it was for many of my young, female colleagues (especially those who are racial minorities) to gain the respect of the students in the classroom. When one of my young, female African-American colleagues (whom I will call Pam), for example, put together an innovative set of materials in collaboration with an older, white female colleague (whom I will call Sheila), which tried to raise issues of race, gender, and sexual orientation, the students responded extremely negatively to Pam but quite positively to Sheila. The student evaluations suggested that Pam was Sheila's research assistant, although in fact, it was Pam who had taken the lead in preparing the materials. In contrast, Sheila was awarded the best-teaching award by the students the next year. It is therefore not possible to objectively say what kind of teaching style is universally effective or even feminist. The efforts of Pam were completely undermined by the racism and sexism of the students, whereas the same efforts by Sheila were strongly rewarded. The students were ultimately so successful in their efforts to undermine Pam's confidence that she left Tulane to teach elsewhere. They therefore successfully exerted the ultimate form of power by forcing her to leave; the efforts of my colleagues to be supportive of Pam could not undo the daily harassment of the students. In choosing an effective feminist teaching style, I therefore believe that we each need to be mindful of the limitations of our situation. In addition, when deciding how to appraise the teaching evaluations of other professors, we need to be mindful of how various factors may be affecting the students' evaluations. The fact that we, as more established female professors, are not experiencing blatant sexism, racism, or homophobia in the classroom does not mean that those factors are not present at our university.

C. Teaching a Large, Mainstream, Required Class

Another very challenging teaching experience that I have had at Tulane Law School is teaching civil procedure as a required course to first-year students. My class has typically been large, with my largest class having 165 students. My attempt at utilizing feminist principles in this class could be described, at best, as modest. There is no way that I can learn these students' names. In fact, there is no way that I will even have a conversation with or probably recognize half of the students in the class. Nevertheless, I have implemented a few techniques in civil procedure that are worthy of mention.

First, I try to pick hypotheticals that involve civil rights issues and to use women in unconventional roles in my hypotheticals. As modest as this attempt may be, it does get noticed by my students. One student reportedly said to another student one day, "I am getting sick of how Colker always tries to ram feminism down our throats. Today, she used a *woman* in her hypo about statisticians!" This exchange made me aware of how little I had to do in the classroom in order to be perceived as a feminist. I realized how close I was to losing my authority in the classroom through modest steps like using women as statisticians in hypotheticals.

Second, I try to teach a very practical civil procedure class. When I practice law, I find that my knowledge of civil procedure is one of the most important skills that I bring to practice. Thus, like Williams, I certainly try to critique the rules, but first, I make sure that my students understand the rules. No matter how much we dislike the rules, they exist and must be used effectively by us as lawyers. I do not think I am doing my students any favors by simply criticizing the rules.

Similarly, I do *not* teach my students that the rules are hopelessly indeterminate as might a strong proponent of critical theory, because in my experience, the rules are not indeterminate. My task as a lawyer is to figure out what is the range of meaning possible for a rule and then to figure out how I can use that range of meaning to benefit my client. There is no point in making an outrageous argument to a judge or magistrate about a rule; limits do exist, even if those limits are not always apparent from the language of the rule. It is my job as a teacher to help my students learn that range of meaning and to become adept at making judgments about the kinds of arguments that are possible.

Finally, I try to make the classroom as comfortable as possible. I usually only call on students who volunteer; I refer to students by their first names; I never belittle a student and always try to find something positive to say about a student's comment; and I try to make myself as accessible as possible outside the classroom. (I also encourage students to call me by my first name.) In that way, I try to conform to the nonauthoritarian feminist party line. Nevertheless, I do view myself as the expert. My students have not practiced law; there is no way they can understand these rules without significant assistance, and I am being paid to "teach" them. There therefore is some "authoritarianism" to my teaching style.

I suspect that my civil procedure class is very different from the property class that Pat Williams teaches. And, in many ways, her class is more authentically "feminist." Nevertheless, I feel comfortable with my traditional classroom, because pragmatically, I believe it represents as much feminism as I can get away with in that classroom. Based on my students' highly positive evaluations, I believe that my students are not plotting my disintegration. More important, based on their final examinations, they seemed to have learned quite a bit of civil procedure.

D. Teaching a Large, Mainstream, Elective Course

In the fall of 1991, I volunteered to teach family law at Tulane Law School for the first time. I decided to teach this course because I realized that much of my legal work—in the area of lesbian and gay rights as well as reproductive freedom—increasingly focused on family law issues in the state courts. I hoped that I could learn more about these issues by teaching a family law course. The first decision that I had to make was what course materials to use. Dissatisfied with the existing casebooks, I sought to compile my own materials. Early in my course preparation, I contacted Professor Martha Minow, who sent me thousands of pages of materials that she used in her family law course at Harvard Law School. I read through the materials that she sent me and hired a research assistant to help me compile my own set of materials. In order to have basic cases and statutory material available for the students, I also assigned a standard casebook.

Before I volunteered to teach the course, we had one section of common-law family law, which typically drew about eighty or ninety students. With two sections of the course now being offered, I figured that I would have no more than forty or fifty students. Since the other section had a course description that did not fit the approach I was planning to take, I wrote a new course description. I stated that the course would focus on what has been called the "nontraditional family," with particular attention to African-American families, poor families, and gay and lesbian families. Further, I stated explicitly that the course would be taught from a feminist perspective. Since another family law course was being offered the following semester, which was quite traditional, I felt comfortable stating my own perspective. On the first day of class, I reiterated my perspective, so I would not have an "attitude" problem in the classroom. I was surprised to note that, in the end, about eighty students enrolled in my section of the course, so I concluded that my use of a feminist approach actually increased enrollment.

One dilemma I faced was how to grade the students. I did not feel that my course would easily lend itself to a traditional law school exam. I wanted my students to write papers for a grade, but I also wanted to be sure that they read the assignments (which were heavy). In such a large class, I also wanted some assurance that the students would attend and be prepared. I did not see how I could run a lively discussion if the students did not read the materials carefully. I also had found that the students were generally less prepared for their classes than they used to be. Their unpreparedness frustrated me in that it made it difficult to teach effectively from *any* perspective.

I therefore made some decisions that would probably horrify some feminists. First, I established a mandatory attendance policy. If a student missed more than four classes (without explanation), she or he would be penalized a half-letter grade per extra absence. In addition, if I called on a student twice and she or he was unprepared on both occasions, I would treat the student as if he or she were absent. I did not expect to have to invoke either of these rules, but by having them in effect, I thought that I would get better attendance and participation. In fact, I only used the rule against one student who missed nearly half of the classes for the first six weeks, until I wrote him a memo criticizing his attendance. I asked him to come by my office to discuss his attendance if he had an explanation. He never visited my office. I believe that I penalized him one letter grade. Because I deliberately never called on any student twice who had not volunteered, I did not have to worry about implementing the other rule. (Its mere existence, however, seemed to encourage preparedness.)

I implemented these rules for many reasons that I continue to believe are valid. In addition to wanting good participation, I did not want my students to take advantage of my "niceness." Probably because of my experience at George Washington University, I was always aware that students take courses for many different reasons. I did not want students to take my course because it was perceived to be a "gut." I work hard to prepare for class, and I want my students also to work hard. Further, I do not feel it is ethical to give students credit for taking a class simply because they turn in a paper. A lot of learning should take place in the classroom as well. (If it does not, then I am doing a very poor job.) In my early years of teaching, I never required attendance, but as students seem less interested in learning and more focused on their grades, I have felt more compelled to institute a mandatory attendance policy. Nonetheless, I probably would not require attendance in the future in such a class, because the students' enthusiasm for the course far exceeded my expectations.

I decided to use a paper as the primary mode of grading the students. I developed a complex set of options from which the students could choose. They could write three papers, two papers, one paper, or take a final examination. The vast majority of the students chose the three-paper option. In that option, I required that their papers touch on most of the topics in the course and that each paper discuss the similarities between two seemingly unrelated topics in the course. I told the students I would be grading them based on originality, clarity, and thoughtfulness. In the future, I will require the three-paper option, because it was the best vehicle for the students to demonstrate their breadth of knowledge and originality. It took me longer to grade these papers than a stan-

dard exam, but I enjoyed reading many of the papers, because they were generally very well written and thoughtful.

A very interesting aspect of the course was the classroom dynamics. I wrote
the following memo to the dean during the course, explaining those dynamics:

> From my perspective, the course is going extremely well. In fact, in my
> seven years of teaching, I don't think that I have ever had a class that I enjoyed
> teaching as much. The students are so lively that I have trouble calling on
> most of the people who volunteer. And the quality of their comments is
> excellent, so that I learn as much from them as they learn from me.
>
> Nevertheless, I understand from my "informants" (gay white men who
> "pass" so that the racists and homophobes feel comfortable talking to
> them), that there is some grumbling going on. I find the examples very
> illuminating. During one class, I gave the students two contrasting hy-
> potheticals involving a lesbian couple who had raised a child together.
> (The hypo was based on the *Alison M.* case which we will read later in the
> term.) I used these hypotheticals after a previous class in which we had
> discussed hypotheticals and cases involving unmarried straight couples with
> children. Apparently, one student complained saying, "Is this a class in
> lesbian law?" (The comment reminded me of one that I had received in
> my second year of teaching after I had used a hypo involving the retention
> of an expert who was a statistician and a female. One student complained
> that I had gone too far in trying to push my feminism on them!)
>
> Last class, we read two cases involving AFDC benefits and the unsuccessful
> attempts by poor people to retain their child support payments and keep
> caseworkers out of their homes. I asked the students why the plaintiff may
> have been so determined to keep the caseworker out of her home. One of
> the dozen or so black students who responded talked about the dignity
> issue—that it is really demeaning to have a caseworker open your drawers
> and see what brand of shampoo you use. She was the only student to
> respond in a way that seemed to draw on personal experience—the other
> students, both black and white, talked about the possibility that she was
> living with a man or owned some expensive furniture, etc. Afterward, one
> student apparently said, "I can see why the black students wanted to talk
> so much since they all know what it's like to be on welfare." I suspect that
> there were equal numbers of whites and blacks talking in a class that is
> probably about 30% black, yet the white student thought that the blacks
> were totally dominating the discussion. In addition, only one black stu-
> dent had made a comment which could have been interpreted as reflecting
> her personal experience. That comment reminded me of one that I re-
> ceived last year in Con Law I on my student evaluations. A student said
> that you could not get called on unless you were gay, black, or female. In

fact, five or six straight white men were dominating the discussion all semester. I tried to make up for this domination by calling on other students to balance out the discussion. I, of course, don't even know which of my students are gay, but obviously some students think that they can identify them.

Numerically, I doubt that the dissenters are very plentiful, especially since family law is an elective and another section will be offered this spring. The overall class dynamic is so wonderful that I was surprised to hear that the dissenters even existed. (I am going to have to try to figure out who they are so that I can call on them to diversify the class discussion.) But it is troubling that simply by *asking* certain questions that students feel compelled to complain. It certainly makes me wonder what stereotypes they would have about me if I were a pregnant, black female standing in front of the class! (They probably would figure that I was a crack addict who planned to abandon her baby in a trash can after birth.)

I believe that my experience says a lot about the power dynamics in a classroom. Students are so unaccustomed to minority students and openly gay and lesbian students speaking in class that whatever they say gets greatly magnified. This phenomenon should not have surprised me in light of my experience in civil procedure, where the use of a female statistician in a hypothetical received so much notice. In contrast, here, rather than make subtle changes, I actually had modified the substance of the course. It is a shame that adding feminist content to a mainstream course receives such notice, although I should note that the vast majority of the students seemed to enjoy the class.

E. Teaching a Large, Required, Feminist Theory Class

Early in 1988, I received a telephone call from the dean at the University of Toronto Faculty of Law, asking me if I would visit in the fall of 1988 to teach a "feminist bridge" to the first-year students. Students at the University of Toronto are required to take four "bridges" during their first year in order for the law school to introduce theory and history in the first-year curriculum. For the first time, the law school would devote one bridge to feminist theory. Unfortunately, one of the leading feminists on the faculty was going to be on sabbatical. The dean therefore invited me to visit at the law school in order to help make this program succeed. (I also visited a second time in the spring of 1990 to help teach the bridge again, as well as Canadian constitutional law.)

When I arrived at the law school the following fall, I learned that I would be one of several faculty members coteaching this one-week intensive course in feminist theory. The students would have sixteen hours of class over four days and then have a take-home exam.

This was one of my most challenging teaching assignments. I was a United States citizen teaching in a Canadian law school. I knew that it was important to have Canadian content in the course, but I knew little about Canadian law. In addition, I knew that some people on the faculty opposed the bridge, and I did not want to be responsible for its failure the first time through. Finally, unlike any other feminist theory course that I had taught, this one would be mandatory. How do you pitch a required feminist theory course to an entire first-year class?

We made several decisions about how to teach the course. We decided that it would have to be personal. Thus, we each introduced ourselves to the class by talking about how we became interested in feminist theory or by talking about our own law school experiences. We wanted to share our own excitement about teaching the bridge, hoping that it would become infectious. I believe that this strategy worked, because we did develop a very warm classroom environment, although I heard that some students felt "embarrassed" by our personal tone. We also decided to try to expose the students to as broad a spectrum of feminist theory as possible. Because we were not confident that we shared enough diversity in views among ourselves, we brought in two outside speakers (one of whom was Catharine MacKinnon) to round out the perspectives. Finally, we tried to use as many practical examples as possible so that the course would not be overly theoretical. I spent a lot of time reading Canadian constitutional law so as to pick examples with Canadian content.

During my lectures, I tried to state my own feminist position forcefully while also appearing open and friendly. I thought that if the students liked me, they would find my lectures more accessible. From what I could see, that strategy seemed to work. At the end of my lectures, I impressed upon the students the need to take feminist theory out of the classroom and into political and legal work. As an outcome of that talk, many students visited my office to discuss pro bono projects that they could begin.

A very difficult aspect of this course was interweaving the MacKinnon lecture. Catharine MacKinnon was invited to give a lecture and then respond to questions by the students. (One decision that we made was to double the amount of discussion time that the bridge usually offered.) I agreed to present a critique to help begin the discussion period. I am a great fan of Catharine MacKinnon's work, although I am also troubled by some of her far-reaching views. To me, her work is like a thought experiment—if I imagine that the world is as bad as she claims it is, I can get a clearer perspective on the actual world.

I wanted to critique MacKinnon in a way that would not cause the students to dismiss her work entirely (which I thought would be the tendency of many of the students). I therefore made some brief critical observations without questioning her basic premises. Afterwards, some students told me that they found my version easier to understand and accept than MacKinnon's version. I was happy to hear that response, because I did not want to do anything to undercut her important work.

I believe that the MacKinnon lecture worked well, because I demonstrated how one could disagree with her in "good faith"—respecting her views while also suggesting their limitations. By making the critique of MacKinnon nonrhetorical, I believe I helped students reject some of her views without feeling that they had to totally dismiss her theory.

The grading process also proved to have its challenges. When requiring exams, I have always preferred take-home exams, because they do not have the false time pressures of an in-class exam. They have seemed to be more feminist to me, because they offer the student the option of taking the exam in a less competitive atmosphere. We chose to give the students a twenty-four hour take-home exam, because we thought that exam technique would give students the opportunity to be more creative and relaxed. We also put a word limit on the exams so that a student would not be inclined to stay up all night to work on the paper. Some women with children, however, complained that they were at a disadvantage, because they could not work in the evenings. We were very sensitive to this problem but did not know how to respond. We said that we did not expect that anyone would need to stay up all night but that we would make exceptions in individual cases. While I do not remember any mother actually approaching us for additional time, I did learn from this experience that even the most benign examination technique can pose problems.

A positive result that flowed from the existence of the feminist bridge was that I found it made it easier for me to interweave feminist theory into my first-year class on Canadian constitutional law, which I taught during my second visit. After the class had the bridge (which occurred in the middle of the semester and in which I again participated), I directly raised with the class the fact that I had noticed that women participated less than men. I said that I would try to overcome that problem by making an extra effort to call on more female volunteers and that I hoped the women in the class would respond by volunteering more. (For a while, at least, more women did seem to volunteer.) I also started offering more explicit feminist analyses of the cases and, in particular, focused more heavily on gay and lesbian issues in some of the cases. I believe that the bridge made me more comfortable with my feminism in the classroom and made the students more comfortable and interested in feminist theory. The bridge therefore truly acted as a "bridge."

F. Teaching Feminist Jurisprudence as an Elective

1. INTRODUCTION

Of all my teaching experiences, teaching feminist jurisprudence as an elective is clearly the easiest, because the class is generally filled with committed feminists. I used to teach Women and the Law, which I abandoned because I decided that it was unteachable. A Women and the Law course requires that the instructor be an expert on every area of the law so that she can then present the special issues involving women. However, my knowledge of the various fields was not sufficient to make me feel that I could do an adequate job.

Feminist jurisprudence can be whatever I want to make it. So much has been written in feminist theory I cannot possibly cover it all. I usually focus the readings around my current research interests. Thus, when I was writing about feminism and theology and abortion, I collected materials on that subject for the students to read. As to pedagogy, I have not been nearly as attentive to group dynamics as Professor Torrey. For example, last spring, I assigned books by Pat Williams, Ruthann Robson, Catharine MacKinnon, Martha Minow, Vicky Spelman, bell hooks, and myself. I had read each of these books many times and believed that I did have substantial expertise to offer the students. On the other hand, I was very careful not to suggest that there is one *correct* feminist theory. My own work, which they read, tries to be open to multiple interpretations and perspectives. In my teaching evaluations, my students sometimes comment on how good I am at presenting views with which I disagree. I believe that if I am going to criticize a view, I should have the strongest version of that view in front of the class. I try to avoid catch phrases like High Objectivity, and instead I try to make my students work hard to understand views with which they disagree. I believe that I can present my views without abusing my power in the classroom by forcing the students to conform to my views. And, if students' views do nevertheless coincide with my own, I feel that it is relatively genuine.

When the class has fewer than twenty students, I teach the first five or six weeks and then have each student present a draft of his or her required research paper and ask another student to serve as the "lead critic." The lead critic provides a response to the classroom oral presentation and offers written comments on the student's rough draft. I also critique each student's rough draft, so each student is provided with two critiques. I use this method so that students will take more responsibility for themselves and others. I believe it is important for students to develop good writing and editing skills, and I hope that my emphasis on their writing will improve those skills. When the class is larger, I dispense with the oral presentations, but I do maintain the system whereby students hand in a draft to myself and a critic, who give them comments.

One dilemma I have often faced in teaching feminist jurisprudence, particularly the material on lesbian and gay rights, is how much to disclose about my own sexuality. In addition, I have often faced a dilemma of trying to figure out how to make my gay and lesbian students feel comfortable in the classroom. The two dilemmas are interrelated. Because of my status as a teacher and my reputation in the field of lesbian and gay rights, the students often seem too interested in my personal life. I feel objectified by being forced to disclose information about my past and present partners. On the other hand, my life experiences are sometimes relevant to our discussions. One way in which I have resolved this dilemma is to provide the students with a copy of a short essay that I wrote in the *Yale Journal of Law and Feminism* entitled "Marriage."[12] This essay puts my personal life on the table without my having to discuss it. Students who want to discuss personal issues relating to their own sexual orientation with me may then feel more comfortable doing so. Some people may view it as odd that I find it easier to write about a subject than to talk with my students about it, but by simply assigning the reading or making it available to them, I feel like I give them the choice to learn as little or as much about me as they choose. I do not have to waste the time of students who do not care to hear about my personal life.

Few professors, of course, have the option of assigning a reading that discloses their life history. And I do not always assign that reading myself. Nevertheless, I usually find ways—often through private conversations in my office—to allow the students to learn about my personal situation, since I believe that it does affect my view of law and feminism.

Similarly, I try to give my gay and lesbian students the space to come out of the closet if and when they want to. I absolutely never pull a student out of the closet in class no matter what I may know about him or her. I would like to share one difficult episode that I had in this regard, however, to show how difficult gay and lesbian issues can be in the classroom. I taught in New Orleans for eight years, where the climate in many law firms is blatantly homophobic. A well-known story in the gay and lesbian community was that a woman who was ranked very high in her class (third, I believe) had a job offer at a major New Orleans firm rescinded after the partners learned she was a lesbian. No one will ever truly know why her job offer was rescinded, but the common belief in the gay and lesbian community is that her sexual orientation was the reason. Understandably, that episode drove many students firmly into the closet.

One of my students was very concerned about her job prospects being damaged if anyone found out she was a lesbian. In my seminar that semester, each of the students had volunteered to lead the discussion on a particular reading. She had volunteered to lead the discussion of Adrienne Rich's "Compulsory Heterosexuality and Lesbian Existence."[13] The point of Rich's essay is to question the meaning of the word *lesbian*. By Rich's definition, all of the women in the class would be on the lesbian continuum due to their commitment to feminism. A few days before the scheduled class, this student came to me and said that she could not lead the discussion, because she was afraid that word would get back to the New Orleans law firms that she was a lesbian. I asked her why teaching that reading would cause anyone to assume she was a lesbian, especially since the essay defines lesbianism in a political rather than a sexual context. (I assume that she was only worried about being labeled a "sexual" lesbian.) She was too upset to provide a coherent answer. I told her that I would think about it. I then got back to her and said that I did not see that I had any options. All of the other students already had chosen a reading to discuss with the class. I had not forced her to pick that particular reading, and I did not think that anyone in the class would particularly care that she had chosen it. Additionally, it was extremely unlikely that what happened in two hours of one class in law school would get back to the New Orleans firms. Further, I suggested that if I changed the class rules and led the discussion myself, that would cause as much attention to be focused on her as if she led the discussion. In fact, it might create even more rumors. Since she had picked the reading, I could only warn her as her professor that I would have to penalize her if she failed to attend class and lead the discussion. I felt horrible to take such a firm position, but I did not want to condone what I perceived to be her self-centered paranoia. In fact, she led the discussion, did a great job, and ultimately landed her dream job in another city (where she decided she preferred to live). She even became a very "out" lesbian in the community. But, at the time, I felt like a cruel, terrible person.

Looking back, I am uncertain what I would do if the situation arose again. I probably would do the same thing, because while I see my role as not invading a student's privacy, I also should not feed needless paranoia. This student was taking steps to get out of the closet but lost courage along the way. I refused to help her shut the door behind her, although I would not have dragged her out of the closet to begin with. If I had Professor Torrey's commitment to making the students run the class, I do not know how I would have handled this situation. I would have had to breach the student's privacy in order to bring this matter to the class's attention. I did try to give the student some control by giving her the option of not showing up and taking a grade penalty, but that was a pretty coercive option. To this day, I can see no good solutions to the problem.

These problems raise the general issue of the need to develop trust in the classroom. Trust is important not only among the students but also between the students and the teacher. Because the issues in this class are inherently sensitive and controversial and because I have found that this class attracts a greater diversity of students than do other classes, potentially troublesome or even explosive discussions often occur. I find that controversial issues can be explored most fully when sufficient trust exists in the classroom. Openness, both by the professor and by the students, seems to foster a trusting and respectful classroom atmosphere. I have therefore structured the class so as to encourage openness and understanding, keeping in mind each individual's privacy interests. I have required students to lead discussions of the materials assigned and have found that this gives students an opportunity to discuss their viewpoints and provides an opportunity for other students to comment based on their own views.

I had never discussed pedagogy with my students, but inspired by Professor Torrey, I did so in the 1993 spring semester. Tulane Law School has a student newspaper in which the students discuss issues that are of concern to them. During the previous semester, the students had filled the pages with discussions of pedagogy, including some references to feminist work. I decided to take advantage of the dialogue that the students had already started in order to make my own classroom more feminist. If I could get the students to take more responsibility, I could become a less central figure in the classroom. I kept a journal of the progress of the class during the semester and will share some vignettes from the class to give the reader a sense of what difficulties as well as rewards can arise when one tries to implement feminist methodology into an elective feminist jurisprudence seminar.

Before I present the vignettes, I need to describe the feminist method that I tried to bring to the class as well as the composition of the class itself. I decided that I would try to have as minor a role as possible in the class—to let the students teach the class by leading the discussion of the readings. I therefore wanted to put a discussion of pedagogy on the table as early as possible. I assigned Pat Williams's book as the first reading in the hope that it would inspire the students to be creative with pedagogy. Because of logistical problems I had to decide what books we would read. Otherwise, there would not be sufficient copies in the bookstore. I therefore chose a cross section of feminist theory, making sure that I included readings by lesbians and African-American women, in particular. I also decided that the students would write a draft and final paper, which I would grade. That was the only way that I could ensure that they did enough work to be deserving of credit. The students would also criticize other students' work in order to improve their writing skills and take responsibility in the classroom.

The composition of the class was also somewhat unusual for a private, American law school. I had thirty-two students in the class. The class had twelve African-American students, one African student, and four Hispanic students. In addition, twelve students identified as gay, lesbian, or bisexual. Twelve students were male. There was only one straight white male in the class; he was Jewish and identified strongly with his oppression as a Jew. Not all of the students identified as feminists; the African-American women seemed the least comfortable with the feminist label. The classroom was therefore a perfect place to explore issues of diversity, and not surprisingly, we had many lively discussions.

2. SOME VIGNETTES

I asked the students what format we should use for class discussion during the semester. One common comment that arose was that after nineteen or so years of schooling, they had little idea about how a classroom *should* be led. They liked the idea of stripping away assumptions by considering that issue but had few constructive suggestions to make. They kept looking to me for guidance. We agreed that three or four students would volunteer to lead each class discussion.

Racism soon reared its head in the class. Four white, female students had volunteered to lead the discussion of Pat Williams's book. One of them, A, was acting in a very dominant way throughout the discussion—cutting people off and controlling the clock. At one point, she made a derogatory comment about her experiences while living in Harlem. She said that living in Harlem had "warped" her. A female, African-American student, B, complained that A had been racist in her description of Harlem and dismissive of an African-American student who had made a comment. That point got us into a lively discussion of unconscious racism, and I suggested that we read Chuck Lawrence's *Stanford Law Review* article for the next class. A dropped the class; we never discussed Lawrence's work, although some students told me in my office that they read it. The classroom was getting somewhat polarized with some white students apparently choosing to remain silent rather than worry about being labeled a racist.

I talked to an African colleague, C, about the racist incident in my class. He said that the issue is trust—that African-American students are wary of what white students will say, so it is easy for white students to offend African-American students.

I thought about C's comment and saw another example that seemed to support his thesis. In one class, another student, D, asked a question about keeping one's name upon marriage, which only referred to the heterosexual students. I was expecting the gay and lesbian students to challenge her on the heterosexual assumptions underlying her question. She was not challenged, because I believe, the lesbian and gay students trusted her. She was an active member of the staff of the gay and lesbian law journal; although she identified as heterosexual, they trusted her to be thoughtful on lesbian and gay issues. By contrast, when I discussed the racial incident with A in my office, I learned that she did not even know B's name. So clearly they did not have a history together that would have created trust. The class probably never developed a fully trustworthy attitude, but we had a party early in the semester, which seemed to help break the ice. One student said that he thought the class finally knew each other well enough to have a good class by the end of the semester. That was probably true and is probably an inevitable aspect of teaching a semester course. By identifying the need for trust, however, one can plan events like parties to help get the class to better interact.

One problem that I soon identified with the class discussion was the bipolar way in which we discussed race. Race was always white or black with no reference to other races; issues were always race or gender without recognition of multiple layers of discrimination. Another problem that I identified was my role in the classroom. I was not sure that my role in the classroom was always the appropriate one; I wanted feedback so that I could modify my role as the class continued throughout the semester. (Some students had told me privately that they wanted me to participate more in the classroom.) I wanted to raise these problems with the class without interjecting my views in a hierarchical way. I began one class with a comment about the bipolar way in which I thought we had been discussing race and gender and explained that I felt some of the reading might help us on that issue. I then asked the students how they felt about my role in the classroom. A student asked me if I had been "holding back." I responded that I had. She then suggested that I should participate on the same basis as a student. I expressed my reservations, explaining that some comments I have held back would have been critical of a student's interpretation of a text and that I was hoping that the students would help each other struggle with the text. I think they better understood my concern, but they reiterated that they would like me to participate on the same basis as another student. They assured me they would tell me if I were dominating or wrong or whatever. I did start to participate more on the basis of those suggestions, and I believe they were correct to suggest that I should not be entirely passive in the classroom.

We then had what I thought was a very good discussion of Pat Williams's book. I introduced my own interpretation of the text, which seemed to help students who were having trouble understanding the book. The content of Williams's book also helped to put anti-essentialism on the table, causing us to be somewhat less bipolar in our discussions.

I came to realize that one aspect of the bipolar nature of the classroom was the seating arrangement. The class had segregated itself along race and sexual orientation lines. I started to move my seat each week and so did some other students, so more intermingling occurred privately before class began.

My question about my role in the class also sparked a confrontation with a student, which reinforced the difficulty of developing trust in the classroom. I had said that I was deliberately keeping quiet in order not to dominate. A student, E, then said, "I pay a lot of tuition, and I won't have any trouble telling you that I think you're wrong." Another student, F, said, "You've been waiting a long time to finally get to tell a professor that we pay their salary." I then took E's comment about tuition and salaries, which I viewed as largely sarcastic or flip, and turned it back to the entire class by commenting that white students often make comments like that on student evaluation forms in order to justify their racist inability to tolerate an African-American professor. I said that it was not in fact an unusual comment at all but one that was often used to disguise racism or sexism—that students can feel justified in being racist or sexist by essentially saying that they have bought their right to believe whatever they want. I had made this comment out of my frustration with the experience of one of my female, African-American colleagues, which I discussed earlier. I did *not* believe that this particular student engaged in such conduct, because I knew that this student was virulently antiracist and antisexist.

Nonetheless, I unknowingly offended F. She soon visited my office to tell me that she was so offended by my comment that she did not come to the second hour of class. She apparently thought I meant to suggest that she was being racist or sexist. I explained that was not what I had meant at all. I also said that I was sorry for hurting her feelings but that I realized I needed to be responsible even for my unintentional conduct. Eventually, I turned the conversation to one of trust. I explained that I felt that a lack of trust was what made the African-American students interpret the white students' comments in a negative way and that I felt that the same lack of trust was causing this student and myself not to communicate effectively. She said that she agreed with my analysis of the race issue, but she saw our problem as "just something personal between the two of us." Frankly, I did not know what she meant by that but dropped the issue. She said she left my office not feeling hurt, so it was a productive conversation. We may even have begun to develop more trust. Later in the semester, a more minor problem occurred between the two of us, and it seemed much easier for us to handle without my hurting her feelings.

I gained more insight into the trust issue when B, the student who had accused A of being racist, stopped by my office to talk. When I asked her how she was enjoying the class, she said that the class was improving a little, and she was enjoying it more than any of her other law school classes, but it was far from perfect. We talked about the issue of trust, and she agreed with my assessment. She also said that people assume she is angry with them just because she has poignantly disagreed with them. That, in fact, is not the case. She gets ideas off her chest and does not stay angry. I suggested that the misunderstanding about anger might be cultural—that it seemed to me that the Jewish and African-American students were more comfortable with those kinds of outbursts but that other students were more uncomfortable. She agreed with my assessment.

She also shared with me a good story about trust. She said that she has trouble with gay issues but that her roommate is gay. He had become her best friend and asked her to share an apartment with him. He also told her he was gay. She told him that was a problem for her, but she did care very much for him and would like to be his roommate nonetheless. She said that because they have such a solid friendship, they can be honest with each other about their differences on gay issues. She said that he is not going to change her mind nor is she going to change his mind, but their conversations are very open and trusting. I came to realize that her gay roommate was a student in the class and also realized that some of the gay and lesbian students probably knew about her "problem" with gay issues. That history may, in fact, have explained some of the lack of trust toward B that I saw in the classroom. Again, I received a lesson in how complicated the trust issue can be. (Her roommate, by the way, was also African-American.)

The most amazing class of the semester occurred when we read Ruthann Robson's book, *Lesbian (Out)Law*.[14] G led the discussion of Robson's book. She began the discussion by saying that she was one of the "S and M dykes" described by Robson. She came to class in classic S and M garb—leather jacket, choke around her neck, greased-back hair, chains, and a whip. The class asked her questions about lesbian S and M, and she was able to handle herself quite well. H then talked about being a white, gay man and said that he had trouble with a lot of the racial stuff that blacks were raising, because as a gay man, he had no protection at all. His family had disowned him; he had to worry about being beaten up, losing his apartment or job, etc. (He held back tears while he talked.) Later, some of the African-American students confronted him about his unwillingness to empathize with their issues; they could not see why he resisted seeing their common thread. Other African-American students, however, sympathized with him, saying that the African-American community was a part of the problem of homophobia.

Although it was not apparent at the time, H was beginning to learn more about racial issues. He wrote a very creative play for his final paper, which really struggled with giving voice to African-American and Hispanic gay characters.

He gave a draft of the paper to B for comments; she was quite impressed by his efforts.

The second class discussion of Robson's book also went well. The leaders of the class discussion decided to do a multimedia presentation. They began class by asking us to close our eyes and listen to a tape (which was largely excerpts from *Torch Song Trilogy*). After listening to the cries of homophobia, they asked us to imagine a world in which gay people were the majority and the norm. They then handed out blue and red poker chips. If one got a blue chip one was gay, and if one got a red chip one was straight. They asked what laws, if any, we should pass on the new island on which we lived. At first, students mimicked the homophobia of our present society by making it heterophobic. But then, we got to more serious questions. Would some people on our island be hateful? What could we do about those people? One of the students, J, role-played that she was a bigot and told us that she would abide by any laws but would teach her children to hate. We could not figure out what to do with J, but her presence forced us to confront basic questions about human nature. (During the role playing, I, of course, objected to the bipolar categories and asked where the bisexuals were.)

One student, later in the class when we were out of role playing, asked why gay people are so concerned about coming out of the closet—why did they feel compelled to tell strangers about their sexual orientation. We then had a good discussion about the many ways in which people's sexual orientation impacts them and the subtle ways in which people communicate sexual orientation through talking about their boyfriend or girlfriend. During the role playing one of the students playing a straight role mentioned wanting to rent an apartment with his wife. Immediately, the class jumped on him and said, "What wife? You can't marry!" The role playing was helpful in making people realize how different their world would be if they were gay or lesbian. I had never before tried role playing in the classroom, but it did seem to work well to get us to have fun while also thinking about difficult issues.

Not all of the classes, of course, were equally lively. For the first time in my teaching experience, the discussion of Catharine MacKinnon's work went poorly. As with the other books, we spent two weeks on MacKinnon's work. The first discussion was pretty lively with some of the African-American women indicating that they did not feel included in MacKinnon's scholarship. The second MacKinnon class was so dull that someone suggested we end class a few minutes early. I ended up directing a lot of that discussion, not feeling that the students were sufficiently paying attention to the text. In the evaluations at the end of the semester, several students commented that we should have skipped MacKinnon.

I think the MacKinnon discussion demonstrated how much the African-American students were "leading" the class thematically. Once several of them identified MacKinnon as insensitive to racial issues, the other people in the class seemed to feel silenced. There is an excellent symposium in volume 4 of the 1992 *Yale Journal of Law and Feminism* that discusses the issue of whether MacKinnon's scholarship is sensitive to racial issues. Next time, I may have the students read that symposium so that we can have several different interpretations of MacKinnon on the table for discussion.

Because the class seemed to be lagging, I decided to get more involved in leading the discussion. For one of the next classes, I handed out a problem in which I asked the students to devise a rape statute that did not need to be constitutional in any way. The statute however needed to respond to the racism, homophobia, and sexism of the criminal justice system. The discussion of the rape problem went well, and the energy level of the class seemed to resume its previous high level. Although I had initially intended to remain relatively passive in the classroom, I discovered that one style of teaching may not be appropriate for the entire semester. I learned to be flexible in response to the varying energy levels of the students.

My book *Abortion and Dialogue* helped generate some excellent class discussions toward the end of the semester. We talked a lot about whether men should have any say in women's abortion decisions. The gay men, in particular, were concerned that they could not contribute sperm to a woman and thereby participate in the woman's decision-making process with respect to childbirth. The men did not want to credit women's gestational role as particularly important. Substantively, I disagreed sharply with their view, yet I learned a lot about the depth of some men's feelings about wanting to be a biological father.

Ironically, although my book is about the importance of engaging in dialogue, I was not sure that the discussion we had about my book was, in fact, dialogic. I had made the snide comment that "sperm is cheap" to discount some of the men's biological arguments. Other students had also made comments in what I viewed as a rhetorical manner. Feeling uncomfortable about the rhetorical nature of the conversation, I raised the question of whether we were talking in a dialogic way. I said that we had agreed in our discussion that dialogue could best occur when the people involved respected each other. I suggested that such respect existed in our class, yet I had not felt like our discussion on abortion was particularly dialogic. The class split on that issue. At first, many of the men seemed to agree with me, whereas the women disagreed. When someone pointed out that there seemed to be a gender difference on this issue, other people spoke up, which eliminated what appeared to be a gendered division. The two people in class who had engaged in the sharpest interchange about abortion said that they had continued their discussion after class and had quite a fruitful discussion. One student suggested that what we had was a "predialogue"—that there was not enough time to really get the discussion going. The fact that two students continued the discussion after class confirmed that was what had happened. Nevertheless, one student maintained that we had not had a real dialogue and that this discussion about whether we had a real dialogue last week only confirmed that fact. She felt that people were only confirming (and rationalizing) their entrenched views.

So did we have dialogue? I really do not know. I am beginning to think that maybe we did if the real test is whether the discussion made people more aware of what other people believe. Such realizations can apparently happen across a rather heated discussion. I also came to realize that different people can have different interpretations of whether true dialogue had existed in the same context. I have always used the word *dialogue* in a rather monolithic way, assuming that we each would agree when dialogue has occurred. But, apparently, each person who participates in a conversation may not have the same view of dialogue.

The women of color seemed to be the least satisfied class members in terms of the productive nature of the class discussion. Some of the African-American women said that they felt that people characterized them as angry and hostile when they had expressed their views in earlier classes. They felt that their cultural manner of speaking was easily misinterpreted. They felt that a white student could make virtually the same comment without being considered hostile.

B told me that she felt that many of the white students were tuning out the race conversations because they did not feel it was about them. Her comment was based on observing the faces of the white students in the classroom. I actually thought that the white students were *very* interested in observing the intraracial dialogue in the classroom. But I was mostly looking at the faces of the people who were speaking, not the white students. So I do not know what she saw when she looked at their faces during class.

A Latina woman, K, was very disappointed with the class discussions, because she felt that they were very bipolar racially—either black or white—without consideration of other racial subgroups. One of the African-American women would often add "and other people of color" to her comments, but K clearly did not feel comfortable with those statements. She usually kept silent (with a red face) during class and vented her frustration to me in my office. I wanted her to talk more but knew it was not appropriate to force her to be a "token." Looking back, I think that I should have taken more responsibility for expressing her point of view. I should not have expected her, alone, to challenge the bipolar nature of the race discussions.

All in all, I thought this was my most successful feminist jurisprudence class because of the probing, honest discussions that we had about race, gender, and sexual orientation. I learned to be more pragmatic in my choice of teaching styles and developed more tools to facilitate trust in the classroom. The student evaluations seemed to parallel my own view. Some of the students, however, offered constructive suggestions, which follow and which will probably help me modify my practice further in the future.

- I like the format (or lack of format) of class discussion but would have welcomed experimentation in different class formats. . . . I would also like to use the energy of the class to come up with some practical suggestions for legal education reform and perhaps submit them to the school/other schools to start the dialogue.
- The class participation format worked well, but I wished you would have interjected more.
- You had a lot more to offer—I read your articles. I wanted to see that in class, though I understood the "idea" behind not taking on "authority" role.
- Focus more on gender/homophobia issues to create an equal balance with race issues. Keep paper presentations from students but maybe ask each to discuss more than their views on a book. . . . Is there a book of exercises for groups to help explore the issues?
- To maximize learning of students, have them pick a topic that they know very little about or have opposite views on; for example, whites presenting black issues; straights presenting gay issues; women presenting male issues.
- With regard to pedagogy, the format of the class was not successful, because the class resulted in a black/white discussion. I would suggest that Professor Colker take a more active role in the class discussions. The wealth of her knowledge was barely tapped. . . . The greatest disappointment was the class's inability to go beyond the "me" experience to elevate the discussion to a theoretical level. The readings were great. I would suggest adding a writing by a Hispanic woman such as Andalzúa.
- Possibly we could have broken into small groups at the beginning (first hour) and met with the whole group later. Each minigroup could deal with a different issue.
- The method of student-led discussion was good but did not involve all the class. We seemed to have experts on our various subjects.
- Some other approaches I can think of are—the instructor meeting with the weekly discussion leaders to help focus discussion. . . . What about an

exercise in taking on perspectives? Such as having every perspective the class wants to encompass represented every week—someone speaks for a foreigner, an aged person, a child, a hetero, a homo, a differently abled. Of course, the perspectives would be endless—but an exercise in forcing people to take on varying perspectives.

There were quite varied views on using MacKinnon's scholarship.

- MacKinnon should be read first.
- I think that "A Feminist Theory of the State" should be utilized in a course such as this and was happy that it was.
- We could have omitted MacKinnon's work.
- I did not like Catharine MacKinnon.

Based on these written comments and the private comments in my office, I think I will try to speak up more in the future while still not dominating. The students seemed to particularly enjoy when I gave them background on an author or placed the work in a theoretical context. I also agree with the Latina student who thought I could have helped the class move beyond a black/white discussion of racial issues. I knew that some of the Latina students were uncomfortable with the black/white polarity of the class, but I was waiting for them to say something about it. As one of them told me in her paper, they did not want to take on that responsibility and felt silenced when they tried to criticize the black/white polarity. As a white person and a professor, I could have made that point in a way that would have been heard. Thus, there may be times when I can and should use my authority to help unsilence some of my students.

I did have one successful experience with helping a student break out of his silence in the classroom, which gave me more insight into how to give students more voice in the classroom. A black South African student had told me privately that he did not feel comfortable contributing to the class discussion, because he had nothing to say about the United States experience, since it was so different from his own. I was very surprised by his comment, since it seemed to me to be so obvious that, as a South African, he would have a great deal to say about race and class oppression. I privately talked to the students who were leading the next class discussion and asked them to try to get him involved by asking him some questions about his experience. In addition, I told the South African student that we would very much value his participation. That tactic worked; the student spoke for the first time. Unfortunately, it was already the last class, so we did not get to benefit from his comments throughout the semester. It provided me with a lesson in how my intervention can be helpful; in the future, I should be more mindful of when such intervention is necessary.

Now that the class is over, I have some perspective on it. I find myself frequently commenting to people about how extraordinary a class it was. The class was extraordinary, in large part, because of the students who self-selected the class. By the end of the semester, I realized that the Caucasian students were actually a minority in the class, which made the classroom a great space for interracial as well as intraracial discussions. There were also a large number of openly lesbian and gay students, as well as a couple of students who, like myself, identify as bisexual. Although not everyone in the class were good friends with each other, there were clearly many discussions going on after class ended. On some level, the classroom became an extension of people's lives. I learned a great deal from my students and find some of their ideas creeping into my most recent scholarship. So it was unquestionably a good learning experience for me and, from the papers I read, a good learning experience for most of the students. Many of them wrote quite original and thoughtful papers.

In thinking about how I might replicate this class experience at my new law school, the University of Pittsburgh, I realize that much of what made the class so successful had little to do with my pedagogical style. The diversity of the class allowed us to have wrenching and probing discussions. At Pitt, I expect my classroom to be mostly comprised of straight, white, female students. In that atmosphere, no matter what pedagogical tools I choose, it will not be possible to replicate these discussions. This experience, therefore, has made me realize that it is not enough for us to choose good pedagogical tools within the classroom, but we also need to be vigilant outside the classroom to try to diversify our classes. We should not think of the classroom as an isolated place but instead see it as part of the larger social framework in which we are teaching.

IV. Conclusion

Sometimes teaching from a feminist perspective seems to constitute an occupational hazard. Even the slightest incorporation of feminist principles into classroom discussions is met with confusion at best and with suspicion or disgust at worst. I have found that the classroom context is important in determining to what extent to employ feminist teaching methodologies. For example, while a large, first-year civil procedure class might not be the best place to adopt a nonhierarchical approach, I found it possible to employ nontraditional examples in the discussions. On the other hand, I found that the small size of my feminist jurisprudence elective, coupled with the nature of its subject matter, makes it possible for me both to adopt a relatively nonhierarchical method and to foster openness. This in turn fosters the trust necessary to engage in full and frank discussion.

I have also found that the generally accepted "canons" of feminist teaching need to be reconsidered and that such canons are not always necessary or appropriate either for teaching from a feminist perspective or for conveying feminist principles. My own experiences in varied situations have taught me that some approaches that may be successful in, for example, a small feminist jurisprudence class, may be either unfeasible or counterproductive in a large, required class. While teaching from a feminist perspective is appropriate in all of these situations, the procedures involved may differ accordingly.

Notes

1. Catharine MacKinnon, *From Practice to Theory, or What Is a White Woman Anyway?*, 4 Yale J. L. & Feminism 13, 13 (1992).

2. Another impetus for thinking about those questions was that I was recently asked if I would be willing to be considered as a dean candidate at a law school. For the first time, I confronted the question not only of how could I be a better feminist in the classroom but also how could I help shape the institution itself into a more feminist environment? In addition, how could I complete this task within the monetary and institutional restraints of the law school environment? These are questions that are beyond the scope of this essay. (I withdrew from the dean search process.)

3. Patricia Williams, The Alchemy of Race and Rights: Diary of a Law Professor (Harvard 1991).

4. *Id* at 12.

5. *Id*. at 13.

6. For further discussion of this problem, see Ruth Colker, *The Female Body and the Law: On Truth and Lies*, 99 Yale L. J. 1159 (1990).

7. Williams, *supra* note 3, at 17.

8. *Id*. at 17.

9. *Id*. at 14.

10. Morrison Torrey, Jackie Casey, and Karin Olson, *Teaching Law in a Feminist Manner*, 13 Harv. Women's L. J. 87 (1990).

11. At the time, I was a full-time trial attorney at the Department of Justice. I believe that George Washington University may have paid me $2,000 to teach this course. I had to put together my own materials and teach twice a week in the evening. I was thinking about going into law teaching (or trying to obtain a position at a women's studies department) and thought that this experience would help me decide. In fact, it is amazing that I decided to go into teaching on a full-time basis, despite this experience.

12. Ruth Colker, *Marriage*, 3 Yale J. L. & Feminism 321 (1991).

13. Adrienne Rich, *Compulsory Heterosexuality and Lesbian Experience*, in Powers of Desire: The Politics of Sexuality 177 (Ann Snitow et al. eds., 1983).

14. Ruthann Robson, Lesbian (Out)Law: Survival under the Rule of Law (1992).

3

The Practice of Writing

The struggle now is how to prevent [Mary Joe Frug's] death from being a
premature closure of the work she was pursuing, how to carry on without one of
our most exciting and challenging feminist legal theorists. The post-modern talk
of "ruptures" and "prying apart crevices" has a horrible, violent ring to me; but
we must not let Mary Joe Frug's death stand as the ultimate rejection of her
position in a discussion that must, somehow, continue.

—Frances Olsen[1]

I. Introduction

IN THE TWO previous chapters, I discussed my practice of law and my teaching.
Another aspect of my "practice" is my academic writing. When I decided to
go to law school, I did not expect to become a legal academic. In fact, I disdained
much of that kind of work, because it seemed too disconnected from the world
of practice. I therefore took a job as a trial lawyer immediately upon graduating
from law school and thought that kind of work would be the focus of my life.

To my surprise, however, I soon found that I was combining the practice of
law with academic writing, because my practice was revealing injustices to me
that I wanted to share with the public. Thus, in one of my first articles "Pornography and Privacy",[2] I shared my frustration of trying to help women like Linda
Lovelace who were allegedly portrayed sexually without their consent. I attempted
to explain the lack of legal remedies from a theoretical perspective. In my next
couple of articles in this area, I tried to suggest new statutory language that
could remedy this problem. My legal writing typically stemmed from my practice, although I often worried that its theoretical tone might make it inaccessible
to the many readers whom I wanted to reach.

Not all of my writing, however, has stemmed directly from my practice of
law. Some of it has been for the purpose of simply exploring theoretical ideas.
Although I am less confident about the value of such writing, it is ironically the
writing that has received the most attention by the academic world. Is that because I am saying what people want to hear, I often wonder? Is pure theory val-

ued over theory-practice work because the latter is so useless politically? These are difficult questions to which I have no easy answer. My current goal is to make my theory pieces as practical as possible, even if they do not directly relate to cases. I try to think carefully about the usefulness of a theory piece before accepting an invitation to write one. (I almost never write a theory piece unless it is solicited.)

In this chapter, I self-consciously describe writing a theory piece that I was invited to contribute to the *Harvard Law Review*. It was called "The Example of Lesbians."[3] I will try to show how I used this invitation to write a theory piece to educate my readers about the practical implications of an anti-essentialist perspective. Despite this political goal, however, I am not sure that I did succeed in really helping many readers move their interest in theory to a more practical plain.

The theoretical nature of this essay was not something I chose. In the fall of 1991, I received a telephone call from the *Harvard Law Review* asking me to contribute an essay to a symposium on Professor Mary Joe Frug's final manuscript. She had been working on the manuscript when she took what turned out to be a tragic evening walk on April 4, 1991—she was murdered while on that walk. The manuscript was entitled "A Postmodern Feminist Legal Manifesto".[4] The editors of the *Harvard Law Review* decided to publish the manuscript as an unfinished work and solicit brief responses from several feminists—Barbara Johnson, Martha Minow, and myself. The manuscript represented Mary Joe's attempt to reconcile feminism and postmodernism. As my description of its thesis describes, it was a highly theoretical manuscript, although she used some concrete examples to further her thesis.

Despite my disenchantment with writing theory pieces, it did not take me long to accept the *Harvard Law Review's* invitation. I had been very upset by Mary Joe's death and hoped that writing an essay on her work would help me deal with her death. I also thought that writing about her work would help her live in our memories. In addition, I was flattered by the invitation and thought it would be good for me professionally to write such an essay. Finally, I saw this invitation as having a lot of potential political mileage, despite the theoretical nature of Mary Joe's work. I had essentially been given a blank check by the *Harvard Law Review*. I wanted to use that opportunity to further my own political agenda.

Upon accepting this invitation, I therefore asked myself the political question, What should I do with the space that the *Harvard Law Review* had allotted to me? A friend of mine, Richard Delgado, had once said to me that the *Harvard Law Review* needed to ask a lesbian or gay man to write an article from a lesbian or gay perspective, as it had previously asked a woman to write an article from a feminist perspective and an African-American man to write a foreword from a civil rights perspective. We both looked forward to the day when such an invitation would occur.

I remembered Richard's remark when I got the telephone call from the *Harvard Law Review*. The *Law Review* was certainly not calling me because of their desire to publish an essay from a lesbian or gay perspective, since I had published virtually nothing on that topic. Nevertheless, they had handed me a blank check. I figured that call—asking me to write a twenty-page essay—was the closest that I, or any other lesbian, gay, or bisexual person, would get to being asked to write an article for the publication. I therefore decided to accept the invitation and to try to use the word *lesbian* in the title—figuring that the *Harvard Law Review* had never published an article with the word *lesbian* in the title in its one-hundred-five-year history.

My own scholarship had been moving in the direction of being very interested in the anti-essentialist critique. This critique was not widely accepted within legal academia but, in my view, was very powerful in allowing us to focus on the lives of the most disadvantaged women in our society. I hoped that if I could give the reader a concrete example of how to apply an anti-essentialist perspective, I could help make that perspective more acceptable in academia. Thus, I made two political decisions: I would write from an anti-essentialist perspective, and I would apply that perspective to the concrete example of lesbians.

That political decision was not made in isolation from Mary Joe Frug's manuscript. As a postmodernist, Mary Joe was very interested in an anti-essentialist perspective. I believe that she would have appreciated my efforts to apply that perspective to her manuscript. In addition, there was a very intriguing sentence in Mary Joe's essay in which she talked about lesbians, but the sentence broke off without being finished. Her husband told me that the sentence was incomplete because she was writing it when she took her fatal walk.[5] Thus, by taking her analysis and applying it to lesbians, I was very much furthering her own thoughts as well as adding depth to her remarks. Had Mary Joe been able to finish her manuscript, she may have made many of the observations that I make in the essay.

The following synopsis and examination of her thesis explain what I learned when I applied an anti-essentialist perspective to Mary Joe's manuscript. The reader can decide whether I achieved my political goals by publishing these conclusions in the *Harvard Law Review*. Because the following discussion is "academic," I will also distance myself from it a bit by referring to Mary Joe as Professor Frug. It was Mary Joe's life as Professor Frug that I discussed in the pages of the *Harvard Law Review*.

When applied to Professor Frug's manuscript, an anti-essentialist perspec-

tive reveals that many of the generalizations she made about women are not accurate when applied to various subgroups of women, such as lesbians. Professor
Frug's central thesis was that law constructs the female body in three ways—by
permitting and sometimes mandating the sexualization, terrorization, and maternalization of the female body. To establish this thesis, she focused on prostitution, family and work, sexuality, and the anti-pornography movement. She had
intended to apply these observations to the abortion rights movement as well.
By applying an anti-essentialist perspective, I found that many of the rules that
Professor Frug described as having a negative sexualizing, maternalizing, or terrorizing effect on some heterosexual women had an enhanced or different effect
on some lesbians. (Lesbians, of course, are not homogeneous. An anti-essentialist perspective requires that we explore differences among lesbians as well as
differences between lesbians and heterosexual women.) In some cases, these
rules had a similar effect on lesbians and heterosexual women, but whereas that
effect was detrimental to heterosexual women, it improved the lives of some lesbians. Nevertheless, the application of an anti-essentialist perspective strengthened Professor Frug's central observation that society constructs women's bodies.
This perspective reveals that legal rules simultaneously have disparate effects
on various groups of women but still reinforce a single definition of "femininity."
Sojourner Truth's famous response, "Ain't I a Woman?,"[6] when confronted with
stereotypes about women's fragility that did not apply to her as an African-
American woman, should remind us that certain women have always been left
out of the category "female" in order for other women to be socialized as female.
Lesbians, the subject of my essay, are but one example of women who traditionally
have been left out of the category "female."

II. Sexualization, Terrorization, and Maternalization

A. Sexualization

The laws relating to prostitution, Professor Frug argued, sexualize the female body by leaving women concerned that they are acting like whores.[7] Women's
attractiveness to men comes, in part, from their acting a little like a whore but
not too much like one. In addition, she argued that prostitution rules, as well as
rules governing the family and social violence, sexualize women by leading them
to believe that they must be sexually monogamous. These arguments were premised on the assumption that all sex workers are heterosexual and that all women
are being sexualized into exclusive, monogamous heterosexuality. By "sexualization," Professor Frug apparently meant "heterosexualization," thereby not
sufficiently recognizing lesbian existence in the construction of her arguments.

Heterosexual women are socialized to make themselves attractive to men, and so they need to be concerned about the whore stereotype. Some lesbians, however, do not orient themselves toward men's standards for attractiveness and sexuality. (I say some lesbians, because there are many lesbians who try to pass as heterosexuals by dressing in a particular "feminine" manner. Other lesbians who are "out of the closet" also dress in ways that conform to societal norms of femininity and attractiveness. My comments best describe the lesbian who is out of the closet and not trying to conform to societal norms.) Lesbians receive a different message from prostitution rules than do heterosexual women, because for lesbians, these rules are part of a larger social order that disapproves of *all of their sexual activity*. If lesbians are sex workers, like heterosexual women, they are criminals. But even if lesbians are not sex workers, their private sexual activities may still make them criminals, unlike heterosexual women.[8] No desired sexual activity is acceptable for a lesbian, irrespective of whether she is a sex worker. Prostitution laws highlight the existence and desirability of a certain type of heterosexuality, while sodomy laws, along with other regulations, hide the existence and desirability of virtually all lesbian sexual activity. Other regulations that hide the existence and desirability of lesbian sexual activity include military regulations that force lesbians to remain closeted[9] and child custody laws that coerce lesbians to hide their sexual orientation in order to attain or retain custody of their children.[10]

Professor Frug's discussion of the sexualization of sex workers was baffling, because she apparently had the stories of lesbian sex workers in front of her when she was writing her essay. (When I refer to lesbians who are sex workers, I am referring to women who sexually arouse men for compensation while choosing women as their sexual partners for uncompensated sex. Although there are women who sell sex to other women and choose women as their partners for uncompensated sex, I do not discuss such women in this chapter. Many of the observations that I make could also apply to them, since both their public and private sex lives are illegal. Nevertheless, their situation is unique, because they do not depend on men for any sexual activity.) For example, she referred to "one sex worker's description of the discomfort she experienced because she sexually responded to her customer during an act of prostitution."[11] Frug concluded that "[h]er orgasm in those circumstances broke down a distinction she sought to maintain between her work and the sexual pleasure she obtained from her non-work-related sexual activity."[12]

A closer reading of the passage, however, reveals that Frug failed to recognize the sex worker's sexual preference. The sex worker to whom Frug referred, Judy Edelstein, described herself as a Jewish, lesbian feminist.[13] After describing her discomfort with having been sexually aroused by one of her customers, she said: "I just can't believe that I had an orgasm with that jerk. I try to forget him, to think about making love with Laura, the woman I'm with right now. But all I can see is the customer's all-American face."[14] Frug interpreted Edelstein's discomfort as a work/nonwork discomfort, but it could also have been a heterosexual/lesbian discomfort. I suspect that Edelstein might have been uncomfortable with experiencing sexual pleasure with any man, irrespective of whether he had compensated her for the sexual activity. (I make this statement, because Edelstein does not describe herself as a bisexual.)[15] Edelstein did not seem to be concerned that her whore image from work would intrude into her private life. Instead, she seemed to want to experience her work life as nonsexual, even if the man was receiving sexual pleasure from her. Sex was what she enjoyed with her female lover; work was what she did with men for compensation. I agree with Professor Frug that Edelstein describes her discomfort with being considered a "whore" in her paid employment. That discomfort may have eventually led her to leave the life of a sex worker. By inducing her to leave, however, society has not induced her to embrace a more acceptable lifestyle of exclusive, heterosexual monogamy.

Rather than sexualizing Edelstein toward heterosexuality, the laws criminalizing prostitution aided in desexualizing Edelstein. Both her public life—providing sexual services while giving massages—and her private life—lesbianism—were illegal. Law discouraged her from engaging in either activity. Contrary to Professor Frug's thesis, the law criminalizing prostitution did not serve to construct her sexuality in a way that society finds desirable.

While prostitution rules may not heterosexualize lesbians, other rules may. Professor Frug argued that our marriage laws and social rules concerning violence induce women to choose heterosexuality. Marriage law is structured as a potential source of financial support for women, making it a plausible substitute or supplement to employment. Social violence, Frug argued, induces women to stay married by leading them to rely on individual men—their husbands—for protection against violence.[16] (I am actually not convinced by Professor Frug's comments about physical security. Given the level of violence against women within the family, it is hard to see how a woman generally benefits physically by living with a man, even if he can serve as a male escort for her.)

Lesbians are not immune from the effects of these rules. They must choose lesbianism in spite of rather than because of these rules. Some lesbians may have relationships with men, despite their inclinations, in order to obtain the benefits of financial security and safety.[17] Anecdotally, I have always found it interesting to see how many women who identify themselves as lesbians (but not bisexuals) have also had serious relationships with men, including marriage. That pattern seems far less true of men who identify themselves as gay. Perhaps this sex difference is the result of women having greater incentives than men to try to be comfortable or happy in heterosexual relationships. Although Professor Frug suggested that it is hard to know how current sexual practices would change if legal rules with respect to sexual conduct changed, I think it is easy to predict. At a minimum, many more women would seek sexual relations with other women. In other words, given the strength of the rules that Professor Frug described, it is surprising that any woman would "choose" lesbianism over the benefits that Professor Frug described for heterosexual women. Not surprisingly, few women find themselves able to live out such a choice within a powerful system of rules favoring heterosexuality, monogamy, and passivity.

So how do lesbians manage to defy the powerful force of these rules that Frug described? As I have discussed elsewhere, the answer lies partly in the "cracks in the wall" of patriarchy.[18] For example, being a sex worker while also being a lesbian may have been a part of Judy Edelstein's strategy for survival within a patriarchal world, because it enabled her to use men to acquire financial security while not conforming her private life to heterosexual norms. The occupation of sex worker may, for some women, serve as a crack in the wall, while for other women, it may serve as a form of subordination and exploitation. By considering the socialization of lesbian sexuality along with the socialization of heterosexual sexuality, we can better understand the full scope of society's construction of the female body and develop law reform strategies to open the cracks wider for a broader range of women.

B. Terrorization

Prostitution rules, Professor Frug argued, also endanger sex workers' lives and make their work terrifying. Thus, Professor Frug argued that women are induced to choose marriage rather than prostitution. There are two problems with this argument, both of which reflect an inattention to lesbian existence.

First, as I discussed with respect to sexualization, lesbians always face terrorization, because both their private and public lives are typically illegal. Moreover, lesbians face the special dangers of violence against lesbian and gay people, irrespective of whether they are prostitutes. The terrorization that a lesbian faces as a prostitute is therefore not a unique problem in her life. A heterosexual prostitute, however, may find prostitution to be a more dangerous activity than marriage. The differential rate of terrorization in the public and private life of a heterosexual prostitute may therefore act as a stronger deterrent to considering prostitution for her than for a lesbian. The existence of prostitution despite terrorization may be best explained by understanding how society makes the lives of certain undesirable women (e.g., lesbians, poor women, women of color) so dangerous that the terrorization inherent in prostitution is an acceptable added danger.

Second, Professor Frug would have better understood the terrorization element in all prostitutes' lives if she had investigated sodomy statutes—an area of the law that is often thought to be inapplicable to heterosexual activity—along with prostitution regulations. (Frug listed six areas of the law that serve to terrorize prostitutes without listing sodomy statutes.) Sodomy statutes permit the state to enhance the penalty for prostitution by also bringing a sodomy prosecution,[19] despite the fact that sodomy (e.g., oral sex) is often safer sex than unprotected intercourse for a female prostitute and her client in terms of potential HIV infection.[20] Although sodomy statutes are an important aspect of the terrorization that many prostitutes face, they are rarely a part of feminist law reform discussions with respect to prostitution. Unfortunately, a heterosexual perspective makes it easy to overlook the impact of an area of the law that is normally associated with lesbian and gay sexual activity rather than heterosexual activity.

C. Maternalization

Finally, Professor Frug described how prostitution rules, work rules, and family law rules maternalize women. Nevertheless, many of these rules have a dematernalization effect on lesbians. In one area, family law, some rules do maternalize some lesbians. Unlike other women, however, this maternalization effect on lesbians may often be beneficial rather than harmful. A key difference between lesbians and heterosexual women is the application of the maternal stereotype. Heterosexual women are viewed as presumptively maternal, whereas lesbians are viewed as unable and unsuitable to bear children. For example, I once shared with a male colleague the fact that I was considering pregnancy. At the time, I was intimately involved with a woman. My colleague was shocked at the idea that I could get pregnant. He seemed to assume that my involvement with a woman had destroyed my biological capacity to bear children. Since I have become intimately involved with a man, however, no one has reacted with surprise at my pregnancies. Somehow, my uterus was figuratively returned when my sexual partner changed from a woman to a man. Similarly, when I have debated lesbian and gay rights issues, my opponent has often assumed that the only way a lesbian could attain custody of a child was through adoption. I find myself needing to point out that lesbians can also attain custody of children through childbirth.

The law goes to great lengths to separate lesbians and gay men from children. For example, even jurisdictions such as Denmark that have begun to recognize lesbian and gay marriage through a registered partnership act, have withheld the benefits of adoption to "married" gay couples.[21] When Massachusetts passed a gay rights statute, opponents of the statute argued that lesbian and gay people should not be able to use the statute in order to adopt children. A compromise was eventually reached when an amendment was added that precluded anyone from adopting a child if their sexual orientation would be "an obstacle to the psychological, or physical well-being of the child."[22] Finally, the legislatures in New Hampshire and Florida have passed legislation barring lesbians and gay men from adopting children.[23] Similarly, our laws and rules with respect to artificial insemination have historically restricted lesbians from eligibility.[24]

Another source of the dematernalization of lesbians is our family-based, workplace rules—rules that Professor Frug described as maternalizing women. Professor Frug argued that discrimination against women in the workplace makes it more likely that women will leave the workplace to raise and care for children, thereby maternalizing women. Other family-based workplace rules, however, dematernalize lesbians, not because they discriminate against women generally but because they discriminate on the basis of sexual orientation. For example, employer-based health insurance is made available exclusively on a family and class basis, and the lesbian family is excluded from recognition and coverage. (I say class basis, because Professor Frug's description of workplace rules typically describes rules that affect middle-class workers who are able to obtain benefits like health insurance. Workers who receive few, if any, job-related benefits would not be maternalized by many of the rules described by Professor Frug.) Thus, it is more difficult for a middle-class lesbian couple to afford to bear and raise a child than for a middle-class heterosexual couple. Our health insurance rules make it financially feasible for some heterosexual women to leave the workplace to raise children while retaining coverage on their husband's plan and make it financially difficult for a lesbian to make a comparable choice.

Family law rules, however, sometimes serve to maternalize lesbians, as well as heterosexual women. Frug assumed that maternalization through legal rules is always bad for women, but for lesbians, that maternalization could be beneficial. For example, Frug argued that it is harmful for women to be maternalized through rules that favor women's parenting roles, as, for example, the "tender years presumption." (Under the tender years presumption, courts assume that it would be in the best interest of a young child to be placed with his or her mother.) But for lesbians, who often face nonmaternal stereotypes in the courtroom,[25] it might be helpful if legal rules would presume that they can be good parents. For example, when Barbara Diehl, a lesbian, sought custody and visitation rights of her child, the court applied a reverse tender years presumption against her. The judge stated that because of the child's "tender years, I feel it is in her best interest not to be exposed to a lesbian relationship." (The court of appeals overturned the restrictions on visitation but affirmed award of custody to the father.)[26] If the maternal presumption were applied to lesbians, it might make it easier for them to undermine the courts' stereotypes with respect to their fitness. Without that presumption, they are simply, like prostitutes, unwelcome criminals.

III. Application to Law Reform: The Anti-pornography Campaign and the Abortion Rights Movement

An anti-essentialist perspective can also help us to develop effective law reform strategies. Professor Frug made the connection between the theoretical and the practical by showing how her thesis applies to the MacKinnon/Dworkin anti-pornography campaign. She hoped that examining the ordinance campaign closely would help "advance the prospects of an abortion reform effort that the Supreme Court might thrust upon us."[27]

One familiar criticism of the ordinance effort, she argued, is the alliance between feminist ordinance advocates and nonfeminist conservatives. Frug, however, claimed that this alliance was positive, because it "successfully engaged nonfeminist political camps."[28] She acknowledged that this engagement came at the expense of feminist unity but "that breaching this unity is a necessary component of feminist efforts against women's oppressions."[29]

Clearly, coalition building is important in any political campaign. However, Professor Frug did not sufficiently probe the basis of the political differences in the anti-pornography ordinance campaign. Among the feminist critics of the ordinance were lesbians who voiced concerns that the ordinance's broad definition of pornography would limit their ability to experiment with new forms of sexuality through the use of pornographic materials.[30] They argued that women have been socialized to be sexually passive and therefore to partake only in what was described as "vanilla" (or bland) sexual behavior. Within a lesbian relationship, where both partners have been socialized female, that problem can be quite acute. Hence, these critics feared that the "Vanilla-Sex Gestapo"[31] would try to encourage lesbians to be even more sexually passive.

Although Professor Frug attributed this disagreement to differences in postmodern philosophy, that is not accurate. As postmodernists, the critics understood that the images of sexuality they might create with their own pornography might help transform women to escape vanilla sex.[32] They wanted to use pornography constructively. Because they were a distinct and invisible feminist minority that had come forward to raise specific objections, the ordinance organizers had an obligation to listen to them and compromise in order to overcome an essentialist understanding of women's views concerning pornography. It was especially important for the feminist proponents to consider the views of the feminist critics, because the critics agreed with the basic postmodern premise of the movement—that pornography can have a transformative effect on society.

An instructive analogy can be found in the abortion rights movement. For more than a decade, African-American feminists have been saying that the abortion rights movement has not been speaking to their concerns;[33] that pro-choice leaders have not been giving sufficient attention to forced sterilization, lack of prenatal care, lack of support for children in poverty, and other policies that limit the choices of poor women. For example, white feminists did not respond with much of an outcry when *Harris v. McRae*[34] was decided, and yet we can anticipate a feminist riot if *Roe v. Wade*[35] is overturned. Instead of addressing the full range of choices in women's lives, the abortion rights movement has narrowly focused on the single issue of the formal right to "choose" an abortion, ignoring issues of affordability.[36] It is not enough for the movement's leadership to acknowledge splintering among women on the abortion issue. Instead, feminists need to ask whether particular groups of disadvantaged women have been left out of the feminist union because of the essentialist way that the priorities of the movement have been constructed.

Professor Frug also argued that the ordinance campaign should have sought to deconstruct pornography rather than destroy it. She criticized the campaign for being too male in its language and rhetorical style. This final observation by Professor Frug brings her in seeming agreement with the feminist critics. Both were trying to open up the discussion of pornography beyond the simplified picture offered by the ordinance advocates. Unfortunately, the feminist critics often used highly dichotomized and hierarchical arguments in expressing their views. But one might argue that they had no choice—it is difficult to respond to a male style of argumentation in a female style.[37]

What, then, is the appropriate lesson for the abortion rights movement? One lesson that I have been trying to develop in my own work is to learn how to talk about the abortion issue in a less dichotomized way. We need to consider, for example, how "choice" and "life" are not bipolar opposites. Women who choose abortions or choose to forego medical intervention during their pregnancies often make those choices out of a respect for life, including the lives of themselves, their families, and their future children.[38] I hope that Professor Frug's manuscript will inspire us to find ways to join in public debates in less polarized ways than we have in the anti-pornography and abortion rights movements.

IV. Conclusion

Professor Frug's manuscript has helped me see more clearly how legal doc-trine constructs women's bodies by sexualizing, terrorizing, and maternalizing them. Other feminists have focused on one or the other of these issues, but no one has brought them together so completely in one work. Rather than being a "linchpin" theorist, she has helped us see the variety of ways that women's sub-ordination is maintained and constructed through law. My critique of her work reflects my concern with the extent to which she deviated from her original in-tention—to provide us with a "localized disruption" rather than a total theory.[39] Many of the rules that she described have an opposing or enhanced effect on lesbians. By exploring the diversity of women's experiences more fully before making generalizations about the effects of legal rules on women's lives, we may get a sharper image of how female socialization actually operates. Certain women are oversocialized as female, while other women are kept out of the category altogether. It is through this combination of effects that socialization tries to steer women toward femininity.

Those are the academic conclusions that I drew about Mary Joe's manu-script in the pages of the *Harvard Law Review*. I still wonder whether those aca-demic conclusions furthered my practice. My misgivings arise on several dif-ferent levels.

First, I worry about the practical insights that I offered in this essay. Despite my anti-essentialist perspective, I worry that my writing suffered from overgen-eralizations or inaccuracies about lesbians. This was not like writing for a spe-cialty journal; I could not expect my editors to have any expertise on the issues I discussed. In addition, I could not expect that they would publish numerous responses to my article if it were filled with inaccuracies or controversial state-ments (as did the *Harvard Women's Law Journal* when I published there). In many ways, I felt like I was writing in a vacuum and might unconsciously further stereotypes and generalizations about the very people whom I was trying to help. When I practice law, I can get feedback on my anti-essentialist perspective from my clients. I can ask them whether I have properly described a problem or dilemma they may be experiencing in their lives. In an academic setting, it is much harder to get such "real-world" feedback.

Second, I worry about how accessible or interesting my conclusions were to many readers. Mary Joe set the stage for me through her use of words like "ter-rorization" and "maternalization." By incorporating her terminology, I may have simply continued an unreadable, detached exercise. In the future, I might try to strive for a more readable text, less filled with jargon.

Finally, I continue to wonder about the overall usefulness of such an exercise in the pages of the *Harvard Law Review*. Earlier in this book, I commented that writers like Betty Friedan seem to be particularly popular because they do not challenge the essentialist fundamentals of our social policy. By writing in a theoretical genre, I, too, may have assimilated myself to a nonthreatening style of discourse. I can rationalize this assimilation by noting that I was self-consciously anti-essentialist, which I believe is inherently threatening. Nevertheless, the theoretical style may have been so limiting that my particular choice of perspective made little difference.

Despite these misgivings, I would probably accept the invitation again tomorrow if it were offered to me. I think there was political benefit in simply having the title, "The Example of Lesbians," appear in the pages of the *Harvard Law Review*. Writing the essay also caused me to reflect more on lesbian, gay, and bisexual issues, making me more determined to have those issues more central to my scholarship in the future. Thus, I decided to use more examples from gay rights issues in this book (in contrast to my last book, which had virtually none); I decided to use an invitation to speak at Yale Law School to raise issues involving bisexuals; and I ultimately decided to write an entire book on bisexual jurisprudence (my next book project after this one). The ultimate benefit of writing the essay for the *Harvard Law Review* is that I educated myself about the blindness of my own scholarship. I came to see that I, like Mary Joe, needed to devote more scholarly attention to issues involving the gay, lesbian, and bisexual communities. Ultimately, I suppose that I wrote for myself, and I learned a lot about the limitations of my own prior scholarship in trying to identify some of the limitations of Mary Joe's scholarship. If the essay was useful in that way alone, I think it was worth doing.

Notes

1. Frances Olsen, *In Memoriam: Mary Joe Frug*, 14 Harv. Women's L. J. i, vii (1991).
2. Ruth Colker, *Pornography and Privacy: Towards the Development of a Group Based Theory for Sex Based Intrusions of Privacy* 2 Law & Inequality: A Journal of Theory and Practice 191 (1983).
3. Ruth Colker, *The Example of Lesbians: A Posthumous Reply to Professor Mary Joe Frug*, 105 Harv. L. Rev. 1084 (1992).

4. Mary Joe Frug, *A Postmodern Feminist Legal Manifesto (An Unfinished Draft)*, 105 Harv. L. Rev. 1045 (1992).

5. *See* Letter from Gerald E. Frug, Professor of Law, Harvard Law School, to Ruth Colker, Professor of Law, Tulane University (Nov. 13, 1991) (on file at the Harvard Law School library).

6. Elizabeth V. Spelman, Inessential Woman: Problems of Exclusion in Feminist Thought 14 (1988) (quoting Sojourner Truth).

7. *See* Frug, *supra* note 4, at 1052.

8. *See, e.g.*, Bowers v. Hardwick, 478 U.S. 186 (1986) (upholding constitutionality of Georgia's sodomy statute as applied to private consensual behavior of homosexuals, including lesbians). The Georgia sodomy statute, like most sodomy statutes, could be applied against heterosexuals who engage in anal or oral sex; however, prosecutions of heterosexuals never occur with regard to private, consensual sex. (Private sex does not include prostitution.) Thus, the United States Supreme Court in *Bowers* did not reach the issue of whether the Georgia statute could have constitutionally been applied against heterosexuals.

9. *See* Michelle Benecke & Kirstin Dodge, *Recent Developments, Military Women in Nontraditional Job Fields: Casualties of the Armed Forces War on Homosexuals*, 13 Harv. Women's L. J. 215, 234–38 (1990).

10. *See* Nan D. Hunter & Nancy D. Polikoff, *Custody Rights of Lesbian Mothers: Legal Theory and Litigation Strategy*, 25 Buffalo L. Rev. 691, 714–15 (1976); Annamay T. Sheppard, *Lesbian Mothers II: Long Night's Journey into Day*, 8 Women's Rts. L. Rep. 219, 241–43 (1985).

11. *See* Frug, *supra* note 4, at 1053 n.7.

12. *Id.* at 1053 n.7.

13. *See* Judy Edelstein, *Contributors' Notes*, in Sex Work: Writings by Women in the Sex Industry 341 (Frédérique Delacoste and Priscilla Alexander eds., 1987) [hereinafter "Sex Work"].

14. *Id.* at 62, 63.

15. *See Id.* at 341.

16. *See* Frug, *supra* note 4, at 1062–64.

17. Professor Frug left us with an incomplete sentence when she turned to the example of lesbians, but she clearly understood that economic and safety incentives "make a male partner more advantageous for non-sexual reasons than a same-sex partner for women." See Frug, *supra* note 4, at 1066.

18. *See* Ruth Colker, *Feminist Consciousness and the State: A Basis for Cautious Optimism*, 90 Colum. L. Rev. 1146, 1160–61 (1990) (book review).

19. *See, e.g.*, State of Louisiana v. Neal, 500 So.2d 374, 376 (La. 1987) (affirming a conviction of the codefendant for a crime against nature and prostitution).

20. Oral sex, without a condom, is not "safe sex," yet studies have found that oral sex is not a major source of transmission of the HIV virus. *See, e.g.*, Marsha F. Goldsmith, *As AIDS Epidemic Approaches Second Decade, Report Examines What Has Been Learned*, 264 JAMA 431, 433 (July 25, 1990); *Letter from Dr. John Petricciani*, 262 JAMA 2231, 2231 (October 27, 1989).

21. *See* Nan Hunter, *Marriage, Law, and Gender: A Feminist Inquiry*, 1 Law & Sexuality: Rev. of Lesbian and Gay Legal Issues 1, 10–11 n.3 (1991).

22. Joyce Cain, *Massachusetts' 1989 Sexual Orientation Nondiscrimination Statute*, 1 Law & Sexuality: Rev. of Lesbian and Gay Legal Issues 285, 298–99 n.93 (1991).

23. *See In re* Opinion of the Justices, 530 A.2d 21 (N. H. 1987) (holding that a proposed New Hampshire law that prevented homosexuals from adopting children or becoming foster parents did not violate the Constitution); Seebel v. Farie, Case No. 90–923-CA18 (Cir. Ct. for 16th Dist., Monroe County, Fla. 1991) (overturning Florida's ban on gay adoptions).

24. *See* Barbara Kritchevsky, *The Unmarried Woman's Right to Artificial Insemination: A Call for an Expanded Definition of Family*, 4 Harv. Women's L. J. 1, 3, 17 (1981).

25. *See, e.g.*, Hunter & Polikoff, *supra* note 10, at 705–14; Sheppard, *supra* note 10, at 241–43.

26. *See, e.g.*, *In re* Diehl, 582 N. E.2d 281, 289 (Ill. App. November 22, 1991).

27. Frug, *supra* note 4, at 1068.

28. *Id.* at 1070.

29. *Id.* at 1070.

30. For an excellent collection on the sex debate, *see* Pleasure and Danger: Exploring Female Sexuality (Carole S. Vance ed., 1984). Many of my comments that follow stem from conversations with lesbians over the years regarding the anti-pornography movement.

31. Although I have found the term *vanilla sex* in lesbian literature, *see, e.g.,* Juicy Lucy, *If I Ask You to Tie Me Up, Will You Still Love Me?*, in Coming to Power: Writings and Graphics on Lesbian S/M 29, 31 (Samois ed., 1982) (distinguishing between S/M sex and "vanilla sex"), I have not found the term *Vanilla-Sex Gestapo*, which I presume is original to Mary Joe. Frug, *supra* note 4, at 1070.

32. *See* Nan D. Hunter & Sylvia A. Law, Brief Amici Curiae of Feminist Anti-Censorship Taskforce et al., in American Booksellers Association v. Hudnut, 21 U. Mich. J. L. Ref. 69, 69–75, 102–105, 128–32 (1987–88).

33. *See, e.g.,* Angela Y. Davis, Women, Race and Class 202–21 (1981).

34. 448 U.S. 297, 326–27 (1980) (upholding Congressional limitations on Medicaid payments for abortions).

35. 410 U.S. 113 (1973).

36. For a discussion of the abortion issue in a reproductive health context, *see* Ruth Colker, *An Equal Protection Analysis of United States Reproductive Health Policy: Gender, Race, Age, and Class, 1991* Duke L. J. 324, 346–50 (1991).

37. For further discussion of this dilemma, *see* Ruth Colker, *Feminist Litigation: An Oxymoron?—A Study of the Briefs Filed in William L. Webster v. Reproductive Health Services*, 13 Harv. Women's L. J. 137, 137–68 (1990).

38. For further discussion, *see* Ruth Colker, Abortion and Dialogue: Pro-Choice, Pro-Life, and American Law (1992).

39. Professor Frug attempted to write a "localized disruption" rather than a total theory. *See* Frug, *supra* note 4, at 1046. Nevertheless, she seems to have been influenced by Catharine MacKinnon's work, which I find somewhat confusing, because MacKinnon does try to write a "total theory" rather than a localized disruption. *See e.g.,* Catharine A. MacKinnon, *Feminism, Marxism, Method, and the State: An Agenda for Theory*, in Feminist Theory: A Critique of Ideology 1, 6 n.7 (Nannerl O. Keohane, Michelle Z. Rosaldo, and Barbara C. Gelpi eds., 1982) ("I aspire to include all women in the term "women" in some way, without violating the particularity of any woman's experience."). The reference to MacKinnon is baffling to me, except to suggest that Professor Frug was possibly torn between writing a total theory rather than a localized disruption.

PART 2
Cases

4

Planned Parenthood of Southeastern Pennsylvania v. Robert P. Casey

Abortion and Private Violence

The Federal Bureau of Investigation (FBI) estimates that domestic violence touches up to 25% of all American families, and that more than 33% of the women murdered in America are killed by their husbands or boyfriends.[1]

[Domestic violence] is the single largest cause of injury to women in the United States—more common than automobile accidents, muggings, and rapes combined.[2]

Pregnancy does not exempt women from being abused. From 4% to 8% of women going to prenatal clinics were abused during pregnancy.[3]

—Antonia C. Novello, United States Surgeon General (1992)

I. Introduction

THEORY CAN BE quite useful when applied to practical problems. Those practical problems, in turn, can help us to refine our theory. In this part of the book, I ask what an essentialist perspective can reveal to us about the legal treatment of the problem of violence against women during pregnancy. I describe the essentialist perspective of the courts in this area as well as discuss how to translate an equality, anti-essentialist perspective into legal doctrine in such cases. I then show how anti-essentialism does not prevent us from generalizing about women's lives.

I became interested in this problem as the result of a request to participate in a symposium on violence against women. The organizer of the symposium suggested that the anti-abortion movement has monopolized the discussion of violence and pregnancy by describing women who have abortions as "murderers." This focus has prevented many people from seeing the real violence that is often visited upon pregnant women including but not limited to women who seek abortions. I agree that we need more public discussion of the problem of

89

violence against women during pregnancy and therefore conducted the research that is the basis of the next two chapters.

The practice/theory dilemma that I face in trying to talk about the problem of "violence against women" is how to talk about women without being essentialist. In other words, how can we talk about women in a way that is inclusive of all women's experiences while also rendering the word *women* meaningful? My anti-essentialist perspective challenges me to consider the lives of all women when I talk about a policy's impact on "women." As we saw in my discussion of lesbians in chapter 3, some women may experience a heightened effect of a policy while other women may experience an opposing effect. All of these women are acted upon by society but can be acted upon in quite different ways. We are essentialist when we assume a priori that certain subgroups such as African-American women or lesbians will experience a heightened version of white, heterosexual women's experience. Instead of making such assumptions, I try to use an anti-essentialist perspective to see the impact of policy on all women's lives.

Essentialism can occur on three different levels. The court itself can be essentialist in not seeing the full range of the impact of a statute on all women or, worse yet, seeing that full range but not caring about it for a subgroup of women. Essentialism develops in reading court opinions if we do not look beyond the court's own description of the impact of its ruling. Finally, as lawyers we can be essentialist in our arguments to courts if we use the word *women* in a way that is not inclusive of all women's lives. Anti-essentialism therefore challenges us in our legal practice while also offering us a tool to criticize courts. These practical challenges can help us make anti-essentialism a useful, constructive tool rather than simply a perspective through which we criticize others.

In this chapter, I explore the phenomenon of private violence and coercion in the lives of pregnant women who desire to terminate their pregnancies and then argue that judicial protection is lacking for the most disadvantaged women in society because of the courts' essentialism in considering women's lives. I start by describing the problem of violence against women when women are pregnant and then discuss the courts' failure to protect disadvantaged women from domestic violence in the *Casey* decision. Finally, I try to show how we could make anti-essentialist, equality arguments to protect pregnant women from violence in the context of the Mississippi case *Barnes v. Moore*.[4]

Although all women face violence in their lives, restrictions on abortion and harassment at abortion clinics impact disproportionately on young and poor pregnant women, because they have the fewest resources to choose an abortion provider. A waiting period rule, for example, is a much more stringent restriction on a pregnant teenager who must surreptitiously schedule an appointment for an abortion (as well as a trip to a judge if there is a parental consent requirement) because of her fear of domestic violence than for an older, middle-class pregnant woman whose decision is supported by her husband. Similarly, the harassment of anti-abortion protestors is much more serious for that same teenager who can only afford to have an abortion at the local clinic, which is the site of abortion protests, than for a pregnant, middle-class woman who can afford the privacy of her doctor's office for her abortion. The pregnant teenager may unfortunately try to self-induce the abortion, have an illegal abortion,[5] or even commit suicide rather than try to schedule two doctor appointments at a clinic, which may not be able to guarantee her privacy. Unfortunately, the courts have demonstrated a systematic disregard for the violence and coercion in the lives of young and poor pregnant women while purporting to protect women from domestic violence.

For the first time, the Supreme Court started to make a connection between restrictions on abortion and private violence against pregnant women in *Planned Parenthood of Southeastern Pennsylvania v. Casey*.[6] Nevertheless, the Court's understanding of the connection between private violence against pregnant women and abortion restrictions was limited. The Court understood the problem of violence in the private sphere for pregnant married women, who are disproportionately older, white, and middle class, but did not understand this problem for pregnant unmarried women, who are disproportionately younger, disproportionately African-American, and poor. Thus, the Court in *Casey* overturned the spousal notification requirement but did not overturn the waiting period requirement. This blindness on the part of the Court is a reflection of the essentialist perspective that the Court uses when considering the reality of women's lives.

II. Domestic Violence against Women during Pregnancy

An anti-essentialist perspective can help us understand the various ways that domestic violence impacts women's lives during pregnancy. We can see the general impact while also recognizing the special aspects of that impact for various subcategories of women.

Violence against women is a serious health threat to women. It is the single largest cause of injury to women in the United States, affecting up to one-fourth of all families.[7] The former Surgeon General of the United States, Antonia Novello, took a major step forward in understanding the seriousness of this problem. She made the following bold statement:

Today, we face two major public health epidemics that represent particular dangers to women. One is the human immunodeficiency virus (HIV) epidemic, and the other is domestic violence. Although these two epidemics might seem unrelated, they are intertwined in ways that pose serious challenges to the health care community. . . . The living situations of both groups are often identical—poverty, decreased access to primary medical care, and relationships with men that are adversarial and demeaning.[8]

Moreover, she noted that pregnancy does not exempt women from being abused; it may even make that abuse more likely.[9]

Despite the statement of the former surgeon general, little progress is being made to use the health care system to detect pregnant women who experience domestic violence. Rather than improving access to reproductive health services, United States policy continues to block access or create barriers to reproductive health services. In addition, groups like Operation Rescue succeed in intimidating and harassing pregnant women, as well as physically blocking access to abortion clinics. These actions cause public violence against women and put women at risk of having their confidentiality lost, thereby subjecting them to violence in the private sphere.

Other scholars have attempted to document the range of violence against women during pregnancy. In a recent article in the *Journal of the American Medical Association*, Dr. Judith McFarlane and her colleagues reported that they found 17 percent of women reported abuse during pregnancy.[10] Abused women were also found to be twice as likely to begin prenatal care during the third trimester of pregnancy, which was explained by noting that they had learned "forced avoidance" from health care.[11]

McFarlane's statistics are about twice as high as those recorded in some other studies.[12] The difference in results appears attributable to her research methodology. Rather than asking women about abuse on a standard medical history intake form, the women in this study were asked about abuse directly by their health care provider. In a related study, about 8 percent of women reported abuse through the use of a standard medical history form, whereas 29 percent of these same women reported abuse when asked directly by a health care provider.[13] McFarlane's research strategy therefore seems to produce more reliable results than strategies used in previous studies because of its more personal approach to questioning.

McFarlane's findings replicate the findings of a 1985 study by the National Family Violence Survey. According to the 1985 study,

154 out of every 1000 pregnant women were assaulted by their mates during the first 4 months of pregnancy, and 170 per 1000 women were assaulted

during the fifth through the ninth months. Approximately 37% of obstetric patients, across class, race, and educational lines, are physically abused while pregnant. Such assaults can result in placental separation, antepartum hemorrhage, fetal fractures, rupture of the uterus, liver, or spleen, and preterm labor.[14]

Moreover, the 1985 study found that pregnant women's risk of abusive violence was 60.6 percent greater than that of nonpregnant women, although that difference appears to be attributable to age rather than pregnancy.[15] Finally, the Second National Family Violence Survey found that the nature of abuse may change during pregnancy, with pregnant women suffering increased blows to the abdomen.[16]

The racial differences among women who suffer domestic violence must be examined carefully. Although health care providers perceive that women most at risk of abuse during pregnancy are African-American,[17] McFarlane's study showed that perception was inaccurate. White women were found to be most at risk, followed by Hispanic women, and then followed by African-American women. These findings confirm previous studies that reported physical abuse was three and a half times higher among white than Hispanic or black women.[18]

Dr. Anne Flitcraft provides a different interpretation of McFarlane's data, because she claims that McFarlane does not give sufficient attention to severity of abuse. She points out that homicide data shows that African-American women are at greater risk of being killed by their partners than Caucasian women. She suggests that it is important to analyze threats with and access to a weapon because of the greater likelihood that such abuse may result in death.[19] Viewing McFarlane's data, she says, "An alternative interpretation may be that severity of abuse differs little across ethnic groups and that threats with and access to a weapon should be ranked in a category with a high probability of significant injury, predictive of severe abuse."[20] The important point from the McFarlane and Flitcraft studies is that all women are at risk of domestic abuse, but that abuse may take different forms dependent upon one's race and ethnicity. White women may suffer disproportionate amounts of domestic abuse, whereas African-American women may face the disproportionate likelihood of paying the ultimate price of death during an episode of domestic violence. Clearly, both problems—quantity and severity—deserve our serious attention rather than stereotypical responses. Health care providers who believe that their white, middle-class patients are immune from domestic violence are sadly mistaken. Similarly, health care providers who do not take seriously the possible outcome from abuse for their African-American patients may fail to prevent their patients' death.

Another important aspect of McFarlane's findings is that women who delay receiving prenatal care until the third trimester are those most likely to face domestic violence. Barriers to reproductive health services, including restrictions on women's health clinics that perform abortions through gag rules, waiting period requirements, abortion restrictions, and Medicaid restrictions on health care services, contribute to the problem of their not seeking timely prenatal care. We have always known that failure to seek prenatal care correlates with harm to the fetus;[21] we now know that it correlates with harm to the pregnant woman as well, such as waiting periods and harassment by anti-abortion protestors.

Our failure to detect and eliminate domestic abuse harms both pregnant women and their fetuses. In calling for a renewed effort by gynecologists to detect abuse of pregnant women, the president of the American College of Obstetricians and Gynecologists (ACOG), Richard F. Jones, has stated that "obstetricians and gynecologists have a double reason for addressing the problem. The first is to protect our patients themselves. The second is to protect the unborn children during pregnancy, because, as brutal as it seems, recent studies show that pregnancy itself may incite violence by the husband or partner."[22] In the name of "life," the pro-life movement has unfortunately harmed the lives of pregnant women and their fetuses.

Reproductive health services could make an important contribution to the detection of domestic violence if prenatal care were more universally available and widely used. The ACOG has begun to understand the importance of gynecologists in determining the existence of domestic violence in women's lives. They have recently sent to their members information about battered women to help them recognize domestic abuse problems. The most important attribute for physicians to use to detect domestic violence is *sensitivity*. When queried directly, most women will answer honestly if the batterer is not present. When talking with women about suspected or even admitted incidents of violence, sensitivity to their needs at that moment and the ability to provide concrete assistance are critical.[23] Barriers to reproductive health care services make it difficult for those sensitive discussions to occur and lead domestic violence to go undetected.

III. *Casey*

A. *The Court's Decision*

In *Planned Parenthood of Southeastern Pennsylvania v. Casey*,[24] the United States Supreme Court considered the constitutionality of a Pennsylvania statute that, among other things, required pregnant women to notify their husbands of their desire to obtain an abortion and make two doctor visits separated by at least twenty-four hours in order to procure an abortion.[25] The Court upheld the waiting period requirement but overturned the spousal notification requirement through a purported sensitivity to the problems of domestic violence. The Court assessed the constitutionality of these requirements applying an "undue burden" standard under which it tried to examine the impact of these provisions from the perspective of the women most impacted by them—asking whether the regulations posed a "substantial obstacle in the path of a woman seeking an abortion."[26] This standard was seemingly sensitive to the anti-essentialist critique while also recognizing the usefulness of the category "woman." It was based on privacy rather than equality doctrine. Unfortunately, the Court's application of this newly announced standard demonstrated a blindness to the impact of abortion regulations on the lives of poor women, thereby making it essentialist in application and not protecting women's equality interests sufficiently.

Although many people, including myself, expected the Supreme Court to overturn *Roe v. Wade* in *Casey* and to minimize the significance of reproductive choice in women's lives, the Supreme Court did just the opposite. It reaffirmed the essential holding of *Roe* that the state cannot ban abortion of a nonviable fetus and explained with surprising eloquence why reproductive freedom is important to women. Its description of the importance of reproductive freedom to women's liberty interest resonated strongly in equality theory. In the Court's words:

> Though abortion is conduct, it does not follow that the State is entitled to proscribe it in all instances. That is because the liberty of the woman is at stake in a sense unique to the human condition and so unique to the law. The mother who carries a child to full term is subject to anxieties, to physical constraints, to pain that only she must bear. That these sacrifices have from the beginning of the human race been endured by woman with a pride that ennobles her in the eyes of others and gives to the infant a bond of love cannot alone be grounds for the State to insist she make the sacrifice. Her suffering is too intimate and personal for the State to insist, without more, upon its own vision of the woman's role, however dominant that vision has been in the course of our history and our culture. The destiny of the woman must be shaped to a large extent on her own conception of her spiritual imperatives and her place in society.[27]

The Court's description of the importance of women being free to make reproductive decisions took into consideration both women's place in society historically as well as women's unique reproductive capacity. It rejected the view that biology must be destiny and placed reproductive decisions in women's hands rather than in society's hands. By making this argument under the liberty component of the Fourteenth Amendment rather than the equality component, the Court did not have to concern itself with the unavailability of similarly situated men. In fact, it could emphasize the distinctiveness of pregnancy without being concerned about finding a male comparator. Thus, the court was able to conclude that women's basic liberty as persons would be infringed if such fundamental decisions were not left to them to make.

Having concluded that abortion decision making is fundamental to women's liberty interest, the Supreme Court did not conclude that the state cannot restrict abortions before the fetus is viable, as it had in *Roe*. Instead, the Supreme Court modified *Roe* by concluding that an abortion regulation is unconstitutional only if it imposes an *undue burden* on a woman's ability to make an abortion decision before the fetus is viable. More specifically, the Court explained what it meant by an "undue burden":

> A finding of an undue burden is a shorthand for the conclusion that a state regulation has the purpose or effect of placing a substantial obstacle in the path of a woman seeking an abortion of a nonviable fetus. . . . In our considered judgment, an undue burden is an unconstitutional burden. . . . Understood another way, we answer the question, left open in previous opinions discussing the undue burden formulation, whether a law designed to further the State's interest in fetal life which imposes an undue burden on the woman's decision before fetal viability could be constitutional. . . . The answer is no.[28]

That definition of an undue burden left open the question of what is "a substantial obstacle in the path of a woman seeking an abortion?" The Court's answer to that question seemed to reflect an anti-essentialist perspective. In order to understand the Court's answer, one must understand it in the context in which it arose.

One of the issues in the case was whether the requirement that a woman notify her spouse of her intent to procure an abortion constituted an undue burden. The district court had entered extensive findings documenting the extent to which the spousal notification requirement might endanger the psychological and physical well-being of women and their children. The Supreme Court reviewed those findings and concluded that "the spousal notification requirement is . . . likely to prevent a significant number of women from obtaining an abortion. It does not merely make abortions a little more difficult or expensive to obtain; for many women, it will impose a substantial obstacle."[29]

The defendants tried to counter that evidence by pointing out that the statute imposed "almost no burden at all for the vast majority of women seeking abortions,"[30] since only about 20 percent of the women who seek abortions are married, and about 95 percent of those women voluntarily notify their husbands of their intention to procure an abortion. Thus, the defendants argued that only about 1 percent of the women seeking abortions would be affected by the statute's notice requirements. They suggested that the impact on "women" should be measured by the impact on the vast majority of women.

The Supreme Court, however, did not accept the defendants' attempt to define women by majoritarian standards. Instead, the Court made the bold statement: "The analysis does not end with the one percent of women upon whom the statute operates; it begins there. Legislation is measured for consistency with the Constitution by its impact on those whose conduct it affects."[31] Since the spousal notice requirement affected married women who did not qualify for one of the statute's exceptions and who did not wish to notify their husbands of their intention to procure an abortion, that is where the analysis begins. Looking at the lives of those women, the Court concluded that the statute operated as a substantial obstacle to a woman's choice to undergo an abortion.

At first glance, the Court's application of its undue burden seems quite sensitive to the lives of disadvantaged women. It focused its inquiry on the women whose conduct was affected by the statute and recognized that these women faced substantial risk of injury as women. Unfortunately, even as the Court made those broad pronouncements, it narrowly applied them to the case at hand. The Court's application of those standards to the waiting period requirement left the most disadvantaged women who face domestic violence through application of that requirement unprotected.

The Court did not overturn the waiting period requirement, although the district court had presented numerous findings concerning the impact that requirement would have on young, poor women who are at risk of facing domestic violence as well as harassment by anti-abortion protestors. The trial court had found that

> [t]wo trips to the abortion provider would subject many women to the harassment and hostility of anti-abortion protestors. . . . For the majority of women in Pennsylvania, delays will range from 48 hours to two weeks. . . . Women who live in any of . . . 62 counties must travel for at least one hour, and sometimes longer than three hours, to obtain an abortion from the *nearest* provider. . . . The . . . waiting period will be particularly burdensome to those women who have the least financial resources, such as the poor and the young, those women that travel long distances, such as

women living in rural areas, and those women that have difficulty explaining their whereabouts, such as battered women, school age women,
and working women without sick leave. . . . In some cases, the delays caused
by the 24-hour waiting period will push patients into the second trimester of
their pregnancy substantially increasing the cost of the procedure itself and
making the procedure more dangerous medically; . . . A delay of 24 hours
will have a negative impact on both the physical and psychological health
of some patients, as well as increase the risk of complications.[32]

Although these findings would appear to be parallel to the findings with
regard to spousal notification, the Supreme Court concluded that they might be
"particularly burdensome" to a particular group of women yet not be a substantial obstacle for the women in that group. Using the semantic distinction between a particular burden and a substantial obstacle, the Court upheld the waiting period requirement while invalidating the spousal notification requirement.

One is therefore left wondering why the waiting period requirement was
less problematic than the spousal notification requirement. The Supreme Court
found that the spousal notification requirement affected women who would not
voluntarily choose to notify their husbands of the desire to have an abortion.
These are likely to be women who fear domestic violence. Similarly, who are
the women who would not voluntarily choose to wait twenty-four hours after
visiting an abortion provider to have an abortion? Poor women who cannot afford transportation costs, the extra child care expenses, or two days unpaid leave
from work would not be able to comply with these requirements. In addition,
women who feared domestic violence if their partner or family knew of their
pregnancy would not voluntarily wait twenty-four hours. Fearful that they could
not afford to surreptitiously visit an abortion clinic twice, they would want to
have the abortion at the same time as they obtained the positive pregnancy test.
The Court, however, could not see that their reasons for failing to comply voluntarily with the statute's waiting period requirement were as compelling as
those of the women who did not voluntarily want to notify their spouse.

B. The Court's Self-conscious Essentialism

I would suggest that it was the Court's essentialism that prevented it from
seeing the equivalent burdens on these two groups of women. Describing the
Court's essentialism is quite complex, because there are two ways to understand
it. First, we can examine the Court's own language to see how essentialism was
a conscious part of its analysis. Second, we can examine the *real impact* of the

Court's decision, looking beyond the impact that the Court intended or understood.

The Court could imagine and sympathize with the burdens on middle-class married women imposed by the spousal notification requirement but could not imagine and sympathize with the burdens on young, poor women who are disproportionately African-American. The difference in the Court's sympathies, I would suggest, was governed by the class and race of the groups that would be most affected by the requirements. Because middle-class women are more likely to marry than poor women, the spousal notification requirement would affect middle-class women more than poor women. (An unmarried woman was not required to notify her partner.) By contrast, the waiting period requirement would most strongly impact poor women who could not afford the extra costs associated with the waiting period requirement. The Court openly used a class-based analysis when it contrasted the two requirements. After affirming the waiting period requirement, while acknowledging that it might increase the costs of the procedure for some women, the Court stated that the spousal notification requirement was invalid, because "it does not merely make abortions a little more difficult or expensive to obtain."[33] The significant word in the quotation is "merely." Why is an obstacle that prevents a woman from obtaining an abortion "merely" an inconvenience rather than a substantial obstacle? For a woman who cannot afford an abortion due to the increased costs of the waiting period requirement, the restriction is as much of an obstacle as for the woman who cannot procure an abortion due to her inability to obtain spousal notification. It is "merely" an inconvenience rather than a substantial obstacle to a court that is determinedly uninterested in considering class-based impacts of legal requirements.

It is also interesting to note that the Supreme Court described the burdens of the waiting period rule only in cost terms, whereas the district court had found that the waiting period rule posed dangers to women who feared domestic violence. In finding of fact 194, the district court had concluded that the waiting period rule subjected women to increased harassment from anti-abortion protestors.[34] And in finding of fact 199, the district court concluded that it would impose burdens on women who had difficulty explaining their whereabouts, such as battered women.[35] Even if one accepted the Supreme Court's presumption that monetary burdens should not constitute undue burdens, there is no reason to overlook the danger to the physical health and well-being of women who face domestic violence, which is imposed by the waiting period rule. Given that the women who face increased domestic violence as a result of the waiting period rule are disproportionately poor, I must therefore reluctantly conclude that their lives and burdens just do not seem to count. Thus, despite the Court's assertion that it would examine the burdens of the statute from the perspective of the women most impacted, some women's burdens—be they financial or physical—appear not to count. They are a mere inconvenience rather than a substantial obstacle.

C. The Real Impact of the Court's Decision

The analysis of the Court's decision that I have just provided emphasizes the importance of the category of economic class. I have argued that the Court treated women differently depending upon their economic class. And I stand by that statement as an accurate portrayal of what the Court *believed* it was doing. In fact, however, the impact of those requirements on women was not quite as distinguishable along class lines as the Court might have thought. Race is an interesting compounding variable. By being vigilant in my use of an anti-essentialist perspective, I was able to uncover the compounding aspect of race in this analysis.

A major factor in the different impact between spousal notification and waiting period rules, as I have argued, is that, by definition, the spousal notification rule only affected married women. The waiting period rule covered all women but had its strongest negative impact on unmarried women who feared abuse from their families or partners. Thus, a married/nonmarried distinction affected which groups were impacted by these regulations. To understand the impact of these rules by race, one must analyze marriage patterns on a racial basis. In the Court's analysis, the focus was on class in understanding the impact of those rules; race, however, also has an effect. Because of my anti-essentialist perspective, I was committed to understanding the racial impact of these rules, which I found to be quite complex.

Although it is true that poor people are less likely to marry than middle-class people, it is also true that race is a very important variable in understanding marriage patterns. Low-income white fathers are two and a half times more likely to marry than low-income black fathers whose girlfriends bear children out of wedlock.[36] Similarly, upper-income white fathers are twice as likely to marry as upper-income black fathers whose girlfriends bear children out of wedlock.[37] Nevertheless, class is also an important variable in understanding marriage patterns. Employed black men whose girlfriends bear children out of wedlock, for example, are 93 percent more likely to marry than unemployed black men.[38]

Knowing that blacks were not permitted to marry under slavery, I was expecting to find that there was a steady historical pattern of blacks not marrying from the time of slavery until the present time. Here, I was flat wrong. In fact, between 1890 and 1950, the black marriage rate was consistently higher than that of whites.[39] Thus, the low black marriage rate is a modern phenomenon, seemingly disconnected from the breakup of the black family under slavery. So, it is accurate to describe marriage rates as being strongly influenced by race but not accurate to attribute those differences entirely to the institution of slavery.

Further research showed that I could not necessarily apply these findings to other racial subgroups. For example, Latino youths have *higher* marriage rates than blacks or whites.[40] These high marriage rates are apparently attributable to the fact that male Latinos are more likely to marry their girlfriends who bear children out of wedlock than are black or white males.[41] I could not find research with respect to other racial subgroups. Therefore, I was left with the knowledge that blacks are less likely to marry than whites but that Latinos are more likely to marry than blacks or whites, and poor blacks and poor whites are less likely to marry than middle-class blacks and middle-class whites. (I did not find information concerning class and marriage rates within the Latino community.)

This research made me aware of how little I actually knew and how dependent my own research was on the categories that others chose to use. Although Latinos are predicted to become the fastest growing population group in the United States, I was able to find little information about their marriage patterns. For blacks I could find ample information, but little of that information was broken down by economic class. Other racial subgroups were entirely invisible. The tentativeness of my own research is therefore necessitated by the inadequacies of the information available to me. I can try to piece together a puzzle, but ultimately I have a hazy picture to look at.

Nevertheless, all of this research brings me back to the question of what image of women did the Supreme Court have in mind in *Casey* when it rendered its judgment? By its own language, it seems that the Court had a class-based image in mind when it created its distinctions. The media portrays married people as being disproportionately middle class and white, which is somewhat accurate. The media does not emphasize the countervailing marriage rates in the Hispanic community. Nor does the media focus on the differences between middle-class and poor blacks. Thus, it is accurate to say that the Court had in mind middle-class white women when it protected them from the abuse of their husbands, even if, in reality, its decision protected a group of women that crosscut racial and class boundaries. We can therefore expose the essentialism of the Court while trying to educate ourselves about the real complexities of the world in which we live.

Of course, some people might say that all I have described is how one should carry out careful scientific research. In part, that is true. But lawyering and careful use of categories are not always consistent. Lawyering requires us to describe issues in stark terms—it is race and and therefore subject to strict scrutiny, or it is class and therefore subject to rational basis scrutiny. Because of the privileging of some experiences over others, lawyering encourages us to emphasize race and then gender and then class in explaining the effects of regulations on people's lives.

More important, what I believe my analysis has shown is that even when the Court *purports* to be allowing disadvantaged women to benefit from its analysis, it is still trying to privilege the experiences of married, middle-class white women. Sometimes, the Court may itself be the victim of a media that distorts reality, so it may accidentally benefit, for example, Latina women while trying to benefit Anglo women. We therefore need to ask questions on many different levels— who did the Court *believe* it was helping as well as who did the Court *actually* help and who *should* the Court help? By asking these kinds of questions, we can have a more flexible and accurate use of categories.

Thus, the Court openly stated that it was not interested in protecting poor women. Nevertheless, the effect of its ruling would also disproportionately impact African-American women. There are therefore two ways to describe the Court's holding from an anti-essentialist perspective. One could say that the Court was essentialist in that it was blind to the impact on young, poor women who are disproportionately African-American. Alternatively, one could say that the Court was quite aware of the impact of its decision on the lives of young, poor women, but it did not choose to protect them from domestic violence. Under the second explanation, the Court is not actually essentialist; instead, it is simply uncaring or vindicative. The application of an anti-essentialist perspective allows us to see the uncaring or vindicative attitude of the Court toward young, poor women. In this chapter, I have generally used the first explanation to describe the Court's action, because it is a "gentler" description; however, I can empathize with the reader who finds the second explanation to be more accurate. The important point for the purposes of this chapter is that the Court's decision left some poor women and African-American women unprotected from domestic violence and unable to procure a legal abortion.

IV. *Barnes v. Moore:* Mississippi

A. Introduction

In my discussion of the *Casey* decision, I provided a strong critique of the Court's analysis through my application of an anti-essentialist perspective. An anti-essentialist perspective, however, is only useful if it can provide the building blocks for making *constructive* legal arguments. Thus, in this section I try to show how one can use an anti-essentialist perspective to argue that a state anti-abortion statute is unconstitutional even under the limited *Casey* undue burden standard. In other words, although the *Casey* decision is deeply flawed, we can and should learn to mold its structure of argument to challenge restrictive abortion legislation. Although the legal argument in *Barnes v. Moore*[42] that I provide in this section was unsuccessful before the Fifth Circuit, I believe that it will ultimately be the basis of a successful challenge to a state waiting period rule. I am therefore sharing it with the reader in the hope that we can refine it to make it a successful, practical, legal strategy. I argue that the undue burden standard should be a fact-intensive standard that provides us with the space to show the impact on discrete groups of women in a state.

The statute challenged in *Barnes* was similar to the one challenged in *Casey*. For example, like the Pennsylvania statute, it contained a twenty-four-hour waiting period requirement. However, the waiting period rule would have a much more dramatic impact on women in Mississippi than it had on women in Pennsylvania. Whereas Pennsylvania is a relatively prosperous industrial state, Mississippi is the poorest state in the United States. If the Fifth Circuit had been willing to truly explore the impact of the waiting period requirement on the women in Mississippi most affected by it, it should have concluded that that burden constituted a substantial obstacle despite the Supreme Court's ruling in *Casey*.

The waiting period requirement in Mississippi increases the health risk of an abortion, raises its cost, and imposes transportation, housing, and child care difficulties on women. Such burdens make it nearly impossible for many women to effectuate their reproductive choices. These burdens are most directly imposed on women who are least represented in the political process and most in need of improved access to health care. I will focus on the effects on poor women, women who are in abusive relationships, adolescents, and women with handicaps, because these requirements will endanger their health and increase the level of violence in their lives.

B. Poverty

Mississippi is the poorest state in the United States. *Twenty-five percent* of the persons in the state live below the poverty line—more than twice the national average and the highest percentage in the United States.[43] The median household income in Mississippi is the lowest in the United States.[44] Welfare payments are also very low in Mississippi. For example, the maximum monthly Aid to Families with Dependent Children benefit for a family of three in 1989 was $120 per month—the second lowest in the United States.[45]

Among the poor of Mississippi, women—particularly young women and African-American women—are the poorest. Overall, 21.5 percent of the households in the state are headed by females; these households are disproportionately poor.[46] In fiscal year 1991, for example, females constituted nearly 75 percent of all of the people in the state on Medicaid. In addition, children under the age of twenty constitute 55 percent of the Medicaid recipients. Seventy percent of Medicaid recipients are African-American.[47] Unfortunately, extreme poverty combined with a shortage of affordable and accessible health care providers places Mississippi at or near the bottom of all states in accessibility of both abortion services[48] and prenatal care.[49]

The mandatory delay in the Mississippi abortion statute increases both the medical risks and the cost of abortions. Because of work, school, or family responsibilities, many poor women can only come to a clinic on Saturdays; the waiting period requirement, therefore, will delay their abortions by at least one week.[50] There is a 30 percent increase in rates of morbidity with each week of delay beyond the eighth week of pregnancy.[51]

Delays of one week can also raise the cost of an abortion by $50 to $200,[52] which, especially for a poor woman, can be prohibitive. As established in the district court, many women pay for their abortions in rolls of dimes, nickels, and pennies.[53] Poor women already unduly delay their abortions as they scrape together the money to pay for them.[54] The additional complications and delay of the statute, therefore, hit poor women particularly hard, because the increase in cost per week is steeper in the second than in the first trimester.

Mississippi's serious transportation problems exacerbate the burdens of the mandatory delay in three ways. First, the difficulty of procuring transportation adds to the delay. This, in turn, increases the cost of the abortion. Finally, making two trips instead of one to the abortion provider will at least double the cost of the transportation itself.

Two of the three abortion providers in the state are located in Jackson. Of the eighty-two counties in Mississippi, seventy-nine have no known abortion providers, although nearly three thousand women from these counties obtained abortions in 1989.[55] Nearly half of all abortion patients travel one hundred miles or more for abortion-related services. For example, Lisa Brown stated in her Declaration: "The average patient travels approximately 2 hours to obtain an abortion at the Clinic, but some travel much longer to arrive at the Clinic. Over 650 of our patients in 1990 traveled over 100 miles total to obtain abortion services."[56] Poor women living in remote rural areas of the state must often travel two hundred miles to obtain an abortion in Jackson. Families living in poverty are likely to be female-headed households in remote rural areas of the state. Six of the seven counties in which more than 30 percent of the families live below the poverty line are located in the northwest corner of the state.[57]

Poor women seeking abortions are also dependent upon a very inadequate public transportation system. For example, at trial, Dr. Morrison testified:

> One case recently had to come from Clarksdale, and you might think that's not a far journey, but if you have to take the Trailways bus you have to go to Memphis. Then you have—to catch the bus you have to leave at 4:00 o'clock in the morning, get the bus to Memphis, then come to Jackson, get here at 12:00. Then that woman would have to go back the same route, get in at midnight, turn around and come back the next morning. And I think that puts a burden on that woman and on me as a physician that would be ridiculous and onerous and certainly is true of no other medical condition.[58]

Virtually no woman on welfare owns an automobile, and exceedingly few have access to a reliable one.[59] Travel expenses to a clinic average $40 to $50; for a woman who has to make two trips, these expenses will be $80 to $100.[60]

The waiting period requirement will often necessitate an overnight stay in Jackson. Poor women, however, find it burdensome to bear the extra expenses of an overnight stay,[61] along with the expenses of an unpaid absence from work and the increased child care costs attendant to an absence from their home. Some women will have no alternative but to spend the night on the street in order to comply with the waiting period requirement.[62]

C. Domestic Violence

These burdens will be further exacerbated for poor women who face domestic violence, because they cannot afford the risk of their partner discovering that they have visited an abortion clinic. One visit to the doctor's office is already a dangerous task for them; two trips will often be extremely dangerous or impossible. Unfortunately, many pregnant women live in abusive relationships in which they cannot inform their partner of their pregnancy and desire to obtain an abortion. Studies indicate that there is a correlation between pregnancy and battering; for example, some men *only* beat their wives when they know that their wives are pregnant.[63] For such women, even one unexplained visit to a doctor may be quite dangerous. For example, Lisa Brown stated in her Declaration in the Mississippi case: "I fear for the health of battered women who need abortions. Battered women seeking abortions already have to reschedule several times because it is difficult for them to get away from their batterers. The Act would only further thwart their attempts to obtain high quality health care."[64] Requiring such women to visit a doctor twice and possibly incur an overnight stay away from home may make the "choice" of an abortion impossible. Although these women's lives or health may be threatened if their partner discovers that they are seeking an abortion, the medical emergency exception does not apply to their situation.

It is impossible to overstate the importance of confidentiality to women who face domestic abuse. Although spousal notification is one way that confidentiality can be lost, waiting period rules pose a serious risk of loss of confidentiality for many women. Planned Parenthood, for example, goes to enormous lengths to protect women's confidentiality when they have *one* office visit (not necessarily for an abortion). Letters are sent to women in "code" in unmarked envelopes, and telephone messages are not left at women's homes. Despite these efforts, women face domestic violence when their male partner calls the post office to find out the source of a postal frank, learns of an unidentified caller's telephone number through special telephone features, or is informed by an anti-choice advocate that his partner's car was seen in an abortion clinic parking lot.[65] Each time a woman must visit an abortion clinic office she takes a serious risk of loss of confidentiality.

D. Adolescents

The waiting period requirement makes it nearly impossible for adolescents to choose an abortion and therefore exacerbates the dramatic health and socio-economic consequences that accompany high adolescent birthrates. Mississippi already has the highest adolescent birthrate of any state in the United States.[66] In a report issued in February 1991, the Mississippi State Department of Health summarized the problems of the high birthrate for adolescents: it leads to a high infant mortality rate, disproportionately high adverse health consequences for the pregnant adolescent, and perpetuation of the cycle of poverty.[67]

Because adolescents are frequently unable to travel to a clinic during the week, they must visit a clinic on Saturdays, with at least a week delay between visits. In addition, if the temporary injunction against the Mississippi juvenile bypass statute were to be lifted,[68] some adolescents would have to schedule two clinic visits after obtaining court approval for their abortion decision.[69] Delays of several weeks could easily occur while adolescents try to schedule clinic visits and court appearances at times when they are not in school and can be away from home. Even the state attorney general acknowledged that such lengthy delays might have negative health consequences.[70] Additionally, to require a waiting period after an adolescent obtains court or parental approval serves no conceivable purpose. The parental or judicial process should have already ascertained that the adolescent has made a thoughtful, mature decision.

Even without the additional juvenile bypass statute, the waiting period requirement causes delays, which will frequently cause an abortion to occur late in adolescents' pregnancies, because unfortunately, adolescents disproportionately delay seeking abortions until the second trimester of pregnancy.[71] As previously discussed, such delays raise the cost of abortion and the health risks. In addition, such delays threaten the adolescent's confidentiality as the physical manifestations of her pregnancy may become more apparent during this delay. Finally, the adolescent must risk loss of confidentiality by missing school or work to surreptitiously visit a clinic; unfortunately, loss of confidentiality may also cause violence against the pregnant adolescent.

E. Women with Handicaps

Finally, women with handicaps or high-risk pregnancies will have their lives and health endangered by being required to travel twice to a physician's office to exercise their reproductive choices. As discussed above, public transportation is generally inadequate in Mississippi and rarely handicapped accessible. Each additional visit to the clinic will therefore be an enormous burden on many handicapped women, as will the costs and difficulties of staying away from home for several days.

Pregnancy itself can be a handicapping condition for many women. The complications associated with pregnancy include nausea, varicose veins, placental abruptio, pre-eclampsia, eclampsia, liver failure, and blood clots to the lungs or brain.[72] These conditions will not exempt women from the waiting period requirement, but they will make it very difficult for a woman to travel twice to a clinic and stay away from home for many days. These women who are experiencing the risks of pregnancy or are quite ill may have to spend the waiting period being cared for as patients in a hospital—at an exorbitant expense.[73]

Women with HIV infection can be particularly harmed by the Act. Unfortunately, this group of women cuts across all of the categories previously mentioned—they are disproportionately poor, members of minority groups, and living in abusive situations.[74] An abortion may often be medically indicated for them, but they have extremely poor access to health care. Creating one more barrier may make it nearly impossible for HIV positive women to choose abortions and will thereby threaten their lives.

F. Summary

Many Mississippi women will be forced to choose illegal abortions, because they will not be able to afford either the increased costs or risks caused by the waiting period requirement. While few abortion-related deaths presently occur, the higher incidence of illegal abortions can be expected to increase abortion-related mortality—particularly for poor and disadvantaged women. Mishandled criminal abortions were the principal cause of maternal deaths in the 1960s, when most abortions were performed illegally.[75] Women of color, who are disproportionately poor, suffered the most from the lack of safe, legal abortions; they accounted for 64 percent of the deaths associated with illegal abortions in this country in 1972.[76] The mortality rates for African-American women were nine times higher than for white women.[77] We can expect the statute to cause poor women, who are disproportionately African-American, to find it difficult to choose a lawful abortion and to face increased rates of death from mishandled illegal abortions.

Thus, the waiting period requirement will act coercively in the lives of poor women by increasing the health risks of abortion procedures while also placing them at increased risk of losing their confidentiality. Loss of confidentiality will increase the risk of domestic violence. Women will also be less likely to seek reproductive health services, which, in turn, will place them at higher risk for lack of detection of domestic violence.

In the brief time that has passed since the Mississippi waiting period rule went into effect, many of the results that I have predicted above have been found to occur. The number of legal abortions being performed in Mississippi has dropped in half, while the number of abortions being performed on Mississippi residents in Louisiana has gone up sharply.[78] Poor women and women who face domestic violence, however, are finding it increasingly difficult to procure an abortion at all. Anti-abortion activists have used the waiting period delay as an opportunity to breach women's confidentiality. One anti-abortion activist, for example, bragged in the local newspaper that he copied down license plate numbers, obtained the person's name illegally from a police department official, and then called the household of the owner of the car to say, "A car registered to you was at the abortion clinic yesterday. They may be there considering having an abortion."[79] One physician who performs abortions reported that a young woman's father became "hysterical" when he received a call "from the people out front."[80] Poor women are reportedly arriving in Jackson for abortions without funds to spend the night or pay for another roundtrip. They receive the abortion "counseling" but are not able to afford to return for the abortion. For example, an administrator at one clinic reported that a twenty-one-year-old woman hitchhiked to the clinic with exactly enough money to pay for an abortion. She then learned of the waiting period requirement and did not have enough money to stay overnight. The clinic staff lowered its fee, put the woman up at a motel, and drove her most of the way home afterward to northern Mississippi. Other women, however, have come in for the first visit and then not been able to afford to return. These kinds of restrictions are not intended to improve the abortion deliberation process; they are intended to prevent women from having abortions. The connection between anti-abortion activists and violence against women will be discussed further in the next chapter.

V. Conclusion

I did not understand the impact that waiting period rules can have on women's lives until I started to work on the Mississippi abortion case in the summer of 1992. In that sense, I think I am like a lot of middle-class people. For example, I recently read an article in the *Tennessee Law Review* in which a Notre Dame law professor reported the results of her interviews with Catholic women concerning their position on abortion.[81] Nearly all of the women identified as pro-choice, but many of them volunteered that they supported restrictions like waiting period rules, because they might improve women's reflections about abortion.

Abstractly, that is a reasonable statement. And in some jurisdictions, such as France, it may even be reasonable in practice. What my practice, however, has shown me is that waiting period rules in the United States are actually a pretext to give groups such as Operation Rescue an opportunity to harass women and even endanger their lives. Such tactics frighten me and make me more committed than ever to overturning waiting period rules in the United States. I have included a copy of my Mississippi brief in the Appendix, so the reader can see how I have combined theory and practice.

France, which also has a waiting period rule, is quite a different jurisdiction. In France, as in most of the European countries, the state pays for abortion services. The state therefore has an incentive to offer abortion services in an efficient manner. It would not make sense for the state to try to increase the costs of abortions just to harm women. Thus, it should not surprise us that France has taken the lead in introducing RU 486, which may ultimately make abortions cheaper and safer, although successful use of RU 486 requires additional visits to the doctor's office. It is a sad reflection on American life that we cannot impose requirements such as waiting period rules because of the hostile atmosphere that women who seek reproductive health services at women's clinics must face.

Unlike myself, the courts have not shown themselves to be educable about the impact that waiting period rules can have on women's diverse lives. Despite the evidence of certain and substantial harm to disadvantaged women in Pennsylvania and Mississippi from the implementation of the states' waiting period requirements, the United States Supreme Court and the Fifth Circuit refused to invalidate the statutes on a facial challenge. Both courts suggested that they would later entertain an "as applied" challenge to the waiting period requirements. In other words, the courts are willing to speculate about the impact of a spousal notification requirement that will disproportionately harm white, middle-class women but are not willing to speculate about the impact of a waiting period requirement that will disproportionately harm poor women. The Supreme Court's promise that it will begin its analysis with the women most impacted by an abortion statute has proven to be a hollow promise for poor and African-American women.

Two hours after the oral argument in the *Barnes* case, the Fifth Circuit rendered its decision upholding the Mississippi statute, finding it indistinguishable from the Pennsylvania statute upheld in *Casey* and denying plaintiffs' request for a factual hearing in the district court to set forth the impact of the waiting period requirement on women's lives. It is hard to know what to hope for next. I can hope that women do face horrible acts of violence through the loss of their confidentiality, so we can present those facts to the court in an "as applied" challenge. But, of course, that means that women's lives will be sacrificed to achieve a challenge to an abortion statute—not something that I could ever desire. Or I can hope that we do not hear of any such violence, so we will not have any stories to report to the court. But, unfortunately, the fact that we do not hear of such stories does not mean that they do not exist. Women who have faced violence in their lives have always been invisible; their continued invisibility would be no victory.

The problem of violence against women is not likely to disappear tomorrow. But maybe we can, at least, start to break down the myth about women who choose abortions and the women who experience violence. All women in society are at risk of experiencing violence in their lives. Neither wealth, age, marital status, nor pregnancy immunize women from violence. Although all women who experience or are at risk of experiencing violence may need judicial protection, that protection is not equally available to all women. Instead, poor, young women who are disproportionately African-American receive the least judicial protection from violence. Moreover, despite attempts by the so-called "pro-life" movement to create distorted images of women in society, pregnant women who seek abortions are not murderers. Instead, they are often victims both of private and public violence themselves. We need to start to value their lives, young or old, rich or poor, white or black.

Notes

1. Antonia C. Novello & Lydia E. Soto-Torres, *Women and Hidden Epidemics: HIV/AIDS and Domestic Violence*, The Female Patient 17 (January 1992).

2. *Id.*

3. *Id.*

4. No. 91-1953 (filed August 5, 1992) (vacating the district court's preliminary injunction).

5. Studies have found that illegal abortion, rather than childbirth, is the most likely result in countries in which safe or legal abortions are not available. *See* Mashalaba, *Commentary on the Causes and Consequences of Unwanted Pregnancy from an African Perspective*, 3 Int. J. Gynecol. Obstet. 15, 17 (1989).

6. 112 S. Ct. 2791 (1992).

7. Novello & Soto-Torres, *supra* note 1.

8. *Id.* at 22.

9. *Id.*

10. Judith McFarlane, Barbara Parker, Karen Soeken, & Linda Bullock, *Assessing for Abuse during Pregnancy*, 267 JAMA 3176–78 (1992).

11. *Id.*

12. *Id.*

13. *Id.*

14. Council on Scientific Affairs, American Medical Association, *Violence against Women; Relevance for Medical Practitioners*, 267 JAMA 3184–89 (1992).

15. Eli H. Newberger, Susan Barkan, Ellice S. Lieberman, Marie C. McCormick, Kersti Yllo, Lisa T. Gary, & Susan Schecter, *Abuse of Pregnant Women and Adverse Birth Outcome; Current Knowledge and Implications for Practice*, 267 JAMA 2370–72 (1992) (but noting that increased risk for pregnant women is probably attributable to age, because women under 25 years of age were more likely both to be pregnant and to be abused by husbands and partners).

16. *See* Richard J. Gelles, *Violence and Pregnancy: Are Pregnant Women at Greater Risk of Abuse?*, 50 J. Marriage & Fam. 841, 846 (1988).

17. *See, e.g.*, Nancy Kathleen Sugg, *Primary Care Physicians' Response to Domestic Violence: Opening Pandora's Box*, 267 JAMA 3157–60 (1992).

18. McFarlane, *supra* note 10.

19. Anne H. Flitcraft, *Violence, Values, and Gender*, 267 JAMA 3194–95 (1992).

20. *Id.* at 3194–95.

21. *See* Ruth Colker, *An Equal Protection Analysis of United States Reproductive Health Policy: Gender, Race, Age, and Class*, 1991 Duke L. J. 324, 338–40 (1991).

22. *ACOG Renews Domestic Violence Campaign, Calls for Changes in Medical School Curricula*, 267 JAMA 3131 (1992).

23. *Id.*

24. 112 S. Ct. 2791 (1992).

25. The Pennsylvania statute contains the following requirements:

§3209. Spousal Notice.

(a) Spousal notice required.—In order to further the Commonwealth's interest in promoting the integrity of the marital relationship and to protect a spouse's interests in having children within marriage and in protecting the potential life of that spouse's child, no physician shall perform an abortion on a married woman, except as provided in subsections (b) and (c), unless he or she has received a signed statement, which need not be notarized, from the woman upon whom the abortion is to be performed, that she has notified her spouse that she is about to undergo an abortion. The statement shall bear a notice that any false statement made therein is punishable by law.

(b) Exceptions.—The statement certifying that the notice required by subsection (a) has been given need not be furnished where the woman provides the physician a signed statement certifying at least one of the following:

(1) Her spouse is not the father of the child.

(2) Her spouse, after diligent effort, could not be located.

(3) The pregnancy is a result of spousal sexual assault as described in section 3128 (relating to spousal sexual assault), which has been reported to a law enforcement agency having the requisite jurisdiction.

(4) The woman has reason to believe that the furnishing of notice to her spouse is likely to result in the infliction of bodily injury upon her by her spouse or by another individual.

Such statement need not be notarized, but shall bear a notice that any false statements made therein are punishable by law.

(c) Medical emergency.—The requirements of subsection (a) shall not apply in case of a medical emergency. 18 Pa. Cons. Stat. Ann. §3203 (1990) (§3209 reprinted at 112 S. Ct. at 2836).

26. *Id.* at 2820.

27. *Id.* at 2807.

28. *Id.* at 2820.

29. *Id.* at 2829.

30. *Id.*

31. *Id.*

32. Planned Parenthood of Southeastern Pennsylvania v. Casey, 744 F. Supp. 1323, 1351–52 (E. D. Pa. 1990).

33. 112 S. Ct. at 2829.

34. 744 F. Supp. at 1351.

35. *Id.* at 1352.

36. Chicago Trib., Nov. 17, 1991, at Cl.

37. *Id.*

38. *Id.*

39. *Id.*

40. States News Service, March 8, 1990.

41. *Id.*

42. 970 F.2d 12 (5th Cir. 1992) (vacating the district court's preliminary injunction).

43. U.S. Dept. of Commerce, Median Income of Households and Percent of Persons in Poverty by State, Based on Three Year Average (1988–90).

44. Mississippi's median household income is $20,414. The next lowest is Alabama's, at $22,610. *Id.*

45. *See* Children's Defense Fund, The Health of America's Southern Children (Table 3.1) (1989).

46. U.S. Dept. of Commerce, 1990 Census of Population and Housing: Mississippi (Table 6) (1990).

47. Mississippi Medicaid Management Information System, Statistical Report on Medical Care: Eligibles, Recipients, Payments, and Services, Section D(2)(1991).

48. Medicaid does not cover the cost of an abortion for a poor woman. Women in Mississippi carry to term quite frequently and have few abortions. Mississippi ranks 49th in its abortion occurrence rate. *See* Abortion Services in the United States, Each State & Metropolitan Area, 1984–1985 17 (Henshaw ed., 1988). It also ranks 45th in the number of adolescents who obtain abortions. *See* Cobb, Selected Facts About Teenage Pregnancy, Mississippi 12 (1991).

49. Mississippi has 12.5 doctors per 10,000 people; the lowest in the United States. *See* U.S. Dept. of Health and Human Services, Health United States: 1990 (Table 87). Mississippi ranked 36th in the United States in its provision of prenatal care from 1984–86. Singh et al., Prenatal Care in the United States: A State and Local Inventory 20 (1989). Mississippi has the dubious distinction of having the highest percentage of low birthweight babies; 8.7 percent of all babies in Mississippi were born at low birthweights in 1986. Carr et al., Report on Minority Health in Mississippi 19 (1990). Mississippi's 1989 infant mortality rate was 11.6 infant deaths per 1,000 live births; the national rate for infant mortality was 9.7. *Id.* at 19.

50. Declaration of Joseph Mitchell, M.D. ¶ 34. (All cites with paragraph numbers are to declarations admitted in the district court in *Barnes*).

51. Declaration of Stanley K. Henshaw, M.D. ¶ 17.

52. Plaintiff New Woman Medical Center charges $200 for an abortion up to 12 weeks gestation, $300 at 13 and 14 weeks gestation, and $400 at 15 to 16 weeks gestation. Declaration of Rogers ¶ 5. At Plaintiff Mississippi Women's Medical Center, the cost of an abortion increases $205 between the eleventh and twelfth week of pregnancy, an additional $50 at week 15, and an additional $100 beyond week 16. Declaration of Lisa Brown ¶ 5.

53. Declaration of Lisa Brown ¶ 6.

54. In one study, 60 percent of women having abortions after 15 weeks attributed the delay to their needing "time to raise money" for the abortion. Torres and Forrest, Why Do Women Have Abortions?, 20 Fam. Plan. Persp. 169, 174 (1988). *See also* Declaration of Joseph Booker ¶¶ 7–8; Declaration of Lisa Brown ¶ 6; Declaration of J. Edward Hill, M. D. ¶¶ 9, 11, 14; Declaration of Karen Jenkins ¶¶ 16–19; Declaration of Joseph Mitchell, M. D. ¶ 38; Declaration of Thomas Walter Tucker, II, M. D. ¶¶ 7–10.

55. Declaration of Stanley K. Henshaw, M. D. ¶ 8.

56. Declaration of Lisa Brown ¶ 7.

57. *See* Gina Stone, Handbook of Selected Data: Mississippi 71 (1989).

58. Trial Transcript in *Barnes* at 108 (Morrison). *See also* Trial Transcript in *Barnes* at 44 (Barnes).

59. Only 3.6 percent of the families on welfare in Mississippi in 1989 owned a car. *See* U.S. Department of Health and Human Services, Characteristics and Financial Circumstances of AFDC Recipients, FY 1989 (1989). *See also* Declaration of J. Edward Hill, M. D. ¶ 12; Declaration of Karen Jenkins ¶ 19.

60. Declaration of Rims Barber ¶ 6.

61. The cost of lodging near the various clinics ranges from $22.50 to $43.00 per night. *Id.* at ¶¶ 8–9.

62. For example, Dr. Hill stated in his Declaration:

> If my patients are required to stay overnight in Jackson they will most likely sleep in the car, if they get the other person [who gave them the ride] to stay overnight, or outside the clinic in the street. None of my patients have ever stayed in a hotel that I know of, and I don't believe they could afford to do so. Declaration of J. Edward Hill, M. D. ¶ 14.

63. *See* Mildred D. Pagelow, Family Violence 314–15 (1984).

64. Declaration of Lisa Brown ¶ 10.

65. These examples are drawn from discussions with my friends who work for Planned Parenthood or local abortion clinics.

66. Declaration of Stanley K. Henshaw, M. D. ¶ 6.

67. Cobb, Selected Facts about Teenage Pregnancy, Mississippi 10 (1991).

68. *See* Barnes v. State of Mississippi, No. J86-0458(W) (S. D. Miss. July 2, 1986) (granting plaintiff's request for a temporary restraining order enjoining juvenile bypass statute).

69. *See* Miss. Code Ann. §§ 41-41-51 to 41-41-55 (juvenile bypass statute).

70. A. G. Br. at 12.

71. Declaration of Stanley K. Henshaw, M. D. ¶ 18.

72. Declaration of John C. Morrison ¶¶ 24-28; Declaration of Joseph Mitchell, M. D. ¶ 42.

73. Declaration of Morrison ¶ 35.

74. Novello & Soto-Torres, *supra* note 1, at 22.

75. Kenneth R. Niswander, *Medical Abortion Practices in the United States*, in Abortion and the Law 53 (Smith ed., 1967).

76. Willard Jr., Cates, & Roger W. Rochat, *Illegal Abortions in the United States: 1972–1974,* 8 Fam. Plan. Persp. 86, 87 (1976).

77. Rachel B. Gold, *Therapeutic Abortions in New York: A 20 Year Review*, 55 Am. J. Pub. Health 964–65 (1965).

78. The Times-Picayune, Nov. 9, 1992.

79. The Times-Picayune, Nov. 9, 1992, at A-8.

80. *Id.*

81. Teresa Godwin Phelps, *The Sound of Silence Breaking: Catholic Women, Abortion, and the Law,* 59 Tenn. L. Rev. 547 (1992).

5

Bray v. Alexandria Women's Health Clinic

Abortion and Public Violence

I was standing near the entrance of the clinic, helping people coming into
the clinic from the street. I was face to face with the anti protestors. . . . A
man was standing by the fence, with 2 young children. The girl was maybe 6
and the boy no older than eight. They stood on either side of this man, just
watching everything. I assumed the man was their father. I was wearing a
hat for protection from the sun and had taken it off to wipe my forehead.
The man yelled out, to me and especially his children, "See that red head? If
you ever see her on the street you can kill her, because she's no good and she
kills babies." I'll never forget those words. He said it with such force, that for
a moment I was scared. I had never been threatened before and I was
nervous. In that one moment this man was teaching his children to hate and
kill anyone who differs from their opinion. As my knees shook, I stood there,
knowing there was nothing I could say.

—Pro-choice activist, excerpt from a letter to the National
Abortion Rights Action League[1]

I. Introduction

WHEN I WAS taking my baby for a walk in the stroller one morning in New
Orleans, a woman passed me on the sidewalk with a T-shirt that read Abortion is Murder with a large picture of a fetus on it. Such T-shirts, which had become
commonplace in that community since Operation Rescue visited for several weeks
in the summer of 1992, typify the excellent job that the anti-choice movement has
done in presenting an image of pregnant women who choose abortions as murderers. What the public, unfortunately, does not always realize is that harassing tactics of groups like Operation Rescue actually increase the level of violence and coercion against pregnant women in society in both the private and public spheres.
Although all women face violence in their lives, applying an anti-essentialist perspective will show that young and poor pregnant women who are disproportionately African-American receive the least judicial protection from such violence.

In the last chapter, I talked about abortion and private violence. The *Casey* decision considered private violence in the lives of disadvantaged women, but it did not discuss the connection between public violence against pregnant women and abortions. The actions of groups like Operation Rescue cause women who use abortion clinics to face a loss of confidentiality and to experience harassment, intimidation, and violence. Because the women who use abortion clinics rather than private doctors' offices are disproportionately poor, these harassing and often violent activities have a dramatic effect on their ability to procure a safe and legal abortion. Although the murder of the Florida doctor, Dr. Gunn, has made people aware of the violent tactics of some members of these groups, the public is not sufficiently aware of the disproportionate impact that these activities have on the most disadvantaged women in our society. I will therefore describe the tactics of Operation Rescue and the systematic way that these tactics deliberately target disadvantaged women. In order to make this discussion as vivid as possible, I will be using the words of the women themselves who have been harmed by Operation Rescue.

From an equality perspective, the tactics of groups like Operation Rescue are very troubling, because their actions prohibit women from exercising their right to choose to have a safe and legal abortion. This is a gender-based problem, because the underlying actions are chosen to target the most vulnerable women, and the effect on these women undermines their ability to live full and productive lives as citizens of our community. The Supreme Court was recently given the opportunity to recognize the gender-based nature of Operation Rescue's tactics in *Bray v. Alexandria Women's Health Clinic*.[2] In *Bray*, the Court was asked to hold that pregnant women and their supporters have the right to use the Ku Klux Klan Act to protect themselves from the public violence of anti-abortion protestors, such as Operation Rescue, as well as to protect themselves from attempts by these protestors to breach their confidentiality, thereby exposing them to private violence. Displaying a lack of concern for women's equality in society and an essentialist perspective that leaves the most disadvantaged women in society unprotected, the Supreme Court ruled against the plaintiffs. I will discuss the assumptions underlying the *Bray* decision later in this chapter and will argue that Congress should pass a statute protecting women from abortion-related harassment and violence when they seek reproductive health services.

II. The Problem

Abortion-related violence is not limited to domestic violence. Some women face public violence and harassment when they seek abortions through the actions of organizations such as Operation Rescue. These groups physically block access to abortion clinics, expose women to violence and harassment as they seek access to abortion providers, and attempt to breach the confidentiality of women seeking abortions (thereby exposing them to violence and harassment in their private lives). Because poor and young women are more likely to use abortion clinics (which offer the lowest cost abortion services) and middle-class, older women are more likely to use private abortion providers who typically escape the wrath of Operation Rescue,[3] this public violence disproportionately impacts poor and young women. It is therefore the most disadvantaged women in society who need protection from the harassment of groups like Operation Rescue.

A. Loss of Confidentiality

Operation Rescue organizes its tactics so as to make women fear a loss of confidentiality. Illustrations of this and other tactics come from a brief recently filed in the Supreme Court by the National Abortion Rights Action League (NARAL),[4] in which they included dozens of letters from women active in the pro-choice movement in an appendix. Excerpts from these letters describe the effect that such loss of confidentiality may have on women:

As an escort I have observed anti-abortion picketers photographing all people who enter clinics. I know of one particular instance in which an anti recorded the license plate number, got the name of the owner and called to preach on the evils of abortion. Sadly, the person who owned the car was the mother of a woman who had not confided her pregnancy to her family.
Everything worked out fine but temporarily destroyed the relationship between mother and daughter. The daughter had been impregnated by the mother's boyfriend. While the patient did not consider her pregnancy a result of rape, she maintained that the mother's boyfriend had taken advantage of her when she arrived home in a drunken state. The incident was the only sexual contact of any sort for the patient in months.[5]

M [ ] writes down the license tag numbers from all the cars parked in the clinic parking lot. Some of the clients who come from small towns are intimidated by this.[6]

The protestors stand on the stairs where there is little room to pass. One of them usually has a camcorder and videotapes patients. This is one of the most intrusive and upsetting things I have seen so far. The patients are afraid that they will see themselves on television, maybe the evening news![7]

Applying the Ku Klux Klan Act against Operation Rescue, Judge Arcara found that Operation Rescue used videocameras as an offensive weapon to intimidate women from having abortions in Buffalo, New York. In the words of Judge Arcara:

> [T]he evidence clearly shows that defendants use cameras as offensive weapons to harass and intimidate patients entering the clinics. Defendants have even pointed the cameras directly into the faces of patients seeking access to the clinics. They have also videotaped patient vehicles and their license plates as they enter the medical facilities. Defendants are well aware that women seeking abortions, especially younger women, are often terrified at the prospect of anyone, especially family members, finding out that they are having an abortion, and that the presence of cameras increases patients' fear that their identities might be revealed.[8]

Applying state law, the Georgia Supreme Court in *Hirsh v. City of Atlanta*[9] found that Operation Rescue illegally used videocameras to harass patients:

> A clinic executive director testified that the protestors' activities caused patients much anxiety, that those who did gain access were visibly upset and some emotionally distraught. Patients' blood pressure and pulse rates were elevated by the impediments they had had to overcome to gain entry, subjecting the women to additional health risk should an abortion, performed under local anesthesia, be done while the patient was in such a shaken state.[10]

These tactics harm women's health while also exposing them to domestic violence through breach of their confidentiality. As discussed in the previous chapter, waiting period requirements give Operation Rescue greater opportunity to harass women, especially when they learn their identity during their first visit by recording their license plate number.

B. Harassment, Intimidation, and Violence

Although Operation Rescue may describe itself as pro-life, its verbal and physical tactics are anything but peaceful.

1. DISRESPECT FOR LIFE

Excerpts from the letters from NARAL's brief describe the anti-life hostility of the Operation Rescue demonstrators.

> These fanatics reveal their true agenda. They demonstrated their disregard of women's health and well being. This becomes evident when they shout to a women [sic] in the driveway "You should die, not your baby."[11]

From the very beginning of my escort work and continuing to this day, I have been subjected to many types of harassment. Verbal assault consists of being called "murderer, butcher, garbage of society, vulture" etc. as well as comments about my personal appearance (hairstyle, clothing) and my life-style (the size of my home, the car I drive, etc.). There were numerous verbal threats made about my daughter, who was 24 years old. Comments such as "we know where your daughter is, we know where she lives." They also learned the identity of her fiancee and in June, 1988 when she was planning to be married, the demonstrators threatened to "publicly embarrass" me by appearing at her wedding, forcing me to have police officers at the church and at my home where the reception was held.[12]

Despite their purported pro-life position, these epithets and slogans by Operation Rescue protestors can hardly be described as respectful of life.

2. VIOLENCE AND HARASSMENT

The NARAL letters also demonstrate the harassment, threats of violence, and actual violence perpetrated by Operation Rescue.

Physical intimidation and verbal assault are the primary tools employed against women by anti-abortion groups. They refrain from accosting men on public streets to demand personal information on pregnancy status, marital status, religion, or his sex life. Instead they assail women. A woman approaching a clinic is first surrounded by anti-choice demonstrators who shout at her to be heard over one another. If she tries to get away from them or says that she is not interested they persist in following, pressing themselves on her, and blocking her every step in order to continue their rebuke and deluge of contempt. Recently I witnessed a so-called 'pro-lifer,' hiss at a woman who was trying to extricate herself from a group of blockaders, "Murderer, Murderer, Murderer. Kill, Kill, Kill."[13]

A man in his late 50's or early 60's, about 6'1" or 6'2", wearing a clerical collar approached me and stood very, very close to me. He was carrying some sort of rolled up cloth which I assumed was a sign and wooden stakes to drive the sign into the ground.

He continued to breathe heavily, as though he were barely restraining himself from hitting me and to move very close to me, within 9" of my body. He said, "You had better get out of here, miss." . . . He said again, "I'm warning you, miss. Leave now." I did not. He then took one of the wooden stakes, which seemed, from my peripheral vision, to be about a foot long made from rough lumber with a point at the end and a metal sheet in the middle, out of his bundle and into his free hand. It was trembling. He brought it up to my left eye, a little to the left of the center of my eye, and about 2 or 3 inches away from my face. He began to twist the stake slowly from side to side, not saying anything, but breathing heavily. Then he said,

"Get out of here!" and he jabbed the stake toward my eye on each syllable.

I did not move, looking back on it, probably because I was too frightened to move. Then a group of escorts came by me and when he saw the orange T-shirts, he slipped back into the crowd and I did not follow him.

The incident also angered me greatly. It was the first time in my life that I had been physically threatened. He was taking advantage of the fact that he was a foot taller than I, at least 100 lbs. heavier, and, for all practical purposes, armed.[14]

The windows in the clinic have been shot out three different times during the night and it is also frightening to arrive in the morning to find windows shattered by bullets and bullets lodged in the walls.[15]

In another incident, a carload of "Operation Rescue" members failed to respond to a police order to stop their car at the mobilization site for a "rescue" attempt in December of 1989. The "Operation Rescue" members actually drove their car into the police officer who was dressed in plain clothes. He got on the front hood of their car while they continued to drive on. All the time he was yelling "Stop, I'm a police officer" and flashing his badge.[16]

Thursday evening I met my partner at the [ ] metro stop, and we headed over to where Operation Rescue was lodged during the D.C. Project II weekend. Our assignment was to photograph people involved with Operation Rescue to update our files. We were making our way through the parking lot when we saw two men approaching us. I agreed with my partner that I should photograph the one on the left, and she, the one on the right. I took my subjects [sic] photo, while my partner focused in on her's [sic]. As I lowered my camera, I saw my partner's subject—a man that we have identified as "Ed", one of Randall Terry's body guards—rush my partner, picking her up, and slamming her against the brick wall of the hotel. She got up off the ground, whereupon, "Ed" rushed her again, forcing her to the ground, kicking her in the stomach, back, face, and breasts. "Ed" then pulled out his metal flashlight and began clubbing my partner on the head and neck with the instrument. During this time, my partner had curled up in a ball, attempting to protect her head and body. I was photographing the entire incident. All the while, "Ed" was screaming at my partner that he was "going to kill her," calling her a "murderous bitch," "cunt," "whore" and "slut." I attempted to intercede, and "Ed" turned towards me with his raised flashlight, until my partner's movements brought his attention back to her, and he continued to beat her. I ran to get help, and upon my return "Ed" had fled off into the parking lot somewhere.[17]

In issuing an injunction against Operation Rescue in Buffalo, Judge Arcar entered findings that Operation Rescue engaged in harassing and violent activ ity.[18] During physical blockading, he found that the demonstrators "trespass on the clinic property and sit or lay in the entrances of the clinic in an attempt to block access to and egress from the clinic."[19] Constructive blockading includes "demonstrating and picketing around the entrances of the clinics, and by harassing patients and staff entering and leaving the clinics."[20] The court also found that Operation Rescue's actions include

> frequently and routinely congregat[ing] in or near the driveway entrances to the facility parking lots in order to impede and obstruct access to the facilities . . . yell[ing] at patients, patient escorts and medical staff entering and leaving the health care facilities . . . [and] crowd[ing] around people trying to enter the facilities in an intimidating and obstructing manner, and grab[bing], push[ing] and shov[ing] the patients, patient escorts and staff.[21]

These are activities of violence rather than peaceful civil disobedience.

3. IMPACT ON DISADVANTAGED WOMEN

As with the *Casey* decision, it is the most disadvantaged women in society who were most affected by the Court's decision in *Bray*—the women who face both public harassment by Operation Rescue and domestic violence through their loss of confidentiality. The NARAL letters document this impact on young and poor women who are disproportionately racial minorities.

> In the summer of 1990, we received a call from the [ ] clinic located in East L.A.; a primarily low-income Hispanic neighborhood. These neighborhoods are favorite targets of Operation Rescue due to the fact that their residents have few health-care options available to them.
> One Saturday . . . a woman in the company of her two children approached the clinic [to take her children to a dentist in the same building who donated his services to children on Saturdays]. They were met by a frenzy of hostile picketers who shoved at them photographs of what they claimed were aborted fetuses and screamed at the mother, "Don't kill your baby!" . . . [O]nce inside the children were hysterical, crying out, "Mommy, don't kill us!"
> The situation at the clinic continued on this way for several months with little help from the local police. It finally ended when the priest and his church group decided to move on to another clinic. Currently, they are harassing women at a health care facility located in [ ], another low-income Hispanic area.
> Most importantly, consider the people who are made to suffer the greatest; the poor and disadvantage [sic] of our community who have so few

options to choose from, and who utilize women's health care facilities for the variety of services they provide.[22]

I remember one young Hispanic couple in particular who came in last December. The woman was carrying a fetus which, through amniocentesis, was determined to be without kidneys. Their doctor told them that the fetus probably would not survive delivery, but would definitely not be able to survive on its own. Because protestors were sitting in front of the doors, myself and another staff member pulled the couple over the protestors and through the doors. You could see the shock and despair, especially on the husband's face, who by now, was in tears. They told me that they wanted to have children, but under the circumstances, felt terminating the pregnancy at that point was the best thing. The people blocking the doors just made a very difficult experience even more traumatic.[23]

N [ ] concentrates on the youngest and most vulnerable looking clients. She tells the young men, "If you love her, you'll get her out of there. She could die. That clinic isn't safe. If she dies, it will be your fault."[24]

The instances of verbal abuse to patients are nearly endless. One of the hardest things I have to do as a volunteer is to keep the men who come in with patients from assaulting the protestors. In one instance, a 17 year-old came in with his girlfriend. The protestors started with the normal "Don't let her kill her baby", "Be a man—that's your baby she's going to kill", "God made her a mother for a reason" nonsense. The patient burst into tears and the boy finally turned to the crowd and screamed, "Let her alone. She was raped!" One protestor shouted, "How do you know it's not your baby she's killing?" The boy replied, "Because I love her too much to sleep with her before we're married."[25]

The husband of a young black woman was also shouting back at the "protestors" telling them that they did not understand the difficulty of raising, supporting, emotionally supporting and giving enough love to the four children he and his wife already had at home. He told the "protestors" how the government was already having to help them financially and that this decision, made by he and his wife, was their personal right giving the "protestors" no right to interfere.

These women are trying the best way they know how to make the most difficult decision of their lives at a time when they are already emotionally stressed by their situation. Before they enter our clinic, they have already had many family discussions and disputes over the situation they are in. This is especially true of parents with young girls who have been on drugs and feel that it is better for a decision to be made now.[26]

A patient . . . told us that she had six children at home and wouldn't be able to get back to the clinic since she lived 2 1/2 hours away and didn't have a car. She had been able to get a ride this time but couldn't get one again. Abortion is no longer available in her community because doctors who did them were picketed and harassed until they stopped doing them.[27]

III. The Ku Klux Klan Act

The Ku Klux Klan Act[28] was enacted in 1871 to provide federal assistance to state and local authorities to assure that private mobs do not destroy the ability of vulnerable groups to enjoy an equal right to live under the rule of law. It prohibits conspiracies "for the purpose of depriving, either directly or indirectly, any person or class of persons of the equal protection of the laws, or of equal privileges and immunities under the laws; or for the purpose of preventing or hindering the constituted authorities . . . from giving or securing to all persons . . . the equal protection of the laws."[29] Until the Supreme Court's adverse decision in *Bray*, lower courts permitted women to use the statute to obtain injunctions against Operation Rescue, thereby keeping clinics open and minimizing the impact of Operation Rescue's harassing and violent tactics.

As the Ku Klux Klan Act has been interpreted to protect African-American travelers from the assault of a white mob,[30] it should also protect women from the mob violence of anti-abortion demonstrators. The tactics of Operation Rescue fit perfectly into the conspiracy requirement of the Ku Klux Klan Act. As a conspiracy, it has a media spokesperson and national mailings announcing, for example, its Summer of Purpose. Its leaders decide exactly what abortion facilities to target; they do not disclose their plans to anyone, including their followers. They then arrange for their followers to board a bus, which they then drive to an undisclosed location where demonstration activity occurs. Their followers make no tactical decisions; those are all made by the leaders of the conspiracy.

I did not appreciate the importance of the Ku Klux Klan Act in protecting women's lives until Operation Rescue arrived in Louisiana. Through mass mailings, Operation Rescue publicly stated that it would target the only abortion clinic in Baton Rouge and suggested that it would also come to New Orleans for protest activity at the dozen or so clinics in the New Orleans area. Working with the NOW Legal Defense and Education Fund as well as with a coalition of Louisiana lawyers, I tried to obtain court injunctions to limit Operation Rescue's tactics in both cities. Because we could not meet the jurisdictional requirement of the Ku Klux Klan Act in Baton Rouge of showing that some of the clinic's patients crossed state lines to obtain abortions, we proceeded in state court under state trespass law.[31] Despite the fact that Operation Rescue was encamped around the Baton Rouge clinic, we could not get an elected state court judge to enter an injunction; in his opinion, neither the clinic nor its patients were in imminent danger. By contrast, in New Orleans, we were able to proceed in federal court, because many of the patients did travel to New Orleans from Mississippi.[32] Despite the fact that Operation Rescue was over sixty miles away from New Orleans in another city, Baton Rouge, we were able to obtain an injunction within twenty-four hours of filing our pleadings. The result was that the Baton Rouge clinic was practically a war zone with Operation Rescue demonstrators blockading, harassing, pushing, and shoving patients as well as surreptitiously taking some patients to fake abortion clinics. The New Orleans clinics were never targeted; the police told me that the injunction intimidated Operation Rescue from entering the New Orleans area. Thus, like African-Americans after the Civil War, women can unfortunately not count on the protection of the state courts. The unavailability of the Ku Klux Klan Act to their lives gives women one less tool to protect themselves from public and private violence when seeking abortion services.

The key difficulty with using the Ku Klux Klan Act is that it has been interpreted to require the finding of a "class-based" animus. Operation Rescue supporters, of course, say they are not anti-woman; they are simply anti-abortion, and they therefore target both men and women who facilitate women procuring an abortion. The Klan, however, was found to have a class-based animus against blacks despite the fact that it targeted both blacks and their supporters. Operation Rescue does not target men's sex lives or reproductive choices. In addition, Operation Rescue does not limit itself to supporters of abortion rights. They typically prevent *any* woman from entering a woman's health clinic, even if she is visiting to undergo a routine prenatal checkup, pap smear, or pregnancy test. Operation Rescue only targets reproductive health choices made by women, focusing their attention on the most vulnerable women seeking to use women's health clinics.

The difficulty in establishing class-based animus under the Ku Klux Klan Act is similar to the difficulty of establishing that pregnancy is a sex-based classification under the Constitution and thereby overturning *Geduldig*. Not surprisingly, a Court that adheres to the correctness of the *Geduldig* decision has found that anti-abortion protestors do not have a gender-based animus. In Justice Scalia's words in the *Bray* decision:

> Respondents' case comes down, then, to the proposition that intent is legally irrelevant; that since voluntary abortion is an activity engaged in only by women, to disfavor it is ipso facto to discriminate invidiously against women as a class. Our cases do not support that proposition. In Geduldig v. Aiello, 417 U.S. 484 . . . (1974), we rejected the claim that a state disability

insurance system that denied coverage to certain disabilities resulting from pregnancy discriminated on the basis of sex in violation of the Equal Protection Clause of the Fourteenth Amendment.... The same principle applies to the "class-based, invidiously discriminatory animus" requirement of § 1985(3).[33]

Applying that test to the *Bray* case, Justice Scalia readily concluded that the plaintiffs could not meet the gender-based animus requirement. In Scalia's words: "Whether one agrees or disagrees with the goal of preventing abortion, that goal in itself (apart from the use of unlawful means to achieve it, which is not relevant to our discussion of animus) does not remotely qualify for such harsh description, and for such derogatory association with racism."[34]

Although the dissent disagreed with Scalia's analysis of the gender-based requirement, the dissent did not understand the particular impact that this statute would have on the most disadvantaged women in society. For example, the dissent stated:

Petitioners, however, are not mere opponents of abortion; they are defiant lawbreakers who have engaged in massive concerted conduct that is designed to prevent all women from making up their own minds about not only the issue of abortion in general, but also whether they should (or will) exercise a right that all women—and only women—possess.[35]

The conduct of Operation Rescue, however, is not designed to prevent *all* women from making up their own minds. Instead, Operation Rescue targets the most disadvantaged women in society and tries to make abortion entirely unavailable to them. Operation Rescue is not likely to change these women's minds about abortion, but it is likely to physically make abortion unavailable to them. That is the essence of its illegal activity, which is not described by the majority or the dissent.

Pro-choice organizations are currently working with Congress to pass a statute banning clinic violence. The recent killing of a physician in Florida, Dr. David Gunn, who performed abortion services, may add momentum to those efforts. There also is precedent in Congress "correcting" the Supreme Court's errors in the sex discrimination area. For example, Congress was able to reverse the Supreme Court's decision under Title VII of the Civil Rights Act holding that pregnancy-based discrimination was not gender-based discrimination through enactment of the Pregnancy Discrimination Act.[36] Nevertheless, the Pregnancy Discrimination Act explicitly did *not* protect women from abortion-related discrimination.[37] If Congress passes the clinic violence statute, it will be the first time that it corrected the Supreme Court's errors with respect to the abortion issue.

Options are also available to women other than getting Congress to pass a clinic violence statute. For example, the President has the authority to send in federal marshals to assist local police if Operation Rescue and their supporters overwhelm the resources of local police forces. Rather than go to federal court, in the future women may go to the United States Attorney's office and request federal assistance. Under either scenario—seeking federal court assistance or executive branch assistance—women are dependent upon the changing politics of the judicial or executive branches of government. No solution appears to be permanent or long lasting. An amendment to the Ku Klux Klan Act to specifically protect women from anti-abortion violence (or a separate statute) would have the most long-term, beneficial effect.

Notes

1. Brief of 29 Organizations Committed to Women's Health and Women's Equality as Amici Curiae in Support of Respondents, Bray v. Alexandria Women's Health Clinic, No. 90-985 (May 13, 1991) App. Letter C79 [hereinafter letters will be cited as "Women's Brief, *supra* note 1, at Letter_____"].
2. 113 S. Ct. 753 (1993).
3. These generalizations are made on the basis of my own experience in Louisiana defending abortion clinics from Operation Rescue.
4. Brief of 29 Organizations Committed to Women's Health and Women's Equality as Amici Curiae in Support of Respondents, Bray v. Alexandria Women's Health Clinic, No. 90-985 (May 13, 1991).
5. Women's Brief, *supra* note 1, at Letter C3.
6. *Id*. at Letter C37.
7. *Id*. at Letter C62.
8. Pro-Choice Network of Western New York v. Project Rescue Western New York, 799 F. Supp. 1417, 1426.
9. 401 S.E.2d 530 (Ga. 1991).
10. *Id*. at 532.
11. Women's Brief, *supra* note 1, at Letter C5.
12. *Id*. at Letter C29.
13. *Id*. at Letter C14.
14. *Id*. at Letter C16.
15. *Id*. at Letter C29.
16. *Id*. at Letter C39.
17. *Id*. at Letter C43.
18. 799 F. Supp. 1417.
19. *Id*. at 1424.
20. *Id*.
21. *Id*.
22. Women's Brief, *supra* note 1, at Letter C8.
23. *Id*. at Letter C26.

24. *Id.* at Letter C37.

25. *Id.* at Letter C38.

26. *Id.* at Letter C59.

27. *Id.* at Letter C62.

28. 42 U.S.C. 1985.

29. 42 U.S.C. 1985(3).

30. Griffin v. Breckenridge, 403 U.S. 88, 95–96 (1971).

31. NOW v. Operation Rescue National, No. 382, 750 (19th Judicial District La.) (July 8, 1992) (Judge Brown).

32. NOW v. Operation Rescue National, No. 92-2289 (E.D. La. July 9, 1992) (Judge Livaudais).

33. 113 S. Ct. at 760–61.

34. *Id.* at 762.

35. *Id.* at 798.

36. Pregnancy Discrimination Act of 1978, 92 Stat. 2076, 42 U.S.C.

37. The Pregnancy Discrimination Act states:

(k) The terms "because of sex" or "on the basis of sex" include, but are not limited to, because of or on the basis of pregnancy, childbirth, or related medical conditions; and women affected by pregnancy, childbirth, or related medical conditions shall be treated the same for all employment-related purposes, including receipt of benefits under fringe benefit programs, as other persons not so affected but similar in their ability or inability to work, and nothing in section 2000e-2(h) of this title shall be interpreted to permit otherwise. This subsection shall not require an employer to pay for health insurance benefits for abortion, except where the life of the mother would be endangered if the fetus were carried to term, or except where medical complications have arisen from an abortion: Provided, That nothing herein shall preclude an employer from providing abortion benefits or otherwise affect bargaining agreements in regard to abortion. 42 U.S.C. § 2000e(k).

6

Pregnant Men

[I]f men could become pregnant, they would not be men (indeed no one
would be a man as we understand that term), and to ask how abortion
would be treated in so fundamentally different a world is to ask a question
that is not subject to meaningful evaluation.
—Cass Sunstein[1]

I. Introduction

IN THE PREVIOUS two chapters, I have tried to show what insights might be
gained from considering the problem of violence against women from an anti-
essentialist perspective. I also showed how difficult it was to make arguments
on behalf of "women" in the reproductive health context because of the courts'
insensitivity to the ways that restrictions on women's reproductive capacity can
contribute to women's subordination. Thus, in chapter 4 we saw that the Supreme Court has used a narrow privacy framework rather than a broad equality
framework in considering restrictions on women's rights to procure an abortion. In chapter 5 we saw that the Ku Klux Klan Act is not available to women
to protect them from the violence of anti-abortion protestors, because the Supreme Court refuses to recognize the anti-woman animus that underlies clinic
violence and harassment.

Doctrinally, a key difficulty to using equality doctrine to protect women from
restrictions on their reproductive freedom is that the Supreme Court has refused
to recognize these restrictions as gender based. Put simply, there are no pregnant men to which we could compare women to show gender-based treatment.
All pregnant *people* are treated alike; it is irrelevant (to the Supreme Court) that
all pregnant people are women. As the examples in the previous chapters show,
however, it is crucial that we convince the courts that pregnancy-based discrimination is gender-based discrimination if we are to improve women's position in
society. We need to find a way to talk about *pregnant men*.

The task of determining how men would be treated if they could become
pregnant is extremely difficult, since it is a counterfactual inquiry. It is made

even more difficult if we take seriously the anti-essentialist critique. Anti-essentialism cautions us not to overgeneralize about "women" or "men." It is very attentive to differences among and between women and men. Although anti-essentialist feminists do not intend to create a theory that might hinder women's likelihood of using the law to challenge their subordination in society, anti-essentialism could achieve that result by supporting the Supreme Court's refusal to make comparisons between women and men when they are not identically situated.

The decisions that are most susceptible to being supported by an extreme anti-essentialist perspective are the decisions in the area of reproductive health. The courts have frequently refused to compare pregnant women to any category of men in society, thereby leaving pregnant women unprotected under equality doctrine. It is difficult to respond to this problem from an anti-essentialist perspective, because an anti-essentialist perspective would have to agree that pregnant women are, in fact, quite different from other groups in society. In other words, anti-essentialism is good at looking at *differences* but not good at seeing *similarities*. Finding similarities, however, is an important component of an effective use of equality doctrine. In this chapter, I discuss how we can use some insights from anti-essentialism while also protecting pregnant women under equality doctrine.

A core difficulty with using equality doctrine to protect women's rights is that the United States Supreme Court has ruled that pregnancy-based discrimination is not per se gender-based discrimination under the equal protection clause of the United States Constitution. In its landmark decision *Geduldig v. Aiello*,[2] the Court ruled that a state-run disability plan that excluded normal pregnancy from coverage did not discriminate on the basis of gender. In the Court's words:

> While it is true that only women can become pregnant, it does not follow that every legislative classification concerning pregnancy is a sex-based classification. . . . The lack of identity between the excluded disability and gender as such under this insurance program becomes clear upon the most cursory analysis. The program divides potential recipients into two groups—pregnant women and nonpregnant persons. While the first group is exclusively female, the second includes members of both sexes.[3]

If the first group, pregnant persons, had included both men and women, the Court would have found it easier to evaluate whether gender-based discrimination was taking place, because it then could have determined whether pregnant women were being treated more disfavorably than pregnant men. But, of course, men, by definition, do not get pregnant.

The *Geduldig* decision gives feminists two choices in developing equality doctrine in the area of reproductive rights. First, we can try to establish that a pregnancy-based rule was "designed to effect an invidious discrimination against the members of one sex or the other." Second, we can try to overturn *Geduldig*'s basic finding that pregnancy-based distinctions are not inherently gender based. In chapter 4, I presented an argument that tried to meet the first requirement; however, it is a nearly impossible requirement to meet. In light of the Court's decision in *Personnel Administrator v. Feeney*,[4] a plaintiff is required to prove intent by showing that a legislature "selected or reaffirmed a particular course of action at least in part 'because of,' not merely 'in spite of,' its adverse effects upon an identifiable group." Legislatures, however, rarely leave such evidence behind in enacting modern legislation. Except in extreme situations like I uncovered in Louisiana, there is rarely evidence that state legislatures consciously harmed women's lives while enacting anti-abortion legislation. In most states, therefore, the only genuine option is to try to convince the Court to overturn *Geduldig*.

One way to overturn *Geduldig* would be to show that men would be treated better than women if they had the capacity to become pregnant. Rather than assume, as does the *Geduldig* decision, that pregnancy is an "objectively identifiable physical condition with unique characteristics," which makes it impossible to compare women's and men's reproductive capacities, I will assume that some limited comparisons are possible. By searching for situations in which women and men are comparably situated with respect to reproductive capacity, I believe that we can begin to answer the counterfactual question of how society would treat pregnant men.

The fact that men do not get pregnant has therefore posed an enormous hurdle for feminist litigators trying to use the Constitution to protect women from pregnancy-based discrimination. With the erosion of privacy doctrine as a way to ensure women's reproductive freedom, it has become increasingly important to find ways to use equal protection doctrine to protect women from pregnancy-based discrimination.[5] But equal protection doctrine is not readily available so long as feminists cannot get over the *Geduldig* hurdle.[6] We need to have ways to show that pregnant women are treated more disfavorably by society than men would be treated if they could get pregnant.

In this chapter, I will try to provide a description of how society would treat men if they could become pregnant, arguing that they would be treated far better than pregnant women are currently treated. Two key problems, however, exist with this line of inquiry. First, some commentators, such as Cass Sunstein, have argued that such counterfactual questions are not helpful or relevant, because they rely on changing one part of reality while keeping the rest the same.[7] But I argue that such counterfactual discussions can be useful and are essential if we are to respond to *Geduldig*. Second, some feminists who consider themselves to be anti-essentialists, such as Angela Harris and Catharine MacKinnon,[8] might disagree with my line of inquiry, because it relies on the use of biological arguments to explain women's subordination in society.

I further argue that feminists can accommodate biological arguments about women's condition in society without engaging in gender essentialism. Gender essentialism is "the notion that a unitary, 'essential' women's experience can be isolated and described independently of race, class, sexual orientation, and other realities of experience."[9] I argue that the litmus test for gender essentialism is whether an author is considering the full range of women's experiences when making generalizations, not whether an author uses biological arguments. Unfortunately, some authors such as Harris and MacKinnon confuse biological arguments with essentialist arguments. This chapter will repeatedly rely on biological arguments to show that society treats women disfavorably due to their capacity to become pregnant. Theorists such as Harris and MacKinnon do feminism a disservice in insisting that anti-essentialism requires that we ignore entirely the role of biology in women's lives.

In this chapter, I discuss the role of biology in perpetuating women's subordination in society and speculate as to how men would be treated if they could become pregnant. I discuss examples in which the courts *ignore* women's biological differences from men and examples in which the courts *exaggerate* women's biological differences from men to perpetuate women's subordination in society. Finally, I examine cases in which the courts try to benefit women by respecting their reproductive capacity. Nevertheless, I argue that these cases really demonstrate situations where what may seem like preferential treatment for some women results in subordinate treatment for the most disadvantaged women in our society.

The cases that I discuss actually reinforce rather than detract from the anti-essentialist critique, despite their emphasis on the role of biology in perpetuating women's subordination in society. They show that society does not treat women monolithically. Society may ignore women's biological differences from men, it may exaggerate those differences, and it may ignore those differences for some women while exaggerating them for other women. The prevailing pattern, however, is that women are treated with respect to their biology in ways that perpetuate their subordination in society. In addition, the most disadvantaged women in society always seem to face the brunt of this mistreatment. This final insight emphasizes the importance of what I consider to be the core insight of anti-essentialism[10]—that when women are treated on the basis of their presumed characteristics, be they socially or biologically created, they are not actually being treated monolithically. Women's treatment is always socially contingent upon women's status in society vis-à-vis class, race, religion, and other group-based conditions.

Thus, the challenge in examining cases involving women's reproductive capacity is to respect women's distinctive reproductive abilities while not overstating the limitations that those abilities place on women. To be true to anti-essentialism, we must examine the effects of such policies on *all* women, especially focusing our attention on the effects on the most disadvantaged women in our society. I will try to engage in such a discussion in this chapter.

II. The Problem with Counterfactuals

Cass Sunstein has argued that the kind of counterfactual inquiry that I will be presenting in this chapter is not particularly useful. He argues that asking how men would be treated if they could get pregnant "has the usual problem of counterfactuals: It can work only if one isolated part of current reality is changed and the rest held constant—an extremely artificial strategy, since the kind of change of that one isolated part of reality changes the rest of it as well."[11] Moreover, Sunstein argues, "[I]f men could become pregnant, they would not be men (indeed no one would be a man as we understand that term), and to ask how abortion would be treated in so fundamentally different a world is to ask a question that is not subject to meaningful evaluation."[12]

Sunstein is correct to observe that asking how men would be treated if they could become pregnant has some troubling counterfactual elements. And this chapter cannot sincerely expect to answer that question. However, there are situations in which men and women are equivalently positioned with respect to reproductive issues due to the new reproductive technology, and interestingly, the men's reproductive interests always seem to prevail. It is helpful, I suggest, for us to explore these situations in which men are "almost pregnant" to see the systematic valuation of men's well-being over women's well-being in society. Sunstein may be overemphasizing the distinctiveness of pregnancy to make his point. By contrast, I think that we should welcome the opportunity to discuss situations in which men are "almost pregnant" in order to demonstrate how much better these men are treated than similarly situated women.

Moreover, feminists have little choice but to try to speculate as to how men would be treated if they could get pregnant if we want to overcome the *Geduldig* hurdle. *Geduldig* leaves feminists with two choices—show how men would be treated if they could get pregnant or show that the legislature acted with the intent to harm women when it created a pregnancy-based category.[13] In other articles[14] and briefs,[15] I have tried to meet the second requirement; however, it is a nearly impossible requirement to meet. In light of the Court's decision in *Per-*

sonnel Administrator v. Feeney,[16] a plaintiff is required to show that a legislature "selected or reaffirmed a particular course of action at least in part 'because of,' nor merely 'in spite of,' its adverse effects upon an identifiable group." Legislatures, however, rarely leave behind such evidence. In fact, in my own research in Mississippi and Louisiana, I found that many state legislatures keep virtually no record of their deliberations. Thus, as difficult as the first line of inquiry may be, we must pursue it until the Court overrules *Geduldig.*

III. The Anti-essentialist Critique of Biological Arguments

I consider myself to be an anti-essentialist feminist, by which I mean that I virulently try to consider the range of women's lives when trying to understand a particular policy's impact on women in society. Because the most disadvantaged women in society—lesbians, poor women, women of color, women with disabilities, and young women (to name a few)—often experience the most dramatic consequences of a policy's impact on women, I also am committed to beginning my analysis with a discussion of the lives of the most disadvantaged women. Thus, in previous chapters, I have discussed how society's rules concerning maternalization and terrorization impact starkly on lesbians,[17] how society's rules concerning reproductive freedom impact starkly on young and poor women,[18] and how society's rules regarding protection of abortion clinics impact starkly on young and poor women as well as women with disabilities.[19] I have learned through these inquiries that the impact on the most disadvantaged women in society is not necessarily a heightened version of the impact on more privileged women; sometimes, that effect is actually an opposing effect or even a comparable effect. The kinds of investigations that I have conducted, I believe, would be consistent with an anti-essentialist critique.

This chapter, however, asks a somewhat different question—it asks how men would be treated if they could get pregnant. When I first started to ask myself that question—stemming from the difficulty in using equality doctrine to assist women in the area of reproductive freedom—I was not expecting this particular chapter to be directly relevant to my anti-essentialist agenda. Since I was asking how privileged men would be treated, it did not seem to me that I needed to have my anti-essentialist lens in sharp focus. What I soon learned, however, is that some feminists might argue that my current inquiry is *essentialist*, because it relies on biological arguments to explain women's subordination in society. For example, Harris[20] and MacKinnon[21] both argue that feminists are essentialists when they rely on that argument. This anti-essentialist critique of biological arguments is so sweeping that one must wonder whether feminists should credit biology with having any role in explaining women's subordination in society.

I therefore learned that I had been using one aspect of anti-essentialism in my previous writings—the aspect that says that we must consider the full range of women's experiences when generalizing about gender—but that I had been ignoring another aspect of anti-essentialism—that we should avoid biological arguments. Thus, I found it necessary to explore the basis of the anti-biological argument in anti-essentialism to decide whether I wished to add it to my own theoretical perspective. As the reader will see, I have chosen not to adopt that position.

A. Angela Harris and Robin West

Angela Harris's pathbreaking work on anti-essentialism has helped the feminist community (and myself) understand how the word *woman* has often meant middle-class white woman within feminist jurisprudence. Thus, I usually begin my articles by quoting Harris's definition of gender essentialism, as I have in this chapter.[22]

Harris's work, however, also contains a strong critique of the use of biological arguments. Her critique of biological premises flows from her definition of the "self," which is integral to her scholarship. She defines the self as follows:

> It is a premise of this article that we are not born with a "self," but rather are composed of a welter of partial, sometimes contradictory, or even antithetical "selves." . . . Thus, consciousness . . . is not a final outcome or a biological given, but a process, a constant contradictory state of becoming, in which both social institutions and individual wills are deeply implicated. A multiple consciousness is home both to the first and the second voices, and all the voices in between.[23]

At its limits, Harris would seem to be suggesting that there is not even a biological self that would distinguish men from women. No aspect of self is innate or given—to the extent that women share commonalities, it is because those commonalities have been constructed by themselves or others.

Harris applies her conception of the self to a critique of Robin West's scholarship. West relies on women's physical differences from men to justify her critique of what she calls the "separation thesis." West argues that women are essentially connected, not essentially separate from the rest of human life, because they get pregnant and breast-feed, but that modern legal theory rests on the separation thesis. In West's words:

> In fact, women are in some sense "connected" to life and to other human beings during at least four recurrent and critical material experiences: the ex-

perience of pregnancy itself; the invasive and "connecting" experience of heterosexual penetration, which may lead to pregnancy; the monthly experience of menstruation, which represents the potential for pregnancy; and the post-pregnancy experience of breast-feeding. Indeed, perhaps the central insight of feminist theory of the last decade has been that woman [sic] are "essentially connected," not "essentially separate," from the rest of human life, both materially, through pregnancy, intercourse, and breast-feeding, and existentially, through the moral and practical life.[24]

West's biological claims are sweeping; aside from using the phrase "in some sense," she makes no attempt to modify her argument for any subgroup of women.

Harris criticizes West's perspective by arguing that it assumes that "every self is deeply and primarily gendered, with its corollary that gender is more important to personal identity than race."[25] It thereby "privileges white women's experience over the experience of black women."[26] According to Harris, "West's essential woman turns out to be white."[27]

I would agree with Harris that West's biological arguments suffer from gross distortions in the lives of women; however, West's theory is problematic for white women as well as for black women. West's scholarship suffers from two problems. First, without citation to case law, she assumes that the courts always rely on the separation thesis to determine how women should be treated in society. As I demonstrate in the latter parts of this chapter, that is not an accurate description of the case law with respect to women's reproductive abilities. At times, the courts emphasize women's reproductive capacity; at other times, they ignore it. But, in either case, they treat women's reproductive capacity in a way that perpetuates women's subordination in society. By assuming that women's reproductive capacity has a unidimensional effect on women's lives by making them feel connected to others, West perpetuates the kind of stereotyping that we will see is the basis of many court decisions. The biological aspects of gender are not necessarily the core defining characteristics of the lives of white women or black women, yet courts often treat them as if they are.

Second, not all women are affected in the same way by society's treatment of their reproductive biology. As we will see in this chapter, society's treatment of women's reproductive biology may benefit some women while harming others. Not surprisingly, the women who are the most harmed are also the women who are already the most disadvantaged in society. By having middle-class women in mind when creating policies, legislatures often clumsily harm poor women while purporting to benefit middle-class women. West's unidimensional thesis does not permit an easy exploration of these multiple effects.

B. Catharine MacKinnon

Like Angela Harris, Catharine MacKinnon argues that it is inappropriate to try to make all women fit into the abstraction "woman" as "a fixed, posited female essence."[28] Whereas Harris identified MacKinnon and West as having such problematic features in their scholarship,[29] MacKinnon identifies Simone de Beauvoir and Susan Brownmiller as using essentialist arguments.[30]

De Beauvoir, according to MacKinnon, is an essentialist, because she defines women in terms of their reproductive capacity. Similarly, Brownmiller is an essentialist because she argues that the accident of women's biology makes women vulnerable to rape.[31] In both cases, their theory is subject to criticism, because "[i]t is unclear exactly how any social organization of equality could change such an existential fact, far less how to argue that a social policy that institutionalized it could be sex discriminatory."[32] According to MacKinnon, feminist theory is therefore essentialist to the extent that it relies on acknowledging women's biological differences from men to explain male dominance.

I agree with MacKinnon that "[t]here is nothing biologically necessary about rape" and that society need not punish women for having a reproductive capacity.[33] In both of those examples, anti-feminist society is trying to attach an unnecessary social meaning to women's biological differences from men. That social meaning must be described for what it is—a socially constructed understanding of women's biology that is not, at all, inevitable. Thus, MacKinnon is correct to urge us to see the *social* meaning of women's biology. Nevertheless, feminist theory may need to refer to the actual facts of women's biology (rather than the social meaning) to explain some aspects of women's subordination in society. MacKinnon relies entirely on examples where society exaggerates the sex differences between women and men to harm women. We can find other examples where society *ignores* the sex differences between women and men to harm women and yet other cases where society tries to help women by focusing on biological differences while actually harming some classes of women. MacKinnon's total critique of the use of biological arguments does not give us guidance on how to look at the full range of society's treatment of women's distinctive biology; it assumes that treatment is one-directional.

C. Conclusion

In sum, Harris's and MacKinnon's critiques of biological essentialism and West's use of biological arguments do not leave us with much guidance about what role biology can or should play in feminist theory. West seems to be giving biology too large a role in claiming that a focus on biology is the "central insight of feminist theory of the last decade."[34] As we will see in the ensuing discussion, *anti-feminists* also often focus on women's distinctive biological capacity to perpetuate women's subordination in society. Thus, it is entirely too simplistic to say that we should construct feminist theory around women's distinctive biological abilities. By doing so, we risk creating a feminist theory that can play into the hands of people who want to use women's biology as an excuse to limit their roles in society.

Rather than abandon biological arguments entirely, I argue that we need to make them in a much more sophisticated way than does Robin West. We need to see when society needlessly exaggerates women's biological differences from men to exclude women from certain roles in society as well as when society ignores women's biological differences when they are truly relevant and important. Finally, we need to be mindful of the differences among women in the meaning of their biological experiences. Pregnancy, for example, is a socially contingent experience in women's lives; we should not expect it to have the kind of universal meaning that West ascribes to it. Harris and MacKinnon, therefore, provide us with an important starting point in suggesting that we should be critical of biological arguments. Ignoring them entirely, however, is no better than privileging them absolutely.

IV. New Reproductive Technology

A. Introduction

Cases involving the new reproductive technology represent examples of the courts ignoring women's biological differences from men in order to perpetuate women's subordination in society. Male sperm donors are considered to have equivalent or superior claims to women who are gestational or biological mothers. Male sperm donors are considered to be "pregnant persons," and not surprisingly, these pregnant male persons are treated much better than pregnant female persons. Such a result occurs because the courts devalue or ignore women's experiences of pregnancy.

Due to the new reproductive technology, women can bear children through in vitro fertilization (IVF) transfer using their own eggs or those of another woman, as well as by artificial insemination (AI).[35] In some instances, the woman is called a "surrogate" mother; however, that terminology is not always accurate. In the famous *Baby M.* case, for example, Mary Beth Whitehead was not a surrogate, because she used her own egg to become pregnant through artificial insemination.[36] In other cases, however, the pregnant woman is more truly a surrogate, because she became pregnant through IVF transfer using the

egg of another woman that was combined with the sperm of a man who is typically the other woman's husband.

For the purposes of this discussion, I will put the reproductive technology
cases into three categories: (1) IVF or AI using the pregnant woman's own egg
and the sperm of her husband; (2) IVF or AI using the pregnant woman's own
egg and the sperm of a contractual stranger; and (3) IVF using another woman's
egg and the sperm of a contractual stranger. In the latter two categories, a woman
can be compensated to relinquish the baby to the sperm donor and his spouse.
In the first category, the woman uses reproductive technology to bear a child
within her own marriage. Of the three categories, the first is the most commonplace.[37] A question that occasionally arises through the use of these technologies
is, Who are the parents?

The problem of defining the family arises in all three categories. A woman
who is sometimes unmarried and sometimes a lesbian can use the sperm of a
man to whom she is not married in order to bear a child. She often intends for
the man not to be considered the father with respect to his legal responsibilities
and burdens; she often does wish her female partner to be considered a second
parent. The male sperm donor has generally donated sperm for compensation
and does *not* wish to have legal responsibility or recognition. States generally
protect men from having any parental obligations and protect women from having to share parental obligations with the sperm donor in that scenario.[38] Further, in some localities (although too few in number), an unmarried woman
can even have another woman become the second parent.[39] Nevertheless, state
statutes sometimes have a loophole—they only provide protection to the sperm
donors of *married* women. Men who have donated sperm to unmarried women
do sometimes seek to be recognized as fathers, despite, in some cases, the parties' initial understanding that the donor would not seek to be recognized as
the father. In such cases, sperm donors have successfully sought recognition
as a parent. They have often been treated better than gestational or biological
mothers. The cases in which male sperm donors obtain parental recognition therefore fit my thesis that "pregnant men" always win.

Similarly, a problem in defining the family can occur when a woman who
gives birth did *not* expect to be considered the legal mother at the time she became pregnant, because she signed a contract stating that she would turn the
baby over to the sperm donor and his family. Irrespective of whether the courts
consider the underlying contract to be valid or whether the pregnant woman is
the "biological" mother, the sperm donor and his family always seem to win.
The sperm donor's claim to fatherhood always seems to trump the pregnant
woman's claim to motherhood irrespective of her biological connection to the

child. Although the courts purport not to be using any categorical rules stating that the pregnant woman always loses and the sperm donor always wins, that seems to be the case in practice. These cases are therefore quite problematic, as further discussion will show.

Before discussing the court's gender bias in these cases, however, it is helpful to remember the kinds of women and men who are being compared in these cases. In the latter two categories, in particular, the women have received compensation from a man to carry a child to term. By definition, the man has superior financial resources, since he can afford to pay for her services. In cases where the woman's own egg is being used, the man will probably want to choose a woman who is of the same race as himself (which is typically Caucasian). However, in cases where IVF transfer is being used and the egg is not that of the gestational mother, a Caucasian man has no incentive to try to choose a Caucasian woman. One could easily imagine Caucasian men disproportionately choosing poor women of color who have few options for productive employment in the workplace to serve as gestational mothers. The gestational mother also does not need to be living in the United States. A physician could conceivably set up a gestational mother "factory" in a third-world country to import babies to the United States. Moreover, in cases where male sperm donors successfully obtain parental rights, the mother is almost always an "unmarried woman," who could also be a lesbian. Thus, it is important not to see the courts' preference for male sperm donors who have paid for their fatherhood as a product of isolated cases. The male privilege in these cases is often accompanied by privileges of race, class, marital status, and sexual orientation, which may become even more heightened in the future as reproductive technology becomes more sophisticated. We are always moving toward a brave new world.

Finally, I should make a technical observation before proceeding to the case discussion. I have often chosen to discuss only one case in each of the categories. I have made this choice for two reasons. First, there are few reported decisions in this area of the law, although at least two of the cases that I will be discussing have received a lot of publicity. Because the new reproductive technology makes these cases more likely to occur in the future, discussion of these early precedents is very important. Second, I am using these cases as much for their symbolic importance as their precedential importance. Each case provides a strong story with a narrative that is potentially very sympathetic to the female plaintiff. Yet, the woman lost in each case.[40] These women were not visible to the courts in terms of the depth of their experience. By telling their narratives, I hope to share these women's lives with the reader and help make them visible in their totality.

B. IVF or AI Using the Pregnant Woman's Own Egg
and the Sperm of Her Husband[41]

Mary Sue Davis desperately wanted to bear and raise a child.[42] During the course of her marriage to Junior Lewis Davis, she suffered five tubal pregnancies, which were extremely painful. Due to reproductive health problems that were causing the tubal pregnancies, she first had one fallopian tube removed and eventually had her other tube ligated. She and Junior Lewis unsuccessfully sought to adopt a child. Eventually, they decided to try in vitro fertilization (IVF) to become parents.

IVF is typically a very painful procedure for the woman, and Mary Sue's case was no exception. On six different occasions, she received hormone injections every day for a month; on five occasions, she was anesthetized for the aspiration procedure to occur. These procedures were particularly painful for Mary Sue because of her fear of needles.[43]

On the last occasion at which IVF was attempted, the physician was able to extract nine ova for fertilization—more than Mary Sue would need for one attempt at pregnancy. By freezing the extra ova, Mary Sue could continue to try to get pregnant without undergoing the aspiration and hormonal stimulation procedure each time. Mary Sue, however, did not continue with the IVF process, because Junior Lewis sued for divorce, and the frozen embryos became the subject of a lengthy court challenge.

The issue in the divorce proceeding was what should be done with the frozen embryos. Mary Sue wanted to have custody of the embryos to transfer them to herself or to donate them to another woman for transfer. (She changed her mind during the course of the litigation.) Junior Lewis was opposed to Mary Sue or another woman making use of the embryos. The court therefore had to determine whose wishes to honor—Mary Sue's or Junior Lewis's.

Both Mary Sue and Junior Lewis presented arguments about their reproductive freedom and why their desires should be honored. Mary Sue wanted the embryos to assist herself or another woman to procreate; Junior Lewis wanted the embryos to prevent himself from being compelled to be a "father." Their views were irreconcilable. Under Tennessee law, the Supreme Court of Tennessee saw its role as acting in equity to weigh the relative interests of the parties in using or not using the embryos; no specific contract or statute bore on the resolution of the issue.

Although the court did not view the case in this way, the case actually presented the court with three options: (1) transferring all of the embryos to Mary Sue, (2) transferring all of the embryos to Junior, or (3) giving half of the embryos to Mary Sue and half to Junior. Although one could argue that the third solution is really a victory for Mary Sue, that is not entirely accurate. Since IVF has a low success rate, there would be a very small chance of success if only half of the embryos were ultimately transferred to a woman's uterus. And if the embryos were donated to an embryo bank to be used by an anonymous woman, neither Mary Sue nor Junior Lewis would know whether they became "parents." The court, however, chose to consider the case as involving only the first two options, thereby viewing it in its most bipolar form. I would suggest that the court's exaggerated sympathy for Junior Lewis made it unable to see the middle grounds available to it.

In reaching its determination, the court purported to view Mary Sue and Junior Lewis as having equivalent claims despite the greater physical burden that Mary Sue had endured to create embryos. In the words of the court:

> We are not unmindful of the fact that the trauma (including both emotional stress and physical discomfort) to which women are subjected in the IVF process is more severe than is the impact of the procedure on men. In this sense, it is fair to say that women contribute more to the IVF process than men. Their experience, however, must be viewed in light of the joys of parenthood that is desired or the relative anguish of a lifetime of unwanted parenthood. As they stand on the brink of potential parenthood, Mary Sue Davis and Junior Lewis Davis must be seen as entirely equivalent gamete-providers.[44]

In fact, this description of Mary Sue's and Junior Lewis's positions understated Mary Sue's discomfort. Not only did Mary Sue experience the pain of IVF, but she also experienced the pain of five tubal pregnancies. That pain is relevant, because had she not experienced the tubal pregnancies, she would not have sought IVF. Moreover, Mary Sue faced the unlikely prospect of being able to get pregnant in the future unless she could use the frozen embryos or underwent IVF again. Thus, a denial of custody in the embryos to her might cause further pain in the future.

Nevertheless, considering Junior Lewis's equitable arguments, the court found that he and Mary Sue had equivalent claims. Junior Lewis had argued that he did not want to be compelled to experience "fatherhood" because of his own unhappy childhood living in a home for boys and having monthly visits with his mother. This is how the court described his situation:

> In light of his boyhood experiences, Junior Davis is vehemently opposed to fathering a child that would not live with both parents. Regardless of whether he or Mary Sue had custody, he feels that the child's bond with the non-custodial parent would not be satisfactory. He testified very clearly that his concern was for the psychological obstacles a child in such a situ-

ation would face, as well as the burdens it would impose on him. Likewise, he is opposed to donation because the recipient couple might divorce, leaving the child (which he definitely would consider his own) in a single parent setting.[45]

On the one hand, the court was faced with Mary Sue's actual pain—the pain of tubal pregnancies, the pain of the IVF procedures, and the future potential pain if she were not provided with the embryos and wanted to try again to bear a child. On the other hand, the court was faced with Junior Lewis's speculative argument about the pain a not-then-conceived child might experience *if* the child were raised in a single-parent setting. In fact, both Mary Sue and Junior Lewis had remarried, so the child might well have had *three or four* adults who considered themselves to be the child's parents. Moreover, the scenario that an adoptive couple might ultimately divorce is a scenario that is, of course, possible for any couple. But Junior Lewis must have weighed that possibility when he decided to participate in the IVF process, especially since he testified that his own marriage had problems during the IVF procedure. It is hard to see how transferring the embryos to Mary Sue or another couple would create a possibility of divorce that Junior Lewis had not already agreed to accept when he participated in IVF.

The court was therefore presented with Mary Sue's real physical pain versus Junior Lewis's speculative and somewhat illogical emotional argument about harm to a future child and himself. Viewing these two pains as equivalent, the court ruled for Junior Lewis. The court concluded that his potential lifetime pain if he were to be coerced to be a father was worse than the physical pain that Mary Sue had already or might in the future experience.[46]

The court's use of language revealed its sympathies in the case. Junior Lewis was consistently referred to as a "father" with an argument (which the court accepted) against coerced "fatherhood." Junior Lewis, however, was no more a father than a man who donates sperm to a sperm bank, never knowing whether that sperm was used to produce a child. Fatherhood should require an emotional bonding, which is difficult to have with one's sperm. Mary Sue wanted herself or another woman to use the embryos to become a mother in the genuine sense—by bearing and raising a child. It is only by distorting the meaning of the word *father* that the Court was able to conclude that Mary Sue and Junior Lewis had equivalent claims. It is a sad reflection on fatherhood if the mere donation of sperm makes one a father.

When I discussed this case with my feminist jurisprudence class at Tulane Law School, I was surprised to hear how strongly some men felt about the legal entitlement that should flow from their donation of sperm. This conversation made me realize the ways in which society socializes men to attribute tremendous social value to their sperm—a value that I would suggest is greatly disproportionate to the availability of the supply. (As I said to my students, sperm is cheap.) I suspect that men are socialized to overvalue their sperm, because their sperm is their only connection to reproduction. Women, on the other hand, have to make a much greater physical sacrifice in order to bring a child into this world. The *Davis* case may therefore reflect an example of how society overvalues sperm in order to put men on an equal footing with women's gestational role in the reproductive process. This discussion with my class also made me realize that my understanding of who is a father—based on an emotional commitment to child rearing—may be inconsistent with the generally accepted understanding of who is a father—based on a genetic contribution to the child.

This case did not literally involve a "pregnant man"; however, the court treated Junior Lewis as having the equivalent childbearing capacity of a woman, Mary Sue, and easily sided with the man. One might argue that that was just happenstance—that he had a more appealing emotional argument in this particular case. In the future, one might argue, a woman might win such a case.

The court, however, did not treat this case as a highly subjective, contextual inquiry. Instead, it treated it as a rule-making case, trying to determine for the future when the woman's wishes rather than the man's wishes should be honored in an IVF transfer case. Thus, the court summarized its views as follows:

> Ordinarily, the party wishing to avoid procreation should prevail, assuming that the other party has a reasonable possibility of achieving parenthood by means other than use of the preembryos in question. If no other reasonable alternatives exist, then the argument in favor of using the preembryos to achieve pregnancy should be considered. However, if the party seeking control of the preembryos intends merely to donate them to another couple, the objecting party obviously has the greater interest and should prevail.[47]

Junior Lewis did not win because of his unusual experience of being raised in a home for boys. All men won who wanted to prevent their wives from using IVF when the particular situation was not the subject of a written contract.[48] The court ended its opinion by stating that "the rule does not contemplate the creation of an automatic veto,"[49] but that is exactly what the court's decision does when there is a "reasonable possibility of achieving parenthood by means other than use of the preembryos in question." Apparently, the fact that a woman would have to undergo the pain, difficulties, and even dangers of IVF to reproduce in the future is considered "reasonable" by the court. Thus, after a woman undergoes the pain of IVF, relying on the fact that she will be able to have the fertilized eggs placed back in her uterus, a man who has donated the sperm, which have already fertilized her eggs, is entitled to prevent her from undergoing the final stage of embryo transfer.

The court tried to describe its rule in gender-neutral terms by referring to the affected individuals as "parties" rather than as men and women. A man, however, is not capable of transferring the embryos to his own uterus. The only person who can take advantage of the transfer is the woman. When one "party" therefore has the power to prevent a transfer, that party is always a man. In other words, the only time an injunction to *prevent* a transfer will be at issue is when a woman wants a transfer to take place and the sperm donor wishes to prevent it; that scenario is quite gender specific. The only aspect of this rule that is, in fact, gender neutral is the provision about giving the embryos to someone else. Either party could desire to make a gift of the embryos to another woman. But interestingly, by allowing either party to veto that gift, he or she would be vetoing another woman's ability to benefit from the IVF procedure. Thus, all the vetoes that are contemplated by the rule will deter a woman from using the embryos—either the biological mother or a surrogate mother. The rule therefore has far-ranging implications in giving men, and sometimes women, the power to prevent a woman from becoming pregnant through IVF transfer. The result in this case—the particular victory for Junior Lewis and the broader rule fashioned by the court—makes sense in a society that respects men's well-being over that of women's. Quite simply, the pregnant man always wins.

When I presented an earlier version of this chapter at the University of Texas Law School, I was interested to hear that many feminists viewed this case as a victory for women, because the court concluded that the frozen embryos were not "life" that should receive a special constitutional status. Had the court taken that view, then Mary Sue Davis would have won easily, since she wanted to sustain that life. Feminists argued that recognizing the frozen embryos as having a special constitutional status would undermine our abortion jurisprudence. I disagree with that argument, because it confuses gestational mothers with genetic mothers. In my view, it is critical to a pro-choice perspective that the fetus lives inside the woman's body; it is not critical to that perspective that the woman has contributed the genetic material for the fetus that resides in her body.[50] Thus, a gestational mother rather than a genetic mother in the case of IVF transfer has the right to decide whether to abort a fetus. In addition, I do not see any problem with acknowledging that the frozen embryos are a form of life. A woman's right to terminate a pregnancy, in my view, is not dependent on our pretending that the fetus inside of her is not "life." Instead, I would say that the termination of that life is an unintended consequence of her desire to terminate the pregnancy. If pregnancies could be terminated without the termination of the life inside of her (and the procedure would not be physically more dangerous to the pregnant woman), then I believe that the woman should have the right to terminate her pregnancy but not have the right to insist that the fetus's life also be terminated. As I have argued elsewhere, one can (and should) be both pro-choice and pro-life.[51]

The Davis case presents the first "abortion" case where the embryo is residing outside of a woman. It therefore represents an example where we can be both "pro-choice" and "pro-life." One can be pro-choice by preserving Mary Sue's right to bring a pregnancy to term, and one can be pro-life by preserving the life of the embryo itself. "Choice" is not always about the choice to terminate a pregnancy; choice can also be about the choice to continue a pregnancy. Because this embryo is not residing in a woman's body, the case gives us a perfect opportunity to distinguish between the right to terminate a pregnancy and the right to terminate a life. In my view, the abortion jurisprudence should only include the former claim. Thus, Junior Lewis should not be able to use that jurisprudence to insist that the life of the embryo be terminated; he should only be able to use that jurisprudence to insist that the embryo not reside in his body. On the other hand, Mary Sue or another woman should be able to use the pro-choice jurisprudence to insist that she be permitted to bring a pregnancy to term. Valuing Junior Lewis's claim over Mary Sue's claim reflects a distorted conclusion from the pro-choice abortion jurisprudence. I believe that distorted conclusion has occurred because a man's reproductive capacity has been valued over that of a woman. Junior Lewis was treated as if he were a pregnant woman who desired to terminate a pregnancy; Mary Sue was not treated as if she were a pregnant woman who wished to bring a pregnancy to term. Thus, the pregnant man prevailed over the pregnant woman.

C. IVF or AI Using the Pregnant Woman's Own Egg and the Sperm of a Contractual Stranger

1. MARRIED MEN WHO ENGAGE IN ARTIFICIAL INSEMINATION TO PARENT A CHILD

In February 1985, Mary Beth Whitehead[52] and her husband, Richard, entered into a contract with William Stern in which Mary Beth agreed to become pregnant through artificial insemination using the sperm of William in return for compensation of $10,000.[53] Moreover, Mary Beth agreed to carry the child to term, bear it, and deliver it to William and his wife, Elizabeth; Mary Beth agreed to relinquish her parental rights and Richard agreed to perform all acts necessary to rebut the presumption of paternity so that Elizabeth could adopt the child.[54] (William would presumably become the father without the need to adopt the child.) In a separate contract, William Stern agreed to pay $7,500 to the Infertility Center of New York for its services in arranging the "surrogacy" contract.[55]

After several artificial inseminations, Mary Beth Whitehead became pregnant and ultimately bore a child on March 27, 1986, which has been referred to as Baby M.[56] (The Sterns named her Melissa; Mary Beth named her Sara Elizabeth.) During the pregnancy and after the birth, Mary Beth had serious misgivings about whether she could relinquish the child to the Sterns. Nevertheless, on March 30, she did turn the child over to the Sterns at their house.[57] Mary Beth then became quite distraught and persuaded the Sterns to allow her to have the baby for one week, after which she agreed to return it to them.[58] In fact, she kept the child for four months until the police forcibly removed it from her parents' home in Florida.[59]

William Stern filed a complaint in New Jersey state court alleging that Mary Beth Whitehead had refused to comply with the surrogacy agreement and that she would flee the state if he attempted to gain custody. The Whiteheads did, in fact, flee the state with the baby, forcing William Stern to commence a supplementary proceeding in Florida state court. Stern was successful in his various state court actions, and Baby M. was eventually handed over to him by the police. Pending final judgment, Mary Beth Whitehead was awarded limited visitation with Baby M.[60]

After a thirty-two-day trial, the trial court issued a ruling from the bench in which it enforced the surrogacy contract, although also finding that vesting custody in the Sterns was in the best interest of the child, and in which it permitted Elizabeth Stern to adopt Melissa.[61] Pending the outcome of the appeal, the New Jersey Supreme Court granted very limited visitation to Mary Beth Whitehead.[62]

On appeal through a grant of direct certification,[63] the New Jersey Supreme Court concluded that the surrogacy contract was not valid, because it violated the state's policy of not permitting payment for adoption.[64] In addition, the court found that the statutory standards for relinquishment of parenthood had not been followed, because the trial court had made no finding of abandonment or neglect with respect to Mary Beth Whitehead.[65]

Having decided that the surrogacy contract was unenforceable, the court then turned to the proper resolution of the custody question. Using the state's Parentage Act, the court then proceeded under a "best interest of the child" standard to determine who should be given custody of Baby M.[66] The New Jersey Supreme Court had to make that determination after the Sterns had already been awarded custody for a one-and-a-half-year period, following the trial court's ruling. Based on the Sterns's extensive involvement with the child, the court concluded that the child's best interest would be served by remaining with the Sterns. In addition, the court concluded that the Sterns offered a more favorable household in terms of emotional support and financial stability.[67]

Despite the court's ruling, it purported to view Mary Beth Whitehead more favorably than had the lower court. The court stated:

> We think it is expecting something well beyond normal human capabilities to suggest that this mother should have parted with her newly born infant without a struggle. Other than survival, what stronger force is there? We do not know of, and cannot conceive of, any other case where a perfectly fit mother was expected to surrender her newly born infant, perhaps forever, and was then told she was a bad mother because she did not.... Her resistance to an order that she surrender her infant, possibly forever, merits a measure of understanding.... And if we go beyond suffering to an evaluation of the human stakes involved in the struggle, how much weight should be given to her nine months of pregnancy, the labor of childbirth, the risk to her life, compared to the payment of money, the anticipation of a child and the donation of sperm?[68]

Moreover, the court criticized the transfer of custody from Mary Beth to the Sterns during the pendency of this case. In the court's words:

> The probable bond between mother and child, and the child's need, not just the mother's, to strengthen that bond, along with the likelihood, in most cases, of a significantly lesser, if any, bond with the father—all counsel against temporary custody in the father. A substantial showing that the mother's continued custody would threaten the child's health or welfare would seem to be required.[69]

Thus, the court seemed to be very sympathetic to Mary Beth Whitehead— noting her substantial risk and discomfort during pregnancy and her strong bond with the child as her mother. Nevertheless, under the standard articulated by the court—best interest of the child—none of those factors were relevant to the custody dispute. They only became relevant to a minor degree in the court's consideration of the visitation issue. Although it did not dictate that the lower court order visitation for Mary Beth, it did suggest that the *five-year delay* in visitation suggested by the child's guardian would seem to be in error.[70]

The result in this case was that William Stern achieved sole custody of the baby, Melissa, and Mary Beth Whitehead was granted some weekend and visitation rights. The father's rights, which arose out of his donation of sperm, trumped those of the mother who donated the egg and actually bore the child.

Although the court does not purport to view this case in gender terms nor propound a rule for the future, it is easy to see an implicit rule in the case. Significant factors in the case were the greater financial and emotional stability of the Sterns. Such financial discrepancy will almost always exist in a "surrogate mother" case given the large amount of money that such cases cost. As for the differing emotional stability, that is also to be expected in such cases. A court is always likely to view a woman as emotionally "unstable" when she has refused to abide by the terms of a contract to which she initially agreed.

It is true that this case presented an unusual element whereby the father obtained custody for a one-and-a-half-year period while the case was pending—a factor that certainly weighed in his favor and a factor that the court cautioned should not occur readily in the future. But interestingly, continuity of custody did not play heavily in the court's analysis; financial and emotional stability played more heavily. Emotional support and nurturance, however, need not be a function of wealth.[71] The court nevertheless seemed to make that assumption. In the future, one would not expect such a case to drag on for such a long period of time, since the validity of the underlying contract would not be arguable. Assumptions about the relationship between emotional support, nurturance, and financial wealth may therefore play heavily in future cases.

The bottom line is that the man's claim to fatherhood based on his donation of sperm trumped a woman's claim to motherhood based on her donation of egg and bearing of the child. The man did not need to be pregnant to win; even when a man has a much weaker equitable argument than the mother in terms of his contribution to the child who is conceived, the man will prevail. The "best interest of the child" analysis pretends to be gender neutral by ignoring parental physical investment in childbirth; ignoring that contribution, however, achieves the gender-specific result of favoring men's disproportionate access to financial resources.

2. UNMARRIED WOMEN WHO USE ARTIFICIAL INSEMINATION TO BEAR AND PARENT A CHILD

In sharp contrast to the successful claims of married men who donate sperm for the purpose of becoming fathers, unmarried women who seek artificial insemination to become mothers do not fare as well. As previously discussed, state statutes typically protect the interests of both men and women when a married woman seeks to use artificial insemination to bear a child whom she wants to parent and whom the sperm donor does not wish to parent. In that case, she is considered to be the legal mother, her husband is considered to be the legal father, and the sperm donor has neither rights nor obligations.

Unmarried women, who are sometimes lesbians, are not treated as favorably by state statutes. Typically, the male sperm donor does have the right, if he so chooses, to seek to become a legal parent when he has donated sperm to an unmarried woman. When male sperm donors have sought to be recognized as the legal parent when the woman is unmarried, they have generally prevailed, irrespective of the parties' understanding at the time that he donated sperm.[72]

The way that I understand the development of the law in this area is as follows: Men who are compensated for donating sperm to unmarried women do not want to have to worry about parental obligations and responsibilities. By passing statutes that eliminate their parental rights, states are therefore protecting men's ability to receive compensation for participating in reproductive activity while avoiding legal liability. Thus, these statutes may incidentally protect lesbians and other unmarried women; however, the purpose of these statutes is to protect male sperm donors. When male sperm donors who donate sperm to unmarried women wish to be recognized as parents, however, the loophole in the state statutes gives them that opportunity. Their act of donating sperm appears to carry much more legal weight than a woman's act of donating an egg and acting as the gestational mother.

Of course, it is theoretically true that unmarried women who have received sperm from a man could sue him for child support, and he would theoretically not be protected by those state statutes. I have, however, not found any such cases. I do not know if that is because women tend to be honest in complying with their initial desire not to have the man recognized as a parent, because women's lawyers tell them that state statutes will probably not be interpreted to accord men parental obligations in such an example, because women are simply less litigious for cultural or economic reasons, or for some other reason.

One important factor, of course, in distinguishing cases like *Baby M.* from cases in which an unmarried woman unsuccessfully seeks to prevent the sperm donor from being recognized as a parent is marital status. The man is almost always married in the *Baby M.* scenario, and the woman is rarely married in the second scenario. (The woman may also be unmarried in the *Baby M.* scenario, although Mary Beth Whitehead was married; being unmarried would certainly not have helped her claim under the "best interest of the child" doctrine.) Thus, one might say that married "pregnant" men are treated better than unmarried pregnant women. True to the anti-essentialist thesis, a factor other than gender— marital status—is relevant to understanding the results in these cases.

D. IVF Using Another Woman's Egg and the Sperm of a Contractual Stranger[73]

Mark and Crispina[74] are a married couple who desired to have a child but were unable to, because Crispina had had a hysterectomy.[75] In January 1990, Mark,

Crispina, and Anna signed a contract, whereby Anna agreed to carry an embryo to term that was created through Mark's sperm and Crispina's egg.[76]

Both parties appeared not to live up to the conditions of the contract. Mark and Crispina did not obtain an insurance policy for Anna, which they had promised to acquire; in addition, they were not sufficiently helpful when she had premature labor during her pregnancy.[77] For her part, Anna had not disclosed her history of stillbirths and miscarriages; before the baby was to be born, she demanded full payment under the contract.[78] She wrote a letter to Mark and Crispina stating that she urgently needed the remaining $5,000 because of housing and health problems she was experiencing; if she did not immediately receive full payment, she threatened to keep the baby, because they would be in breach of the contract.[79] The situation sufficiently deteriorated so that both Mark and Anna filed lawsuits before the baby was born to establish parentage. When the child was born a couple of months later, blood samples confirmed what each of the parties knew—that the baby was the product of the sperm of Mark and the egg of Crispina.[80]

As in the *Baby M.* case, the court ordered that the baby live with the father and his spouse (Mark and Crispina) pending the outcome of the case; Anna was permitted limited visitation.[81] Unlike the *Baby M.* case, however, Mark's spouse had a biological claim to the child. As in the *Baby M.* case, the trial court ultimately determined that the contract was legal and enforceable against Anna's claim; the court also terminated the order permitting visitation to Anna.[82]

The appeals court upheld the custody award and visitation decision but based its decision on California law rather than the terms of the contract. It did not determine whether the contract was valid.[83] The California Supreme Court upheld the surrogacy contract.[84]

The appeals court tried to apply California law in a gender-neutral way: thus, because a man can only demonstrate paternity by proving that his sperm was used to produce the embryo then a woman can only demonstrate maternity by proving that her egg was used. The problem with this analysis, of course, is that it ignores the other substantial contributions that a woman makes to a fetus other than through her genetic material. The court did generally note the contribution that a gestational mother makes to her fetus:

> While the woman is pregnant, she shares most of her major bodily functions with the child. For some time after birth the child retains and uses the woman's life-preserving tissue, cells, blood, nutrients and antibodies. The woman protects and nourishes the child during pregnancy, and, for good or ill, can permanently affect the child by what she ingests. The contribution to the child's development by the woman who gave it birth is indeed, as amicus curiae points out, profound.[85]

The court's description, however, was incomplete. It ignored the discomfort that Anna experienced in order to have the embryo implanted in her, as well as the physical difficulties of her pregnancy. Like Mary Sue Davis, she would have had to undergo IVF transfer with the hormone injections and invasiveness of that procedure. Unlike Mary Sue Davis, she also experienced pregnancy and child-birth. Moreover, the court described the contribution of Anna in entirely impersonal terms. Although ample evidence existed in the record of Anna's specific physical problems during pregnancy and the toll that pregnancy took on her body, the court only described her contribution in generic terms as "a woman." There was no reason for the court to use a generic woman in its description; Anna's personal situation was amply described in the record.[86] It appears that the court tried to depersonalize Anna's situation by ignoring the actual facts.

The court discounted all the facts regarding Anna's physical discomfort and physical contribution, because Anna did not fall into a category of "traditionally protected" biological mothers. Moreover, state law was not seen as infringing her liberty interests, since she voluntarily created her own predicament. In sum, the court was not willing to use statutory or constitutional arguments on behalf of Anna to deprive Mark and Crispina of the "traditional parental relationship which they might otherwise be able to enjoy."[87]

The court never defined exactly what it meant by "traditionally protected" parental relationships. Its definition of a traditional family, however, served the interests of a white man and his wife over that of an African-American woman. Anna was African-American, whereas Mark was Caucasian and Crispina was Asian-American.[88] As Charlotte Rutherford has noted, Anna's situation unfortunately is *traditional* for African-American women harkening back to memories "of slavery and the days of the breeder woman whose feelings for her child, whether born out of love or out of rape, were disregarded when men with power over her made decisions about the child."[89] Although the court rendered its holding in race-neutral language, it is not difficult to see the implications of this decision for other African-American women. Because a white man can compensate an African-American woman to bear a "white baby" through the use of IVF transfer, the economic disparity in the United States on the basis of race makes African-American women a likely source for IVF transfer gestational mothers. By denying this category of women parental rights, the courts may be perpetuating yet another vehicle by which poor African-American women become the "wet nurses." Through IVF transfer, African-American women can serve as paid incubators for rich white women as well as wet nurses after birth. IVF transfer can therefore further the subservient experiences of African-American women with respect to reproduction.

Although the court did not consider the broader implications of its decision, they are quite dramatic for surrogate mothers. The court's result did not require that Anna be actually compensated for her services, since the case was not decided on the basis of the contract. If Mark and Crispina had wanted to do so, they could have sued Anna for custody as soon as the child was born and withheld all compensation. Thus, Anna could have delivered the child, lost custody, lost visitation rights, *and* not have been compensated. (In this particular case, Anna was to be paid six installments with the last to be paid six weeks after the child was born. She had apparently been paid $5,000 and had another $5,000 payment forthcoming. In the *Baby M.* case, Mary Beth Whitehead was not to be paid until after the child's birth.) In other words, the court's ruling creates a unilateral contract, with the gestational mother having no enforceable rights after giving birth.

The analysis by the California Supreme Court was no more sensitive to the rights of Anna. The court found that both Anna and Crispina had some legal claim to motherhood. It used the parties' initial intent as the "tie breaker," thereby ruling in favor of Crispina. The court noted in passing that "some commentators have expressed concern that surrogacy contracts tend to exploit or dehumanize women, especially women of lower economic status"[90] but found that "there has been no proof that surrogacy contracts exploit poor women to any greater degree than economic necessity in general exploits them by inducing them to accept lower-paid or otherwise undesirable employment."[91] As in the *Davis* case, the court refused to engage in a factualized inquiry to see if this *particular* contract exploited Anna. Anna apparently felt exploited by the contract and therefore preferred to keep the child rather than live up to the terms of the contract. Presumably, that was an expensive choice for her but one that she felt compelled to make. The court was presented with a specific factual situation where a surrogate sought out of a contract, and the court pretended that failing to enforce such contracts would harm surrogates! The court therefore chose an analysis that benefited the "traditional" couple while purporting to consider the interests of economically exploited surrogates.

E. Conclusion

An underlying question in two of these cases is, What is in the best interest of the child? Since clear statutory directives regarding alternative reproductive technology are absent, that question dominates the courts' analyses. That analysis always favors the more prosperous and mainstream party, which is invariably the man. Not recognized by any of the courts are the assumptions underlying the "best interest of the child" analysis. For example, Anna J. loses in the court of appeals, because she supposedly does not bring a "traditional" family to the child, whereas Mark C. does represent such a family. But what is so traditional about a couple who contracts with another woman to carry their "child" to term rather than adopting one of the many children available for adoption? Why is Anna as a surrogate less traditional than Mark and Crispina who contract for the use of the services of a surrogate? In fact, this case represents a common double standard whereby a woman is blamed for sexual conduct when a man is equally blameworthy. If such a double standard were not employed under the guise of "the best interest of the child" standard, women's claims in these cases would seem to be more meritorious. The courts' decisions perpetuate the double standard by defining the man's behavior as traditional and the woman's behavior as nontraditional. These standards are then passed to the next generation through the courts' custody decisions. Imagine the day when a child goes to school and explains that her "mother" was her gestational mother, because another couple donated the egg and sperm. When a child can make that statement without fear of ridicule, pregnant women will have gained increased respect in society.

These cases—particularly the latter category in which the pregnant woman is a gestational but not a biological mother—also present enormous risk of upper-middle-class white men's race and class privilege being vehicles for them to make superior claims over poor women. Men are therefore able to purchase their reproductive freedom; they can use their financial resources to insulate themselves from the risks and discomforts of pregnancy and child rearing. Elsewhere, I have criticized the class-based privilege of privacy doctrine when it is applied to women who are seeking reproductive freedom.[92] Poor women, for example, do not truly have the choice to "choose" abortion so long as privacy doctrine does not compel the state to pay for abortion services. Middle-class women are granted far more reproductive choices through privacy doctrine. The parallel experience as reflected in these cases is that upper-class men can choose to utilize extremely expensive reproductive technology, including compensation for women to serve as gestational mothers, in order to pursue their reproductive freedom. Poor women have few choices about the societal and economic conditions under which they become gestational mothers or the contractual choices that are available to them as gestational mothers. Pregnant men, to the extent that they are privileged by class, therefore constitute the paradigm of favorable treatment under the law.

V. Women's Exclusion from Employment Based on Biology

In the previous cases, we saw that the courts' refusals to consider the distinctive burdens that fall on women due to their reproductive capacity caused them to lose arguments for custody of the child they had borne. Nevertheless, we should not generalize from those cases that courts or society always ignore women's distinctive reproductive capacity when deciding cases or social policy. That same reproductive capacity is often emphasized when it is in fact *not* truly relevant in order to exclude women from jobs that are also sought by men. In this section, I will examine four such examples—women's exclusion from the practice of law, women's exclusion from the military draft, women's exclusion from contact guard positions in a maximum-security penitentiary for men, and women's exclusion from jobs that purportedly create a health risk for the fetus a woman might be carrying. Despite the fact that these biological arguments were overstated by government policymakers, they were generally accepted by the courts.

A. Bradwell v. Illinois[93]

Although numerous cases preceding the 1970s reflect the use of biological arguments to justify women's exclusion from employment, one of the most famous is *Bradwell v. Illinois*.[94] In that 1873 case, the Supreme Court upheld Myra Bradwell's exclusion from the bar by the state of Illinois in a brief opinion. In a more lengthy concurrence, Justice Bradley explained why that exclusion was appropriate, referring explicitly to women's "natural" biological condition. In Justice Bradley's words:

> [T]he civil law, *as well as nature herself,* has always recognized a wide difference in the respective spheres and destinies of man and woman. . . . *The natural and proper timidity and delicacy which belongs to the female sex* evidently unfits it for many of the occupations of civil life. The constitution of the family organization, which is founded in the divine ordinance, *as well as in the nature of things,* indicates the domestic sphere as that which properly belongs to the domain and functions of womanhood.[95]

By contemporary standards, it is easy to see that Justice Bradley's concurrence is filled with exaggerated notions about the physical differences between women and men. In the context of the case, however, that exaggeration is particularly repugnant, because Justice Bradley had before him the example of a woman who clearly did not fit the description that he provided. She had gone to law school, passed the bar exam, and edited a legal periodical.[96] She did not limit herself to the domestic sphere and apparently prospered in the so-called male sphere. Thus, Justice Bradley could really offer no explanation for why Myra Bradwell should be excluded from the practice of law; even by Justice Bradley's own yardstick, she possessed none of the so-called limitations of her sex.

Myra Bradwell was not pregnant nor was there any indication that she planned to become pregnant soon. The *Bradwell* case therefore demonstrates how *all* white women were viewed as frail due to their potentiality to become pregnant during the Victorian Era. (As Sojourner Truth reminded us with her famous statement, "And ain't I a woman?"[97] stereotypes concerning women's frailty have been applied to white women and not to African-American women.) What I take from this example is that all white women (certainly in late nineteenth-century America) were pregnant persons in the eyes of the law irrespective of whether they were actually pregnant. *Nonpregnant* white women were therefore not compared to nonpregnant white men. Pregnancy was an excuse for the treatment of women, not a genuine concern with women's physical condition.

The *Bradwell* case is in many ways no different from modern cases arising out of women's exclusion from employment, because it rests on the need to exaggerate the sex differences between women and men even when the record is full of facts that contradict that exaggeration. Unlike the 1908 decision in *Muller v. Oregon*,[98] where the Supreme Court upheld a restriction on women's working conditions because it was deliberately misled into believing that all women possessed a scientifically demonstrable frailty, the Court in *Bradwell* upheld a restriction on women's working conditions despite the fact that the plaintiff's life was testimony to the inaccuracy of the stereotypes that justified the law. Some members of the *Bradwell* Court, however, chose to articulate a stereotype about women rather than deal responsibly with the facts in the record about the plaintiff. In such cases, one can see the Court has helped to perpetuate stereotypes about the biological differences between women and men. If men could get pregnant, stereotypes about women would not be so dependent on their perceived biological frailty.

B. Rostker v. Goldberg[99]

In this case, the United States Supreme Court and Congress's consideration of the physical differences between men and women was much more subtle. The issue in the case was the constitutionality of Congress requiring men but not women to register for the draft—a policy that was reinstituted during President Carter's administration. The justification for excluding women was that women and men were not similarly situated due to another level of discrimination—that only men were eligible for "combat" positions. The military therefore argued that it need only draft those people who were "combat-ready," which included a class comprised entirely of men. Due to women's intrinsic unavailability for combat, they could therefore be excluded from the draft entirely.

Assumptions about women's capabilities exist at two levels in the Court's opinion. First, the Court had to assume the validity of the combat exclusion—an exclusion that is historically justified in physical terms. This assumption was not challenged by the plaintiffs, because they viewed it as irrelevant to the case.[100] Second, the Court had to conclude that people who are drafted must also be people who are "combat-ready."

It is easy to see how the first assumption relied on an exaggerated sense of the physical differences between men and women. Since the military does individualized testing for military service during which it excludes many men from eligibility, it would not be particularly onerous to do the same testing for women and determine which are fit for military service. The combat exclusion allows the military to use a blanket rule for fitness through a gender proxy, although that proxy is not accurate.

The second assumption, however, also relied on an exaggerated sense of the physical differences between men and women. Assuming (as does the Court) that women are not qualified to serve in combat (or, more accurately, that Congress is constitutionally allowed to disqualify women from combat roles), it does not necessarily follow that every draftee in the military be combat-ready. In fact, draftees work alongside volunteers, including many women who are, by definition, not combat-ready. The image that is evoked by the Court's opinion is that the dominant character of the military must be combat-ready even if particular jobs contain no combat role. Somehow, the military's machismo would be softened if women became a large portion of the noncombat members of the armed forces. What is therefore exaggerated through the second assumption is the usefulness of combat-ready draftees. This exaggeration serves to further the importance ascribed to men in society.

As noted by the dissent, the second assumption bore little support in the record:

> I perceive little, if any, indication that Congress itself concluded that every position in the military, no matter how far removed from combat, must be filled with combat-ready men. Common sense and experience in recent wars, where women volunteers were employed in substantial numbers, belie this view of reality.[101]

Yet, out of deference to Congress in matters of national defense, the Court preceded under an absurd assumption—that the military would not benefit from having women drafted who would not be eligible for combat duty even though, in the dissent's language, "the serious view of the Executive Branch, including the responsible military services, is to the contrary."[102] Deference to national security interests therefore became a way to undermine the level of scrutiny that the courts would ordinarily utilize to question Congress's actions. In this case, such deference protected outmoded stereotypes about women's abilities in society.

Although Congress has expanded the number of job classifications for which women are currently eligible in the military, only men are still required to register for the draft. If a challenge to male-only registration is brought again, the Court will probably have to contend with what I believe to be the true justification for women's exclusion from mandatory registration—the public's distaste for *women* (and particularly potentially or actually *pregnant* women) being killed during war[103] and the exaggerated privacy concerns that currently foster the exclusion of gays and lesbians from the military.[104] Hiding behind biological arguments permits the military to avoid putting their stereotypes about women's role in society on the table for discussion.

C. Dothard v. Rawlinson[105]

The plaintiffs in *Dothard v. Rawlinson* challenged an Alabama prison's policy of only hiring men to be contact prison guards in a men's maximum-security prison. Again, biology came to the surface to justify this exclusionary practice.

The defendants made numerous biological arguments: (1) the inherent danger to women themselves of working as guards, (2) the special problem of women being raped by prisoners, and (3) women's inherent physical weakness. Of these three arguments, the Supreme Court accepted the second. The possibility of female guards being raped was found to create genuine security risks at the prison, because 20 percent of the male prisoners were estimated to be sex offenders, and prison conditions could cause aggressive behavior.[106] Thus, in this case, women's "rapability" rather than women's ability to get pregnant was used to justify this rule. In the Court's words: "The employee's very womanhood would thus directly undermine her capacity to provide the security that is the essence of a correctional counselor's responsibility."[107]

The exaggerated sexual differences that are a part of the Court's reasoning should be obvious. Although the Court mentioned that 20 percent of the inmates were sex offenders, it did not specify whether their sex offenses were against women or against men. The victims of sex offenses are not limited to women. In addition, irrespective of the sex of the victims of sex offenses outside prison, men are routinely raped in prisons. Thus, rape is not a sex-specific offense. A male prisoner could as easily rape a male guard as a female guard, but more likely, a male prisoner would rape another male prisoner given their more ready availability and the greater tolerance for the crime.

At its core, the *Dothard* decision reflected unfounded stereotypes about women and their "essence." As the dissent noted, there was no evidence in the record concerning the likelihood that inmates would assault a woman because she was a woman.[108] In the words of Justice Marshall, "[T]his rationale regrettably perpetuates one of the most insidious of the old myths about women—that women, wittingly or not, are seductive sexual objects."[109] Society and employers rather than women are therefore allowed to control women's decisions about their bodies; men can decide to expose themselves to risks through combat military service or work as a prison guard but not women.

D. International Union, UAW v. Johnson Controls[110]

The plaintiffs in *International Union, UAW v. Johnson Controls* challenged a company policy of excluding women with childbearing capacity from jobs that might cause lead exposure. Johnson Controls won in both the trial court[111] and the court of appeals[112] despite evidence disputing the sex-based justification for the policy.

Plaintiffs offered several arguments to challenge Johnson Controls's rationale for barring women from employment. First, they argued that there was no strong correlation between exposure to lead at the plant and women bearing children with defects. Second, they argued that to the extent that any risk to reproductive health does exist, men are as vulnerable to those risks as women. Finally, they argued that individual women rather than Johnson Controls should determine whether they want to attempt to bear children despite their exposure to lead. They argued that Johnson Controls's responsibility was to make the workplace safe for all of its employees by following the standards set forth by the Occupational Safety and Health Administration rather than to bar certain employees from the workforce.

The trial court used a distorted analysis of the phrase "as a woman" in order to conclude that the policy of excluding women from the workplace was not facially discriminatory. First, the court observed that there is a presumption that the policy was facially discriminatory because it applied only to women. It noted, however, that such a presumption could be rebutted by a showing that there are "significant risks of harm to the unborn children of women workers from their exposure during pregnancy to toxic hazards in the workplace [which] make [it] necessary for the safety of the unborn children, that fertile women workers be appropriately restricted from exposure to those hazards and that its program is effective for the purpose."[113] In other words, a facially discriminatory policy becomes nondiscriminatory if one can show that the employer only treated a woman in that particular way due to her distinctive reproductive capacity. Despite the language of the 1978 Pregnancy Discrimination Act (PDA)—which states explicitly that "women affected by pregnancy, childbirth, or related medical conditions shall be treated the same for all employment-related purposes . . . as other persons not so affected but similar in their ability or inability to work"[114]— the court defined gender discrimination as only including those aspects of women's lives which do *not* relate to their reproductive capacity. The court's reasoning turns the PDA on its head by allowing the employer to defend his treatment by saying that he was genuinely concerned about how women handled their reproductive capability. Amazingly, the trial court, writing in 1988, never once mentioned the PDA. Similarly, the court of appeals largely ignored the PDA.[115]

The lower courts were therefore using a male model of person (taking women's reproductive capacity out of their definition of womanhood) to engage in the inquiry of determining what it means to be treated as a woman. Thus, women were women only so far as they were *not* being treated on the basis of their distinctiveness as women—a rather odd and illogical definition of womanhood.

Somewhat surprisingly (given the previous cases discussed), the Supreme Court found in favor of the plaintiffs, relying heavily on the PDA. Citing *Muller v. Oregon,*[116] it noted that concern for a woman's ability to become pregnant has historically been an excuse for denying women equal employment opportunity. By passing the PDA, Congress changed that result. The Court therefore concluded: "It is no more appropriate for the courts than it is for individual employers to decide whether a woman's reproductive role is more important to herself and her family than her economic role. Congress has left this choice to the woman as hers to make."[117]

Before concluding that the Supreme Court "finally got it," we need to look at this case in the historical context. Congress passed a very strong and explicit Pregnancy Discrimination Act in 1978 *after* the Supreme Court had ruled that pregnancy-based discrimination did *not* constitute sex-based discrimination in *General Electric v. Gilbert.*[118] Had Congress not spoken so forcefully on the issue of pregnancy and women's employability, it is clear that the Supreme Court would have ruled otherwise (as it did in *Gilbert*). And remarkably, despite the strong language of the PDA, the lower courts had all ruled *against* the plaintiffs. Even a vigilant Congress cannot insure that women will be expeditiously protected by the courts; the plaintiffs only won *Johnson Controls* after a lengthy court battle, which ended in the Supreme Court.

E. Conclusion

Since the nineteenth century, courts have exaggerated white women's physical differences from men in order to justify women's exclusion from traditionally male occupations. (Women of color have always been permitted to work under

the most arduous circumstances with no concern at all for the toll on their reproductive capacity.) In the nineteenth century, women were excluded from the
practice of law; in the twentieth century they are still excluded from some contact prison guard positions and mandatory registration for the military draft.
With the passage of the Pregnancy Discrimination Amendment to Title VII, it is
increasingly difficult for employers to use stereotypes about women's reproductive capacity to exclude women from employment; nevertheless, it still takes
lengthy court suits to get those rules enforced. Thus, the true physical hardships
on poor women of color are ignored while the physical hardships on middle-
class white women are exaggerated. Both invisibility and exaggeration serve to
perpetuate women's subordination in society.

VI. Counternarratives?

In the preceding discussion, I argued that society and the courts either ignore women's biological differences or exaggerate them to perpetuate women's
subordination in society. Sometimes, one might argue the courts "get it right,"
in that they seem to acknowledge women's biological differences from men in
order to benefit women in society. In this section, however, I will show that a
close examination of those cases reveals that seeming victories for women were
in fact not victories for the most disadvantaged women in our society. Although
the minority of middle-class women who worked outside the home and could
afford to work less than ten hours per day may have benefited in some of these
cases, poor women were the victims of a statute that left them underemployed
or unemployed. These cases suggest that when the legislatures or courts try to
give preferential treatment to women on the basis of their reproductive capacity,
they have middle-class rather than poor women in mind. Gender essentialism,
when rooted in biology, therefore strikes hardest at the most disadvantaged
women in society.

A. Muller v. Oregon[119]

Muller v. Oregon is the classic case of judicial paternalism. The state of Oregon had passed a statute forbidding the employment of women "in any me-
chanical establishment, or factory, or laundry" . . . more than ten hours during any
one day.[120] The Supreme Court upheld this statute through the arguments made
in Louis D. Brandeis's infamous "Brandeis" brief, in which he argued that the
"widespread belief that woman's physical structure, and the functions she performs in consequence thereof, justify special legislation restricting or qualify-
ing the conditions under which she should be permitted to toil."[121]

Although the Court reached its decision in order to protect women from stressful work, the effect of its decision was to further impoverish women who needed to work more than ten hours per day to support themselves and their family. While middle-class women may have benefited from the improvement in their working conditions, poor women would have been hurt. By having a middle-class image of women in mind, the Court could ratify such treatment.

For the purposes of the present discussion, the important point about *Muller* is twofold: first, the Court exaggerated the physical differences between women and men; and second, that exaggeration furthered the subordination of the most disadvantaged women by leaving them further impoverished by limitations on the hours they could work. Unfortunately, *Muller* does not represent the last occasion in which the Court acted in such a paternalistic manner.

B. *Michael M. v. Sonoma County Superior Court*[122]

The plaintiff in this case challenged California's statutory rape law under which he had been convicted for having intercourse with a sixteen-and-one-half-year-old female, Sharon. The plaintiff was a seventeen-and-one-half-year-old male, Michael. Under California law, only the male could be convicted of statutory rape.

To justify the statute, the Supreme Court relied on its exaggerated notions about the sex differences between men and women. In the Court's words:

> We need not be medical doctors to discern that young men and young women are not similarly situated with respect to the problems and the risks of sexual intercourse. Only women may become pregnant, and they suffer disproportionately the profound physical, emotional, and psychological consequences of sexual activity. The statute at issue here protects women from sexual intercourse at an age when those consequences are particularly severe.[123]

Of course, one does not need to be a medical doctor to know that only women can become pregnant. But the consequences that the Court is speaking about do not flow inevitably from that fact. First, women only become pregnant when they have unprotected intercourse (or contraceptive failure). Nevertheless, a male who has sex with an underage female who is using contraceptives is criminally liable for his conduct. Second, many of the consequences of pregnancy are socially created rather than inherent. The reason, for example, that the consequences are "particularly severe" for underage females is social rather than physical. For females between fifteen and eighteen, pregnancy is no more dangerous than for older women. Lack of prenatal care, poverty, poor educational opportunities, a lack of publicly funded day care, and a disproportionate lack of male involvement in child rearing make the pregnancies of underage females particularly problematic.[124] These are socially created conditions rather than physical ones.

The fact that these differences are socially rather than physically created is important, because Court decisions can influence those differences. Were the Court, for example, to insist that abortions be funded under Medicaid, poor teenagers would find it much easier to obtain abortions, thereby avoiding the consequences of childbirth.[125] Similarly, were the Court to invalidate parental notification and waiting period restrictions for adolescent females, abortions would also become easier to obtain.[126] When faced with those restrictions, however, the Court does not choose to point out the "fact" that childbirth is particularly problematic for those age groups; instead, it allows the state to use policies that favor childbirth over abortion for teenagers.

Looking at all of the cases involving female adolescents and pregnancy, one sees a distinct pattern, which is society's attempt to *control* their lives. *Michael M.* fits into that pattern, because the underage female has no authority to determine whether a statutory rape prosecution should be brought. Statutory rape laws do not empower her; they make her the pawn of the state if it decides to prosecute her male companion.[127]

Of course, not all sexual activity by an underage female is voluntary. The facts in the *Michael M.* case suggest, for example, that Sharon did not voluntarily have intercourse, because Michael hit her several times before they had intercourse.[128] If California, however, wanted to truly protect *and empower* females, it would have required that the female consent to the prosecution in order for it to occur. In criminal cases, however, the state rather than the victim of the crime decides whether a prosecution should take place.

Some people might argue that *Michael M.* represents a situation where men are treated more coercively than women with respect to their role in the reproductive process, thereby undermining my "pregnant men" thesis. There are several problems, however, with that conclusion. First, it ignores the reality that statutory rape prosecutions rarely occur when the sexual activity was consensual.[129] Statutory rape offers the prosecution a convenience—not having to prove force or lack of consent. As in the case of *Michael M.*, there is often evidence of coercive sexual activity that may not be sufficient to meet the standards of proof for rape. By contrast, there will almost never be evidence that the female forced herself upon the man. (That is why virtually no woman has ever been convicted of raping a man.[130]) The male and female are therefore not similarly situated; however, their dissimilar situations are far different from that described by Justice Rehnquist. The difference is not women's ability to become pregnant; the problem is the likelihood of women being raped. A second and related difficulty, however, is that the woman does not have to consent to the statutory rape prosecution. She does not have to acknowledge that there was something problematic about the sexual activity. Thus, it is possible that men will be prosecuted who did not coerce underage females into having sex with them. The solution, I would suggest, however, is to empower women by making them consent to prosecution for sexual coercion rather than to free men from the responsibilities of their conduct.

Nevertheless, I must acknowledge that some men will be disadvantaged through California's statutory rape scheme. One might then ask, Which men are likely to be disadvantaged? I would suggest that it is poor men who are most likely to face prosecution. The class-based dimension of *Michael M.* is present although subtle. To see this dimension, one must ask who needs to have sex in public view? (Sharon and Michael had sex in a public park.) Poor people are most likely to live in crowded conditions where sexual activity cannot easily occur in privacy, and they certainly cannot afford to purchase a room in a hotel or motel for a few hours. In addition, poor people are more likely than middle-class people to be victims of prosecutorial decisions, because they have less power to bargain about the conditions of their lives. Thus, the coercive aspects of statutory rape convictions are most likely to strike the groups in society with the least amount of power. I therefore suspect that Sharon and Michael will rarely be rich white kids from the suburbs.[131]

That analysis is very important to help us refine the "pregnant" man thesis. White, middle-class, heterosexual "pregnant" men are likely to be treated very well by the law. We have seen that pattern in all of the cases involving married white men who purchased gestational services from women. Poor, young, unmarried men, like Michael M., however, do not fare as well under our system of law. Thus, if there were such an entity as poor, young, unmarried "pregnant" men, they might not be treated much better than poor, young, unmarried pregnant women. The class, race, and sexual orientation biases of our legal system will operate here as well as elsewhere.

C. Johnson Controls *Revisited*

The one case in which the Supreme Court seemed to "get it right" was the *Johnson Controls* case. It is true that the Supreme Court correctly interpreted Congress's intent—that employers are not permitted to decide what reproductive risks individual women wish to take at the workplace by precluding them from employment. Nevertheless, it is difficult to see *Johnson Controls* as a victory for the most disadvantaged women in society. Recognizing that African-American

women and men are overrepresented in jobs that involve exposure to toxic sub-
stances, the NAACP Legal Defense Fund had argued in *Johnson Controls* that
"employers should be required to reduce hazardous exposures to safe levels for
all workers or to find product substitutes."[132] Although the Supreme Court recognized the dangers that toxins pose to women's reproductive capacity, its decision did not require Johnson Controls to change its work behavior except to
allow women to work at the plant. Poor women were therefore free to make the
"choice" of working in an unsafe environment or foregoing employment. Neither of those options were true choices.

   In many ways, *Johnson Controls* is a modern day *Muller* decision. In *Muller*,
the legislature protected women but not men from the physical toil of working
ten hours per day. Rather than make the workplace tolerable for all workers, it
was made tolerable for women. In *Johnson Controls*, the legislature also protected
women by guaranteeing them access to jobs that might injure their reproductive
capacity but not that of men's. Rather than make the workplace safe for all workers, it was made safe only for men.[133] Both *Muller* and *Johnson Controls* left poor
women with unacceptable options—unemployment in *Muller* and poor reproductive health in *Johnson Controls*. When, one must wonder, will poor women be
able to have employment *and* safe working conditions? The courts' and legislatures' focus on middle-class women makes that day seem unlikely anytime soon.

VII. Conclusion

   These cases show that society does not treat women monolithically. It may
ignore women's biological differences from men; it may exaggerate those differences; and it may exaggerate those differences for some women while ignoring
them for other women. The prevailing pattern, however, is that women are
treated with respect to their biology in ways that perpetuate their subordination
in society. In addition, the most disadvantaged women in society always seem
to face the brunt of this mistreatment. This final insight emphasizes the importance of what I consider to be the core insight of anti-essentialism—that when
women are treated on the basis of their presumed characteristics, be they socially or biologically created, they are not actually being treated monolithically.
Women's treatment is always contingent upon their status in society vis-à-vis
class, race, religion, or sexual orientation.

   These cases demonstrate that courts systematically discount the pain and
experience of childbirth in order to find that men's reproductive claims are equivalent to or superior to those of women. The theoretical issue that emerges from
these cases is what to make of the biological differences between men and women.
When anti-essentialists equate gender essentialism with biological essentialism,

they do us a disservice, because they make it difficult to explain why it is wrong for the courts to ignore women's biological role in the reproductive process.

By taking a historical view of the courts' treatment of women's reproductive capacity, we can get a much sharper understanding of these cases. When it suits society to emphasize women's frailty due to women's reproductive capacity in order to disqualify women from certain roles in society, it does so. On the other hand, when it suits society to discount women's reproductive capacity so that men can be considered to have superior or equivalent reproductive claims, it also does so. Moreover, either emphasizing or ignoring women's biological differences from men can have a disproportionate effect on certain groups of women: such policies need not act monolithically on women's lives. By considering both phenomena simultaneously, one can improve on the anti-essentialist critique of biological essentialism. Ignoring women's reproductive capacity when it is relevant is as bad as exaggerating women's reproductive capacity when it is irrelevant. The challenge for feminists is to get society to view women's reproductive capacity *accurately and compassionately* rather than to insist that it is irrelevant in women's lives.

Notes

1. Cass R. Sunstein, *Neutrality in Constitutional Law (With Special Reference to Pornography, Abortion, and Surrogacy)*, 92 Colum. L. Rev. 1, 35 n.129 (1992).
2. 417 U.S. 484 (1974).
3. *Id.* at 496–97 n.20.
4. 442 U.S. 256, 279 (1979).
5. In Planned Parenthood v. Casey, 120 L. Ed. 624, 748 (1992) (June 29, 1992), Justice Blackmun invoked the first mention of gender-based equality theory in a Supreme Court reproductive freedom case, concluding that "State's restrictions on a woman's right to terminate her pregnancy also implicate constitutional guarantees of gender equality." Blackmun, however, ignored the *Geduldig* decision entirely, never dealing with the conceptual problem that men cannot get pregnant. No other member of the Court joined his concurring opinion.
6. This problem became compounded recently when the Supreme Court reaffirmed *Geduldig* in Bray v. Alexandria Women's Health Clinic, No. 90–985 (January 13, 1993) at 4.
7. Sunstein, *supra* note 1, at 35 n.129.
8. *See, e.g.,* Catharine A. MacKinnon, *From Practice to Theory, or What Is a White Woman Anyway?*, 4 Yale J. L. & Feminism 13, 16 (1991) (arguing that Angela Harris wrongly applies the label anti-essentialism "to socially-based theories that observe and analyze empirical commonalities in women's condition"); Angela P. Harris, *Race and Essentialism in Feminist Legal Theory*, 42 Stan. L. Rev. 581, 590–601 (1990) (arguing that MacKinnon's dominance theory is flawed by essentialism).
9. Harris, *supra* note 8, at 585.

10. *See Id.* (describing the core insight of anti-essentialism as our inability to describe women independently of race, class, sexual orientation, and other realities of experience).

11. Sunstein, *supra* note 1, at 35 n.129.

12. *Id.*

13. In *Geduldig*, the Court made a brief reference to the fact that plaintiffs could demonstrate that "distinctions involving pregnancy are mere pretexts designed to effect an invidious discrimination against the members of one sex or the other." *Geduldig*, 417 U.S. 484, 496–97 n.20 (1974).

14. *See, e.g.*, Ruth Colker, *An Equal Protection Analysis of United States Reproductive Health Policy: Gender, Race, Age, and Class*, 1991 Duke L. J. 324 (1991).

15. *See, e.g.*, Brief for Black Women of Choice et al., Sojourner T. v. Buddy Roemer, No. 91–3677 (5th Cir. filed October 18, 1991) (*reprinted in* Ruth Colker, Abortion and Dialogue: Pro-Choice, Pro-Life, and American Law 163–75 (1992)).

16. 442 U.S. 256, 279 (1979) (Supreme Court affirmed constitutionality of Massachusetts's Veteran's Preference Statute despite its disparate impact against women).

17. Ruth Colker, *The Example of Lesbians: A Posthumous Reply to Professor Mary Joe Frug*, 105 Harv. L. Rev. 1084 (1992).

18. Colker, *supra* note 14.

19. Ruth Colker, *Abortion & Violence*, Law & Social Inquiry (forthcoming 1994).

20. Harris, *supra* note 8, at 602–605.

21. *See e.g.*, MacKinnon, *supra* note 8, at 16–17.

22. *See supra* text accompanying note 9.

23. Harris, *supra* note 8, at 584.

24. Robin West, *Jurisprudence and Gender*, 55 U. Chi. L. Rev. 1, 2–3 (1988).

25. Harris, *supra* note 8, at 604.

26. *Id.* at 603.

27. *Id.* at 605.

28. MacKinnon, *supra* note 8, at 16.

29. Harris, *supra* note 8, at 585–605.

30. MacKinnon, *supra* note 8, at 16–17.

31. *Id.* at 17.

32. *Id.*

33. *Id.*

34. West, *supra* note 24, at 3.

35. During in vitro fertilization, eggs are extracted from a woman and fertilized outside the uterus; the fertilized egg is then implanted in a woman's uterus—not necessarily the same uterus from which the egg came. During artificial insemination, a man's semen is injected into a woman's uterus. Fertilization occurs in the woman's uterus; the egg is that of the gestational mother. *See* Lisa Hemphill, *American Abortion Law Applied to New Reproductive Technology*, 32 Jurimetrics J. 361, 362 (1992).

36. *See* In the Matter of Baby M. 537 A.2d 1227, 1234 (N.J. Sup. Ct. 1988) (noting that Mary Beth Whitehead, the biological mother, was inappropriately called a "surrogate mother").

37. Artificial insemination by husband and by donor have been in use for several decades. *See* Hemphill, *supra* note 35, at 362.

38. *See, e.g.*, Jhordan C. v. Mary K., 179 Cal. App.3d 386, 224 Ca. Rptr. 530 (Super. Ct. 1986) (enforcing California Civil Code, section 7005, which provides that "the donor of semen provided to a licensed physician for use in artificial insemination of a woman other than the donor's wife is treated in law as if he were not the natural father of a child thereby conceived"). At least twenty-four states have statutes that cover some facet of artificial insemination. *See* Areen, King, Goldberg, and Capron, Law Science and Medicine 1307 (1984).

39. *See, e.g.*, *In re* Petition of L.S. and V.I. for the Adoption of T. and of M., Adoption Nos.

A-269–90 and A-270–90 (Super. Ct. of D.C., Family Division 1991), *reprinted in* Judith Areen, Family Law 1565–67 (1992) (interpreting D.C. code to permit same-sex adoptive parents). *But see* Opinion of the Justices, 129 N.H. 290, 530 A.2d 21 (1987) (holding that a state statute that barred homosexuals from being adoptive parents was constitutional).

40. It is important to recognize that the wife of the male sperm donor does *not* necessarily win in these cases. Whether she has any legal claim will depend upon whether she has donated genetic material. Thus, if a man donates sperm to another woman who uses her own egg to get pregnant, the wife of the male sperm donor has no legal standing to make a custody or visitation claim for the child. This is true even if the wife of the male sperm donor is the person who takes on major child rearing responsibilities after the child is born. *See, e.g.,* Sonni Efron, *Estranged Wife Is Denied Custody of Surrogate Baby,* The L. A. Times (April 9, 1991), Metro Section, B1, Col. 2 (describing a court ruling that a woman who helped raise the child born to her husband and a surrogate mother had no legal rights to the ten-month-old girl whom she helped raise).

41. *See* Davis v. Davis, 842 S.W.2d 588 (1992) (father prevailed in "custody" dispute over frozen embryos); York v. Jones, 717 F. Supp. 421 (E.D. Va. 1989) (frozen embryo is property of biological parents so that embryo dispositional agent only creates a bailment relationship between the parents and the IVF clinic); Del Zio v. Columbia Presbyterian Hosp., No. 74 Civ. 3588 (S.D. N.Y. Nov. 9, 1978) (unpublished opinion) (parents sued hospital for destroying embryos created through in vitro fertilization without notice).

42. 842 S.W.2d 588 (Tenn. Sup. Ct. June 1, 1992).

43. There is also, of course, the possibility that we will learn someday that such massive injections of hormones to prepare a woman's body for IVF has adverse effects on women's health, e.g., causes cancer. I know of no such evidence at this time; however, that issue was raised by several participants at the University of Texas Women and Law Conference, which I attended in March 1993.

44. 842 S.W.2d at 601.

45. *Id.* at 604.

46. Junior Lewis makes his arguments based on the premise that he does not want to be "coerced" into being a father. I could appreciate such an argument if he had been tricked or coerced into donating sperm. In this case, however, he is the only party who one might say "tricked" the other party, because he apparently did not confide in Mary Sue that he thought the marriage was troubled while she was undergoing a painful IVF process. The court's sympathy for Junior Lewis's desire not to be coerced is therefore a disproportionate sympathy in that the court seems entirely oblivious to the genuine ways in which Mary Sue may have been tricked or coerced.

47. 842 S.W2d at 604.

48. Under the court's decision in *Davis,* the frozen embryos are considered to be "property." Thus, if the Davises had provided for the disposition of the frozen embryos in their contract with the Fertility Center of East Tennessee, the institution that stored the embryos, then the legal issue in this case would have presumably been resolved with reference to the contract. Because there was no written agreement between the parties with respect to the issue that arose, the court had to proceed in equity to resolve the matter.

49. 842 S.W.2d at 604.

50. For further discussion, *see* Ruth Colker, Abortion and Dialogue: Pro-Choice, Pro-Life, and American Law 108–11 (1992).

51. *See Id.* at xiv–xv, 144–57.

52. In the Matter of Baby M., 109 N.J. 396, 537 A.2d 1227 (N.J. Sup. Ct. 1988).

53. 537 A.2d. at 1234.

54. *Id.* at 1235.

55. *Id.*

56. *Id.* at 1236.

57. *Id.*

58. *Id.* at 1237.

59. *Id.*

60. *Id.*

61. 217 N.J. Super. 313, 525 A.2d 1128 (1987).

62. 537 A.2d at 1238.

63. 107 N.J. 140, 526 A.2d 203 (1987).

64. 537 A.2d at 1240.

65. *Id.* at 1242.

66. *Id.* at 1256.

67. *Id.* at 1258–59.

68. *Id.* at 1259.

69. *Id.* at 1261.

70. *Id.* at 1262.

71. *See* Martha Fineman, *Dominant Discourse, Professional Language, and Legal Change in Child Custody Decisionmaking*, 101 Harv. L. Rev. 727 (1988).

72. *See* In the Interest of R.C., 775 P.2d 27 (Colorado 1989) (court found that the parental rights of a known sperm donor who gave semen to an unmarried woman who was artificially inseminated with the assistance of a physician were not extinguished by a Colorado statute); In C.M. v. C.C., 152 N.J. Super. 160, 377 A.2d 821 (1977) (court found that a known donor of semen who gave semen to an unmarried woman who artificially inseminated herself without the aid of a licensed physician was entitled to visitation rights of the resulting child); Jhordan C. v. Mary K., 179 Cal. App. 3d 386, 224 Cal. Rptr. 530 (1986) (court determined that the parental rights of a known donor of semen to an unmarried woman who artificially inseminated herself without the help of a licensed physician were not extinguished by a California statute).

73. *See* Anna J. v. Mark C., 234 Cal. App.3d 1557, 286 Cal. Rptr. 369 (Cal. App. 4 Dist. 1991); Surrogate Parenting Associates v. Armstrong, 704 S.W.2d 209 (1986) (upheld surrogacy service's right to arrange surrogacy adoptions).

74. *See* Anna J. v. Mark C., 234 Cal. App.3d 1557, 286 Cal. Rptr. 369 (Cal. App. 4 Dist. 1991).

75. 286 Cal. Rptr. at 372.

76. *Id.*

77. *Id.*

78. *Id.*

79. *Id.* at 372 n.11.

80. Technically, the blood tests excluded the possibility that Anna could be the "genetic mother" of the baby. *Id.* at 373 n.12. In addition, Anna stipulated that Crispina was the biological mother. *Id.* at 376.

81. *Id.* at 373.

82. *Id.*

83. Because the result that the court reached under California law was identical to the result dictated by the contract, the court did not have to reach the difficult question of whether the contract was invalid under California law because it constituted "baby selling."

84. Johnson v. Calvert, 851 P.2d 776 (Cal. Sup. Ct. May 20, 1993), *reprinted in* 61 U.S.L.W. 2721 (June 1, 1993).

85. 286 Cal. Rptr. at 378.

86. For example, Anna's letter to Mark and Crispina described in some detail the physical, financial, and emotional problems that she experienced during pregnancy. *Id.* at 372 n.11.

87. *Id.* at 380.

88. *See* Charlotte Rutherford, *Reproductive Freedoms and African American Women*, 4 Yale J.L. & Feminism 255, 268–73 (1992).

89. *Id.* at 272.

90. 851 P.2d at 784.

91. *Id.* at 785.

92. *See* Colker, *supra* note 50, at 58–80.

93. 83 U.S. (16 Wall.) 130 (1873).

94. *Id.*

95. *Id.* at 141 (emphasis added).

96. Her lawyer noted that Mrs. Bradwell had been admitted to the bar and that coverture had been abandoned in the state of Illinois. *Id.* at 136–37.

97. Elizabeth V. Spelman, Inessential Woman: Problems of Exclusion in Feminist Thought 14 (1988) (quoting Sojourner Truth).

98. 208 U.S. 412 (1908) (upholding exclusion of women from more than ten hours of employment per day in factories or bakeries). For further discussion, see *infra* text accompanying notes 114–16.

99. 453 U.S. 57 (1981).

100. *Id.* at 87 n.2 (Marshall, J., dissenting).

101. *Id.* at 83 (White, J., dissenting).

102. *Id.*

103. I always find it interesting, when listening to the news, to hear how news commentators often talk—with great horror—about how many "women and children" have been killed during a military skirmish. What I think they mean by these reports is that *unarmed civilians* have been killed, assuming that all women and children are unarmed civilians. If women served in combat, news commentators would have to develop new linguistic ways of describing when "innocent" people are killed during war.

104. I believe that sexual relations are crucial to understanding the exclusion of heterosexual women as well as lesbians from the military. Heterosexual women need to be excluded from the military because they might get pregnant (through the acts of men in the military). Lesbians need to be excluded from the military because they refuse to make themselves available to men sexually. No woman is therefore sexually appropriate for military service; hence, all women are excluded. But the military will not talk about "sex" to justify the exclusion; instead, they stand behind biological arguments. For an excellent discussion of women in the military, *see* Michelle Benecke & Kirstin Dodge, *Recent Developments, Military Women in Nontraditional Job Fields: Casualties of the Armed Forces War on Homosexuals,* 13 Harv. Women's L. J. 215 (1990).

105. *See* Dothard v. Rawlinson, 433 U.S. 321 (1977).

106. *Id.* at 335.

107. *Id.* at 336.

108. *Id.* at 345 (opinion by Marshall, J.).

109. *Id.* at 345.

110. *See* International Union, UAW v. Johnson Controls, 111 S. Ct. 1196 (1991) (reversing trial court and court of appeals that had concluded that Johnson's policy of excluding women of reproductive age from being employed at certain jobs due to the alleged risk to their fetus were they to become pregnant was nondiscriminatory).

111. International Union, UAW v. Johnson Controls, 680 F. Supp. 309 (E.D. Wisc. 1988).

112. International Union, UAW v. Johnson Controls, 886 F.2d 871 (7th Cir. 1989).

113. International Union, UAW v. Johnson Controls, 680 F. Supp. at 315 (quoting Wright v. Olin Corp., 697 F.2d 1172, 1190 [4th Cir. 1982]).

114. Pregnancy Discrimination Act of 1978 (PDA), 92 Stat. 2076, 42 U.S.C. § 2000e(k).

115. The Pregnancy Discrimination Act received passing reference, without quotation. *See* International Union, UAW v. Johnson Controls, 886 F.2d at 893.

116. 208 U.S. 412 (1908).

117. 111 S. Ct. at 1210.

118. 429 U.S. 125 (1976).

119. 208 U.S. 412 (1908).

120. *Id.* at 416.

121. *Id.* at 420. For further discussion, see Kenneth Karst, *Legislative Facts in Constitutional Litigation*, 1960 Sup. Ct. Rev. 75 (1960).

122. 450 U.S. 464 (1981).

123. *Id.* at 471–72.

124. *See* Colker, *supra* note 14.

125. *See* Harris v. McRae, 448 U.S. 297 (1980).

126. *See* Hodgson v. Minnesota, 110 S. Ct. 2926 (1990).

127. *See* Frances Olsen, *Statutory Rape: A Feminist Critique of Rights Analysis*, 63 Tex. L. Rev. 387 (1984).

128. 450 U.S. at 483–88 n.* (Blackmun, J., concurring) (providing excerpts of court transcript in which Sharon testified that Michael "slugged" her in the face several times before she "agreed" to have intercourse).

129. *See generally* Lawrence Friedman, A History of American Law 588 (1985) (noting that morality laws were enforced only sporadically, on the occasion of a "crackdown" or to "get" an unusually flagrant or unlucky offender).

130. *See* Sourcebook of Criminal Justice Statistics 1991 442, 544 (Timothy J. Flanagan & Kathleen Maguire eds., 1992) (reporting that 98.9 percent of persons arrested for "forcible rape" are male and that 99 percent of persons convicted for "rape" are male).

131. The Justice Department does not appear to collect separate statistics on statutory rape. It includes statutory rape under the generic category "sex offenses (except forcible rape and prostitution)." Nearly three times as many people are arrested for "sex offenses" as for "forcible rape," so it is impossible to learn anything about statutory rape from the general statistics on sex offenses. *See* Sourcebook of Criminal Justice Statistics 1991 442 (Timothy J. Flanagan & Kathleen Maguire eds., 1992).

132. *See* Rutherford, *supra* note 88, at 255, 277 (discussing Brief for the NAACP Legal Defense and Educational Fund, Inc., and the National Black Women's Health Project, UAW v. Johnson Controls, 111 S. Ct. 1196 (1991) (No. 89–1215) (1992)).

133. In fact, it is not clear that the workplace in *Johnson Controls* was safe for men. If, in fact, the workplace did harm men's reproductive capacity, I would suggest that the case represents a devaluation of the reproductive health of working-class men.

PART 3

The Practice of Theory

7

Anti-essentialism and Equality
Theory Revisited

Don't misunderstand me: I've never met a generic woman I didn't like. But I
wouldn't want my brother, or my sister, to marry one. And I certainly wouldn't
want to be one: generic women don't eat rice and beans, collard greens, samosa,
challah, hot dogs, or Wonder Bread; even in Cambridge, Massachusetts, I've never
seen one eating a croissant. And while it is true that generic women don't have
bad breath, that is hardly any consolation, I should think, for having no breath at all.

—Elizabeth V. Spelman[1]

I. Introduction

PROPONENTS OF THE anti-essentialist critique have suggested that we cannot
speak about what it means to be treated "as a woman" in society and cannot
make biological arguments to explain women's subordination in society without creating a false, unitary view of women.[2] In this book, however, I have tried
to engage in both kinds of discussions while also applying an anti-essentialist
perspective. I believe that anti-essentialism and equality theory can be used together; they each need to be modified to make them as practical as possible.

In this chapter, I examine some theorists closely who have purported to apply an anti-essentialist perspective to see how their theory may need to be modified
in light of my practice. Close examination reveals that the anti-essentialist critique contains some conflicting and unclear elements. Proponents of that critique often criticize our ability to speak about "women," yet they talk about subgroups of women, such as black women.[3] Their work is unclear in that they do
not give us guidance to determine which categories are appropriate to use and
which are not. In addition, they often seem to equate gender essentialism with
biological essentialism, suggesting that it is inappropriate to ever rely on the biological differences between women and men to describe the causes of women's
subordinate treatment in society.[4] Having a categorical rule that biological issues can never be relevant to the subordination in women's lives, however, can
be as essentialist as the opposing view. In addition, such a categorical view flies

in the face of the reality that men and women are defined by their biological differences. Anti-essentialists do not provide us with a way to discuss those differences. As I argue in this chapter, anti-essentialist feminists can speak about women's treatment "as women" and acknowledge the biological differences between women and men. They will still be utilizing an anti-essentialist perspective so long as their scholarship reflects consideration of the differences among women.

Similarly, equality theory can and should be available to protect women in the area of reproductive freedom. In the third section of this chapter, I examine the theoretical work that has developed on using equality theory to protect women's reproductive freedom. I will show how much of that work fails to address the "pregnant men" problem that I discussed in chapter 6. Nonetheless, I will also show how some of that work, particularly the work by feminists such as Justice Ruth Bader Ginsburg, which describes women's current situation in society, can help us resolve the "pregnant men" problem. Concretely, I end this chapter with examples from court cases in which courts have, in my view, used equality doctrine to further women's reproductive freedom while also protecting the most disadvantaged women in society.

II. Anti-essentialism

A. As a Woman

Although many theorists have propounded an "anti-essentialist" perspective, I will use the work of Angela Harris and Elizabeth Spelman to suggest how this theory must be modified to be more practical. I have chosen Harris, because she applies anti-essentialism to a legal context. Also, I find her work to be a very powerful version of the theory. If I am going to offer a critique of anti-essentialism, I believe I should offer a critique of one of the strongest versions of that theory. I have chosen Spelman, because her work is probably recognized as the foundational work in this area. Many of Harris's conclusions derive directly from Spelman. In no way are my words intended as a personal attack on Angela Harris and Elizabeth Spelman; instead, I hope to be paying them a compliment by taking their work seriously and providing a serious response to it.

Angela Harris's[5] path-breaking work on the anti-essentialist critique strongly criticizes our ability to use the phrase "as a woman." Harris argues that when feminist theorists have referred to women's treatment "as women," they have often been really referring to white, straight, and economically privileged women's treatment as women.[6] Relying on the work of Elizabeth Spelman, she criticizes the following propositions that she associates with gender essentialism and feminist theory: "women can be talked about 'as women'," and "women's situation can be contrasted to men's."[7]

E. christi cunningham, in turn, criticizes Harris for relying improperly on Spelman. Cunningham claims that Spelman, unlike Harris, does believe in the meaningfulness of the word *woman*. She simply criticizes feminism when it is essentialist and thereby assumes that the word *woman* "is the same in each of us and interchangeable between us."[8] Harris, cunningham argues, conflates feminism and essentialism, thereby suggesting that all feminists are also essentialists. Spelman supposedly does not make that error.

Cunningham's attempt to distinguish Harris and Spelman relies on a very subtle reading of Spelman's text, which is not entirely supportable. Cunningham is correct to observe that Spelman cited the before-mentioned propositions as basic to *feminism* rather than *essentialism*; however, Spelman's discussion of those propositions quickly leads to the conclusion that feminism and essentialism are nearly identical. For example, Spelman concluded that those propositions coupled with others found in feminism "lead inevitably to a focus on women who are not subject to any other form of oppression than sexism, that is, women who are white and middle-class."[9] The word *inevitably* does not leave much room for nuance or qualification; it suggests a direct correlation between feminism and essentialism (to the extent that feminism contains the characteristics that Spelman describes for it). Nevertheless, in other passages, Spelman is a bit more ambiguous. For example, she says that phrases such as "as a woman" "*typically* operate to obscure the race and class identity of white middle-class women."[10] *Typically* is, of course, not the same as *inevitably*. Cunningham seems to emphasize *typically*, whereas Harris seems to emphasize *inevitably*. Because the paragraph begins with *typically* and ends with *inevitably*, I would tend to agree with Harris's rather than cunningham's interpretation of Spelman. In any event, Spelman certainly questions the ability of feminism to use the phrase "as a woman" and its ability to contrast that treatment with "as a man."

If Harris and Spelman are correct to note the problematic nature of the core assumptions within feminist theory, then it would be rendered meaningless to the extent that it tries to compare women's situation to men's. How can one create sex-based equality theory without talking about women and comparing women's situation to men's? One could talk about the basic conditions of *humanity* and show how certain specific subgroups have been denied participation in this humanity, but that would be humanism rather than feminism, because such a theory would not focus on male dominance or gender inequality.

Similarly, if Harris and Spelman are correct, then my legal practice that I have described in this book would not be in the best interest of women. It would be furthering the interests of white, straight, and economically privileged women. I believe, however, that my legal work has exposed the *courts'* essentialism and thereby made it more possible that the most disadvantaged women in society would receive legal protection. Although Harris is certainly correct to observe that some people, especially some judges, have had a narrow view of women, that indictment is not true of all feminists or even all judges. What we need instead is a more sensitive method to determine when the phrase "as a woman" is being used in a way that only serves the interests of the most privileged women in society.

Close examination of Harris's and Spelman's critiques reveal that they suffer from two major problems. First, Harris and Spelman have often overstated the extent to which feminists, as opposed to other members in society, have engaged in essentialist arguments. For example, Harris and Spelman employ the famous example of Sojourner Truth asking "And ain't I a woman?"[11] after a white man had said: "[w]omen need to be helped into carriages, and lifted over ditches, and to have the best place everywhere."[12] Harris and Spelman claim that this example shows how gender essentialism has caused white and black women to be unable to work together effectively. What the Sojourner Truth example, however, reveals is how a particular man (who I presume was white and upper class) rather than women or feminists tried to create a false unity of "woman." If I consider that man to be representative of men within powerful institutions in society such as the courts or legislatures, then we can see that it is on the basis of a false unity that courts or legislatures create law and social programs. Harris and Spelman blame feminists for this false unity, but the blame often belongs elsewhere, such as in male-dominated courts or legislatures. For that reason, I have been careful in this book to distinguish between essentialist arguments made by courts and by feminists. Most of the essentialist arguments that I have uncovered have come from courts rather than feminists.

Second, their critique of feminists' use of the phrase "as a woman" assumes a kind of symmetrical comparison that feminists do not purport to make. For example, when feminists make the assertion that women are discriminated against on the basis of their gender when society creates abortion regulations, that claim is not based on an equality argument that compares women directly to men.[13] Men, of course, do not get pregnant, so a perfect comparator is never available. Nevertheless, feminists argue that restrictions on women's reproductive freedom are at the core of their gender inequality in society, because those restrictions make it difficult for women to work, raise children, support themselves, protect themselves from sexual abuse, and otherwise attempt to achieve full citizenship in society.[14] Thus, feminists feel comfortable in saying that abortion restrictions act on women "as women" and that society would be unlikely to treat a dominant class, such as middle-class men, in that way.

Despite the fact that there is no perfect comparator between pregnant women and men, I do nonetheless believe it is useful to make the best available comparison between pregnant women and men to demonstrate that "pregnant men" would never be treated as disfavorably as society has treated pregnant women. The anti-essentialist critique always asks us to focus on *differences* among women and does not challenge us to find *similarities* when those similarities may serve a strategic purpose. Thus, in this book, I have tried to use the anti-essentialist critique to note differences among women while also struggling to find the best comparator for pregnant women.

In other areas of the law, outside the area of reproduction-based restrictions, there are more parallel examples between women and men. But the parallel is always between the treatment of some women and a dominant subclass of men. Neither all women nor all men are in either category. For example, when employers prohibited women from becoming firefighters, those restrictions only impacted on the subcategory of women who desired to perform that work.[15] Similarly, it only benefited the subcategory of men who desired to perform that work. Although these two subcategories of women and men may have been similar in their desire to become firefighters, they also would have differed enormously among themselves and between the two groups. And those differences changed over time. When African-Americans and Hispanics were barred from such positions, the dominant group who benefited from barring women would have included mostly white men. When firefighter positions were opened to African-Americans and Hispanics but still unavailable to women, the dominant group included men of nearly all races. The fact that we can see how these policies impacted various and changing subcategories of women and men, however, does not detract from the usefulness of describing how women and men were treated. The gender-based story, however, can often only be told with reference to other variables such as race.

Harris seems to understand some of these shortcomings of her work, because she does not entirely dismiss the importance of categorization. She says:

> I do not mean in this article to suggest that either feminism or legal theory should adopt the voice of Funes the Memorious, for whom every experience is unique and no categories or generalizations exist at all. Even a jurisprudence based on multiple consciousness must categorize; without categorization each individual is as isolated as Funes, and there can be no moral responsibility or social change. My suggestion is only that we make our categories explicitly tentative, relational, and unstable, and that to do

so is all the more important in a discipline like law, where abstraction and "frozen" categories are the norm.[16]

Similarly, Spelman says:

I am not saying that we ought never to think about or refer to women "as women" or to men "as men." I am only insisting that whenever we do that we remember which women and which men we are thinking about. . . . Whenever we feel tempted to talk about women "as women," we might remember what the poet Gwendolyn Brooks once said in a somewhat different context: "The juice from tomatoes is not called merely *juice*. It is always called TOMATO juice." Even the most literal reading of Brooks ought to make us ask whether we're more careful about what we order in a restaurant than we are in thinking of women as the particular women they are.[17]

Harris has to acknowledge the usefulness of categories, because she uses the category "black women" in her own scholarship. Moreover, her own use of categories would seem to be essentialist. For example, when Harris refers to "black women," she seems to be exclusively referring to *poor* black women. One could therefore criticize Harris for holding a unitary view of black women, which is similar to the problem of theorists holding a unitary view of women. Rather than abandon categories, it appears that the important task is to find accurate ways to employ the use of categories. Unfortunately, neither Harris nor Spelman provides the reader with much assistance in understanding when categories are useful rather than problematic; Harris only suggests that we should be "tentative" in our use of categories without explaining what she means by "tentative." By sharing my own research methods with the reader, I have tried to show how we can create a hypothesis and revise it as we acquire new data. I have also tried to provide examples of situations in which I used forceful rather than tentative argument for strategic, rhetorical purposes. It is not enough to say we should be "tentative;" we need to consider concrete situations that call for different styles of argumentation.

I believe that we can use the category "woman" in two different ways. First, we should try to understand the view of women that is held by society when it develops laws and policies; that view may be essentialist and, if so, needs to be acknowledged for its essentialism. To the extent that we are convinced that society has that particular view of women in mind, I see no reason to be tentative. In fact, we may want to incorporate many of these understandings into legal argument on behalf of women who are outside that essentialist view of women; legal argument can rarely be effective if it is tentative rather than rhetorical.

Second, we should try to understand the varieties of ways that law and policies do impact on women; to be accurate we will have to consider subcategories of women and not assume that all effects are in the same direction. Some women might experience negative effects while others experience positive effects, yet they all may be acted upon "as women." In explaining the ways that laws and policies affect women, I do see room for "tentativeness." In order to understand the impact of policies on women, we generally need to have a hypothesis, such as that the policies particularly impact on poor women. In the course of our research, however, we may determine that race has a larger effect than class in explaining the effects of particular policies on women. By being tentative, we can leave our hypothesis open to revision and not try to mold the data to fit our preconceived categories. Moreover, even after we have described the effects that we have seen in class or race terms, we should be open to further revision in the future as new data comes to light. Thus, we need to be careful not to throw around phrases like "black women" without having examined whether class and marital status, as well as race and gender, may explain the particular life conditions that we are trying to describe.[18] Although Harris embraces tentativeness in her own work, she does not seem to embrace an openness to categories, which would allow her to see the operation of factors other than race and gender.

B. Relational Feminism and Biology

One branch of feminist theory that is often criticized as being essentialist is relational feminism. The most prominent relational feminist is Carol Gilligan.[19] Gilligan argued that women's relational qualities lead them to develop a moral perspective and moral identity different from men's. This version of feminist theory can be essentialist in two different ways, both of which can be seen in the following quotation from Robin West, another relational feminist: "[P]erhaps the central insight of feminist theory of the last decade has been that woman [sic] are 'essentially connected,' not 'essentially separate,' from the rest of human life, both materially, through pregnancy, intercourse, and breast-feeding, and existentially, through the moral and practical life."[20]

West's version of relational feminism is essentialist in two different ways. First, she purports to have found an aspect of women's lives that is universal. She fails to consider how the experiences of pregnancy, intercourse, and breast-feeding as well as the other aspects of women's lives vary according to race, class, sexual orientation, disability, or age. Why would a lesbian who has not given birth feel connected to society in the way that West describes? Why would a poor woman who has been coerced to maintain a pregnancy, and has had her behavior dictated by society throughout her pregnancy, feel connected in the way that West describes? By purporting to describe women generally, West's argument is a classic essentialist argument.

Angela Harris has observed that essentialist aspect of West's argument but also points out that West is essentialist because of the biological basis of her argument. West's thesis relies on a universality about women's biological experiences, which is simply not true. Women are not perpetually pregnant; most American women are pregnant about three times in their life. And few women get pregnant until they are, at least, a teenager. Yet, West would probably argue that women are connected irrespective of whether they have yet borne children or breast-fed. And even for women who do experience these biological conditions, their responses vary enormously. Many women choose to terminate the pregnancies that they do experience; other women find themselves facing an unwanted pregnancy but do not have the means to terminate the pregnancy. Many women do not breast-feed. Although lactation is physically required to breast-feed, it is not sufficient. Women must be at home with the child or be able to "pump" if they are to breast-feed. (Is "pumping" even breast-feeding in that the connectedness is with a piece of machinery? Someone other than the mother typically feeds the child if the woman "pumps.") To the extent that women do breast-feed, they usually do so for no longer than six months. Why should any of these physical experiences, which women experience in many different ways, *cause* women to feel connected to others? For example, women who face unwanted pregnancies and must breast-feed because they are too poor to afford formula may *resent* these physical experiences. West's comments seem to presuppose women identifying with and choosing to take advantage of their physical capabilities to become pregnant and breast-feed. That identification and choice, however, is socially constructed. Other options are available and are experienced by some women.

A personal example may illuminate this point. When my child was a few weeks old, I mentioned to a colleague that I had breast-fed her twelve times the previous day. He responded with horror, saying that I was allowing the child to make a slave of me! Until he made that comment, I had thought of breast-feeding as I had been socialized to think of it—as an experience of connectedness with my infant. But the connectedness of *servitude* was not what I had in mind. Based on his comment, I then took steps to insure that I fed my child seven or eight times a day rather than twelve, beginning to see myself as having control over the meaning that breast-feeding would have in my life. Had I continued to feed her twelve times a day, I doubt that I would have continued to see breast-feeding as a wonderful opportunity to connect with my child. Thus, not only was I able to modify the *meaning* that breast-feeding had in my life, I was also able to modify the physical experience (i.e., frequency of breast-feeding). Neither the biological experience nor the social meaning attached to it are inevitable or static.

West's thesis is weakened by her failure to explore the variety of responses that women may have to their capacity to become pregnant. Bell hooks's statement, for example, "I am most passionate in my relationship with mama. It is with her that I feel loved and sometimes accepted,"[21] may reflect a connectedness based on the birthing experience. Linda Hollies, by contrast, who describes herself as an incest survivor, seems to have an entirely different feeling of connectedness. For example, she recounts: "I saw in my mother's death the story of many Black women, wives, mothers, sisters, and daughters. They exist in an empty place, full of a vast interior emptiness."[22] Although Hollies had three children of her own, she did not appear to feel connected to her family. Instead, she found that the connectedness she did feel was an unhealthy connectedness—of dependency and abuse. She therefore worked in therapy for many years to become more *separate* from her family. Hollies came to understand the connectedness to others imposed upon her by society, including that of her father's repeated rape of her, but also came to understand that connectedness was not inevitable or healthy. Thus, for bell hooks the connectedness of pregnancy and family may be a strong metaphor of sisterhood; whereas, for Hollies it may be a strong metaphor of subordination. West assumes the ideal metaphor of connectedness for all women, not seeing the socially constructed aspects of that metaphor.

One reason that West seems to be unable to discuss the variety of ways women respond to their capacity to become pregnant is that she does not sufficiently explore the socially constructed aspects of pregnancy. She makes a passing reference to the fact that women are socialized to do nearly all of the child care but does not connect that fact to society's construction of women's biology. In other words, I would suggest that it is impossible to separate women's socialization to perform child care from their biological capacity to bear children and lactate. It is unlikely that women's subordination would take the particular form that it does in our society if women did not have the biological capacity to bear children and breast-feed.[23] On a socialization basis, it is easy to see that African-American women are strongly socialized to bear and take care of children. That socialization is probably part of their subordination in society. By entirely disavowing the usefulness of biological arguments in her criticism of West, Harris seems to be denying the role that mothering plays in the socialization of African-American women.[24] The weakness of West's scholarship—her oversimplification of what is biology and her failure to tell stories to reinforce her thesis—may have caused Harris not to see the applicability of her scholarship to the lives of some black women.

Relational feminists, however, are not the only theorists to use biological arguments, which are criticized as essentialist. For example, Catharine MacKinnon gives two examples of theorists who she believes are essentialists—Simone de Beauvoir and Susan Brownmiller—because they each rest their theories on biological sex differences between men and women. These theorists, in

MacKinnon's view, are essentialist in using biological explanations, because they assert that there is nothing we can do about the inherent biological differences between men and women. If those biological differences cause sex inequality, then, in MacKinnon's words, "[i]t is unclear exactly how any social organization of equality could change such an existential fact."[25] By focusing on *biological* rather than *socially created* determinants of sex inequality, these theorists do not offer a possibility for eliminating that inequality. MacKinnon, by contrast, emphatically resists giving any significance to biology; by showing that women's experiences are socially constructed rather than biologically necessary, she attempts to offer solutions to the problems of sex inequality.

MacKinnon therefore believes that it is appropriate to look for commonalities in women's condition in society but that it is not appropriate to look to biology for those commonalities. It is inappropriate, because if biology were the source of women's inequality, then there would be no way to eliminate the inequality. It is not so, because it would be very inconvenient for it to be so.

That explanation is not very helpful. After all, it is MacKinnon who has said that we should not reject her stark description of women's inequality in society because we do not want to believe that it can be that bad.[26] Similarly, if biology does have some role in women's inequality in society, then we need to acknowledge that it is true and, hard as it may be, try to find strategies to overcome that inequality. The *meaning* that society ascribes to those biological differences may not be inevitable even if the differences themselves are inevitable. For example, the fact that women can become pregnant and men cannot does not mean that abortion must be criminalized. Society does not have to treat the difference coercively, thereby furthering the subordination of women in society. Instead, that difference could be respected and women could be treated such that the difference is accommodated rather than coerced. Feminists should not be so afraid to talk about biology as having *something* to do with sex inequality. Given that men and women are, by definition, biologically different, it would be very surprising if biology had *nothing* to do with sex inequality.

C. Pre-conditions to Anti-essentialism

If the use of biological arguments does not inherently make one an essentialist and talking about "women as women" does not make one an anti-essentialist, then what are the pre-conditions of anti-essentialism?

My practice of anti-essentialism has led me to the following conclusions about how to talk about "women" while being sensitive to the anti-essentialist critique. I believe that we need to make three distinctions in order to discuss the category "woman" in a meaningful way. First, it is important to distinguish between how society acts upon a category that it perceives to be "woman" and how women themselves respond to those actions. Law and society often are essentialist, by which I mean that they have a narrow, unitary view of women in mind when they create policies and programs. Women, in fact, are quite diverse. Law and society's failure to see that diversity creates different kinds of problems for different women, depending upon how closely they fit law and society's false image of women. Thus, a crucial question we should ask ourselves in constructing feminist theory is, What view of women does law and society have in mind when it creates various policies and programs? If that view is a static, unitary view, then it is an essentialist view and should be described as such. The fact that feminists may identify that society has an essentialist view of women does not make feminist theory itself essentialist. In addition, identifying society's essentialist view of women may help us to understand how policies affect different women in different ways. Thus, in part 2 of this book, I explored the courts' essentialism. In *Casey*, we saw how the Court consciously decided to protect middle-class women rather than poor women. The fact that I could expose the unitary view of women held by the courts does not mean that I, as an author, hold such a unitary view.

Second, we need to distinguish between biological arguments and essentialism. Feminist theorists may rely on women's biological differences from men to explain some aspects of women's subordination in society without being essentialists. Their biological arguments will not be essentialist so long as they make reference to the biological variation among women as well as to the different ways that society treats the same biological traits within women. Some theorists, such as Catharine MacKinnon,[27] suggest that one is only being essentialist if one relies on biological arguments in constructing feminist theory. Such a view cannot be correct within feminist theory, because it would prevent us from discussing the biological differences between women and men. By definition, women and men do differ biologically—that is the basis upon which society assigns people to the categories "male" and "female." By insisting that feminists entirely ignore such differences, feminists are being as essentialist as they accuse their critics of being. In other words, by denying categorically that the differences between men and women are relevant to feminist theory (and society), one is rigid, unitary, and universal—the purported evils of essentialism. Rather than avoiding biological arguments entirely, the challenge for feminists is to sort out innate biological differences between men and women that have some bearing on women's position in society and those purported differences that have been exaggerated by society; moreover, we should examine differences among women in terms of their biology as well as differences among women in terms of how society treats their biology.[28] We should not be afraid to consider the impact of pregnancy on women's lives while recognizing that society can distort biological reality. Thus, in chapter 6, I consciously looked at the role that biology (and society's treatment of women's biology) has played in women's reproductive lives while not assuming that that role has been uniform or static over time.

Rather than examining an author's use of biological arguments to determine whether she is an essentialist, I would prefer to look at what stories the author tells. Feminists must read voraciously about the lives of as many women as possible, because none of us can know all women through our daily experiences. And because we are more likely to know women who are "like us," it is especially important that we read about women who are different from ourselves in race, class, physical ability, sexual orientation, and other group-based characteristics. Only by becoming constantly vigilant and curious can we hope to think and talk about all women as we try to understand the nature of women's subordination in society. When authors are *not* inclusive, we should be quick to criticize. But when an author, such as Catharine MacKinnon, consistently tells stories about many different kinds of women in her scholarship, we should read those stories and try to learn from them. Of course, we might disagree with her interpretation of the stories. Storytelling, by itself, is not sufficient. We need to reflect closely on the stories that are told. Why are those particular stories told rather than others? Are other interpretations available of those stories? Do counternarratives also exist? Thus, in chapter 4, I used women's narratives to teach us about the connection between abortion and violence.

Finally, when we talk about a policy's impact on women, we do not have to feel compelled to describe a unitary effect of that policy on women. Some women may experience a heightened effect of the policy, while other women may experience an opposing effect. All of these women are acted upon by society but can be acted upon in quite different ways. We are essentialist when we assume a priori that certain subgroups, such as African-American women or lesbians, will experience a heightened version of white, heterosexual women's experience. Thus, in chapter 3, I used the example of lesbians to show the many different effects that a policy can have on a subgroup of women. Such discussions are important if we are to hold an anti-essentialist view of women.

I hope that readers will conclude that I have tried to consider the lives of all women, particularly the most disadvantaged women in society, when I wrote this book. I, too, however, have probably made inaccurate generalizations and insulted some women. I can only hope that readers who disagree with my conclusions will engage in dialogue with me, so we can all move to a more inclusive understanding of women's lives.

III. Equality Theory

Q. What were you thinking that you would have had to do if welfare had not paid for your abortion?

A. Well, when you are in such a situation, you . . . do crazy things really, you know, even though you do not have the right to do it or anything. I would have probably done something very dumb.

Q. What would you have done?

A. You know, in Columbia [*sic*], people do a lot of dumb things that I know. I probably would have. I know people who does this. I would have done it. I could have grabbed a handle and make a wire and put it over there and do something.

Q. You would have tried to abort yourself?

A. I would have done it, yes. I would have tried. I don't know. Because you have to do something if it was going to be a torment. I was not physically ready to have a baby. And, it was going to be a big, big, problem. I don't know how I would have handled it, but I would have done something real bad. (Plaintiff's testimony, *Doe v. Maher* [Connecticut 1986])[29]

A. Introduction

A central premise of this book has been that reproductive freedom cases ϡould be decided from a gender-based equality perspective rather than from a rivacy perspective, because privacy doctrine has been essentialist in that it has ot been able to protect the most disadvantaged women in society. Nonetheless, ϡrprisingly little has been written about what an equality perspective would)ok like in the area of reproductive freedom. Moreover, little of this writing is ɔnsciously anti-essentialist. In this section, I survey the existing literature on quality theory and reproductive freedom and then suggest a new direction for ιe development of a reproductive freedom equality theory, which will also be ϡnsitive to the anti-essentialist critique.

As we saw in chapters 4 and 5, the federal courts have virtually never ap-lied gender-based equality doctrine to reproductive freedom cases. In *Planned 'arenthood v. Casey*, Justice Blackmun invoked the first mention of gender-based quality theory in a Supreme Court reproductive freedom case. He said:

A State's restrictions on a woman's right to terminate her pregnancy also implicate constitutional guarantees of gender equality. State restrictions on abortion compel women to continue pregnancies they otherwise might terminate. By restricting the right to terminate pregnancies, the State conscripts women's bodies into service, forcing women to continue their pregnancies, suffer the pains of childbirth, and in most instances, provide years of maternal care. The State does not compensate women for their services; instead, it assumes that they owe this duty as a matter of course. This assumption—that women can simply be forced to accept the "natural" status and incidents of motherhood—appears to rest upon a conception of women's role that has triggered the protection of the Equal Protection Clause. *See, e.g., Mississippi Univ. for Women v. Hogan*, 458 U.S. 718, 724–726 (1982); *Craig v. Boren*, 429 U.S. 190, 198–199 (1976). The joint opinion recognizes that these assumptions about women's place in society "are no longer consistent with our understanding of the family, the individual, or the Constitution."[30]

Blackmun's recitation of equality theory is sketchy. It suffers from major problems, but I will focus on one—that he does not respond to the existing pregnancy-based equality case law. In particular, he does not try to distinguish *Geduldig v. Aiello*,[31] in which the Supreme Court ruled that pregnancy-based discrimination is not per se gender-based discrimination. By not citing *Geduldig*, Blackmun does not attempt to distinguish it.

Blackmun, however, does refer to some legal scholarship on equality theory in the abortion context. It therefore might be useful to examine that underlying scholarship to see if it does a better job than Blackmun in distinguishing *Geduldig* and in offering a full explanation for why pregnancy-based discrimination should be viewed as gender-based discrimination. Blackmun cites Cass Sunstein's article in the *Columbia Law Review*,[32] Larry Tribe's treatise *American Constitutional Law*,[33] and Jeb Rubenfeld's article from the *Harvard Law Review*,[34] which never uses an equal protection analysis (and which I do not discuss). Interestingly, aside from Reva Siegel's article in the *Stanford Law Review*,[35] he fails to discuss any of the feminist writings on this subject, including Sylvia Law's early article in the *Pennsylvania Law Review*[36] and Justice Ruth Bader Ginsburg's article in the *North Carolina Law Review*,[37] in which they argued forcefully that pregnancy-based discrimination is gender-based discrimination. Had he looked more closely at the feminist writings on this subject, I believe he would have had a much stronger foundation for his argument.

B. The Law Review Commentary

1. CASS SUNSTEIN

Justice Blackmun's opinion in *Casey* is highly derivative of Cass Sunstein's article "Neutrality in Constitutional Law."[38] Sunstein attempts to respond to the shortcoming that I noted in Justice Blackmun's opinion. He would excuse Blackmun's failure to discuss *Geduldig* by saying that it is not useful to inquire about "pregnant men." He argues that such counterfactual questions are not helpful or relevant, because they rely on changing one part of reality while keeping the rest the same.[39] Moreover, all of reality, he argues, would be fundamentally changed if such a transformation in men's abilities occurred. In addition, the question is somewhat meaningless, since if men could get pregnant, they would not be men (since the capability to become pregnant is the basis of our sex-based classification system). Rather than respond to the problem of having little evidence about how society might treat "pregnant men," one might say that Sunstein "fights the hypo."

Although Sunstein is certainly correct to note that it is not plausible for men to become pregnant and society to maintain its current structure, that does not mean the counterfactual question is entirely useless. The usefulness stems from practical rather than theoretical considerations. As we saw in chapter 6, there are situations in which men and women are similarly situated with respect to reproductive health, but men are treated better than women. It is helpful, I believe, for us to explore the situations in which men and women are similarly situated in the reproductive health context to see the systematic valuation of men's well-being over women's well-being in society. Sunstein may be overemphasizing the distinctiveness of pregnancy to make his point, as have some courts. Unlike Sunstein, however, when courts overemphasize the distinctiveness of pregnancy, they often do so to deny women their rights in the reproductive health context. Thus, I suggest that we should welcome the opportunity to discuss situations in which men are "almost pregnant" in order to demonstrate how much better these men are treated than similarly situated women. Equality theory should not prevent us from engaging in such an inquiry if it is to be useful.

2. LARRY TRIBE

Larry Tribe offers an equality theory that does purport to distinguish *Geduldig*, but still suffers from major problems. Tribe tries to use some of the insights of relational feminism to make his argument and therefore suffers from some of the essentialism that is basic to relational feminism. In his treatise, Tribe describes the abortion issue as embedded in *relational* concerns—those between the women and men, and between pregnant women and the fetuses they carry.[40] Unfortunately, he tends to see pregnant women as unidimensional without exploring the variety of responses that women have to their pregnancies. Noting that 96 percent of unmarried teenage mothers keep their children, although two-thirds of those births were unintended, Tribe argues that a ban on abortion requires "women to sacrifice their liberty in order . . . to create lifelong attach-

ments and burdens."[41] His use of statistics in this way, however, is very mislead-
ing in terms of the realities of women's lives. Both married and unmarried women
often become pregnant unintentionally yet choose to give birth, because their
unintended pregnancies become wanted pregnancies. Tribe's analysis is insensitive to the range of responses that women have to an unintended pregnancy;
not all of those pregnancies are carried to term due to coercion.

Tribe's more recent writings on abortion are no less essentialist. He uses a
narrow pro-choice perspective, which looks at abortion rights in isolation from
reproductive health and women's lives, in his book *Abortion: The Clash of Absolutes*.[42] The purpose of Tribe's book is to examine the highly rhetorical abortion
rights debate to see if there is any common ground on abortion. He examines
proposed areas for compromise, such as waiting period rules and parental consent, and concludes that these purported areas of compromise are not really compromises at all, because they would take away the right to have an abortion for
certain groups of women.[43] His recognition of this disproportionate impact is
an important anti-essentialist insight that was missing from his prior work. Nevertheless, in searching for common ground, Tribe starts from a very narrow
premise regarding the concerns of the pro-choice movement—that they simply
want to make abortion more accessible to women who face unwanted pregnancies. His discussion is almost entirely focused on the choices available to women
after they have already experienced an unwanted pregnancy. By starting at that
point, and relying very heavily on the possibilities of medical technology,[44] he
entirely misses a discussion of the social conditions that make some women have
to conclude that they cannot afford to carry the fetus to term or that some
women experience an unintended pregnancy through rape or sexual abuse. The
existence of unwanted pregnancies is a given for Tribe and not a problem he
considers linked to the abortion issue. Writing by women of color on the abortion issue, however, has repeatedly emphasized that it is essential that we look
at reproductive freedom in the entire context of women's lives so arguments for
abortion rights are not simply a subterfuge to compel poor and minority women
not to bear children. Given the history of sterilization abuse that has existed in
this country, it is essential that pro-choice arguments be developed in as broad
a framework as possible. By taking unintended pregnancies as a given and by
relying heavily on the possibilities of expensive medical technology, which is
unlikely to ever be available to poor women, Tribe makes an argument that is
based in the lives of privileged rather than disadvantaged women.

Unlike Sunstein, however, Tribe makes a modest attempt to compare men
and women with respect to the burdens imposed by society through compulsory childbirth. He argues, for example, that "the law nowhere forces *men* to

devote their bodies and restructure their lives even in those tragic situations (such as organ transplants) where nothing less will permit their children to survive."[45] Nevertheless, Tribe recognizes that there are no perfect analogies between pregnant women and nonpregnant men. Whereas men are not required to take affirmative steps to save a fetus, Tribe observes that a pregnant woman is not being asked to take affirmative steps to save fetal life; instead, she is being asked to refrain from extinguishing life.[46] He responds to this lack of a parallel argument by noting that the "grossest discrimination can lie in treating things that are different as though they were exactly alike."[47] It should be sufficient, he argues, to note that the state is *indifferent* to the "biological reality that sometimes requires women, but never men, to resort to abortion if they are to avoid pregnancy and retain control of their own bodies."[48] Not only is the state indifferent, but citing Ruth Bader Ginsburg, he observes that the state *exploits* this special vulnerability to reinforce women's subordination in society.[49] This intent to subordinate can be determined by examining the history of anti-abortion laws and learning that they were generally enacted in the late nineteenth century to keep women in their place.[50]

Tribe responds to arguments about the fetus's vulnerability and dependence by noting that the relationship of woman and fetus is unique. Citing Sylvia Law, he argues that until the fetus is viable, "*only* the pregnant woman can respond to and support her fetus's 'right' to life."[51] Thus, he argues that the state of medical technology is a relevant moral and constitutional fact. As technology enhances the point at which a pregnant woman can be relieved of the burden of her pregnancy and transfer nurture of the fetus to other hands, Tribe argues that "the state's power to protect fetal life expands—*as it should*."[52]

Although Tribe makes some important and intriguing observations, he does not really attempt to deal with the equality-based case law in the area of reproduction. Despite his fondness for extensive footnoting, he never even mentions *Geduldig*. His argument that restrictions on reproduction are an attempt by society to perpetuate women's subordination is based on a historical argument that is not relevant to many contemporary restrictions on abortion. For example, in chapter 4, I argued that waiting period requirements impose substantial burdens on women who fear physical abuse from their partners. Those restrictions, which are becoming increasingly common, are quite modern restrictions. Despite the enormous burdens that they will impose on some women's lives, they could not be invalidated under Tribe's historical analysis.

Finally, Tribe's reference to the moral significance of viability makes little sense in the lives of women. One could easily reverse Tribe's argument by saying that a woman only has to maintain her pregnancy *until* the fetus is viable;

at the point of viability, she can choose to abort it, and the state can decide whether it wants to take steps to maintain the fetus's life. A woman would therefore have no responsibility to maintain her pregnancy until the fetus is viable, because at the point of viability, she could choose to abort it, leaving the state with the responsibility to take steps to maintain the life of a viable fetus. In other words, Tribe's "moral" solution leaves women rather than the state with all of the responsibilities to maintain a fetus's life, both before and after viability. The fact of viability does not answer the moral question of who should take responsibility for maintaining that viability.

I would suggest, by contrast, that the state should *never* be able to impose *all* of the responsibility of sustaining fetal life (and borne children) on women, because those burdens are enormous. Thus, a state should not pass all of those burdens on to women by regulating abortion when it is not willing to offer free prenatal care, paid pregnancy leave, free child care, and compensation for the physical burdens of pregnancy. Rather than look historically at why the state chose to criminalize abortions, I believe that we should look at contemporary society and the state legislatures to see how insincere the state has been when it says that it values prenatal life or children. Why has the United States been the only industrialized country without *any* paid or, until recently, even unpaid pregnancy leave? How can a society that is so willing to impose the costs of waiting period rules on disadvantaged women be able to say that it would be too expensive to impose the costs of *unpaid maternity leave* on employers? Why are states that refuse to increase funding for women and children under Medicaid also the states that restrict abortions substantially? Interestingly, under a Clinton-Gore administration, we can probably expect the state to provide more services for pregnant women and their children while *also* liberalizing abortion law. These steps would be consistent with the pattern that I have described; it is only by looking at the larger picture—funding of services for pregnant women and their children as well as restrictions on abortion—that one can ascertain whether the state respects women's lives. Although Tribe sees the historical picture, he misses the contemporary picture and provides an argument against abortion restrictions that is not relevant to the modern restrictions that have been recently imposed on women.

C. The Feminist Commentary

1. REVA SIEGEL

Reva Siegel has offered the most sustained equal protection analysis of abortion regulations of any of the law review commentators cited by the Supreme

Court, although little of her analysis was incorporated into Blackmun's opinion. In contrast to Tribe, she does an excellent job in collecting evidence that shows contemporary society's failure to value the lives of pregnant women and mothers. She points to the following three probative examples: (1) President Bush's veto of the Family and Medical Leave Act, which would have provided parents with unpaid leave after the birth or adoption of a child; (2) our failure to provide prenatal care to pregnant women who lack health insurance, which contributes to an extremely high infant mortality rate; and (3) the fact that more than half of the children living in female-headed households are born into poverty.[53] Those contemporary facts can be much more probative of the legislature's attitudes about women and children than historical evidence from the nineteenth century. Moreover, she lists in great detail all of the burdens of pregnancy and motherhood—burdens that our society takes for granted rather than respects or compensates.[54] None of these examples, however, were featured in Justice Blackmun's opinion in *Casey*.

Nevertheless, Siegel glosses over the key doctrinal hurdle, *Geduldig v. Aiello*. She blithely says at the outset of her analysis: "I assume, as most commentators have, that when the Court revisits *Geduldig v. Aiello*, it should modify it to accord with the common social understanding and the amended terms of the Civil Rights Act of 1964, that regulation concerning women's capacity to gestate categorically differentiates on the basis of sex, and so is facially sex-based."[55] In a footnote, she supports her view that *Geduldig* was wrongly decided. Evidence of the sex-based character of abortion regulations is that the state does nothing to regulate the conduct of men in order to avoid the need for abortions; instead, it only regulates the conduct of women who desire abortions.[56] In addition, she argues that laws restricting abortions shape "the social horizons of every woman who believes herself capable of becoming pregnant. Thus, for reasons physiological and social, such regulation affects women's lives in ways it simply cannot affect men's."[57] Finally, she argues that legislatures "are not interested in regulating the conduct of men except insofar as men are instrumental in effectuating women's decisions respecting abortion."[58] In what ways could we expect legislatures to regulate men's lives that would be more parallel to the ways that they regulate women's lives? And, if legislatures regulated men's lives more, would that make restrictions on women constitutional or not sex based? Unfortunately, Siegel does not answer those questions and therefore does not provide us with strong arguments to demonstrate to the Court that *Geduldig* was wrongly decided.

Like Tribe, Siegel relies on a historical argument to show that abortion restrictions have the purpose of confining women to maternal roles in society. She recognizes, however, that "[i]t may be claimed that the gender code informing the nineteenth century campaign was a product of its era, and that today a legislature might restrict access to abortion to protect the unborn without entertaining any similar assumptions about women."[59] Although she recognizes that history alone cannot refute that objection, she argues that the "historical record supplies strong evidence that this argument should not be readily credited."[60]

Not relying entirely on a historical argument, Siegel uses the example of Louisiana to discuss contemporary abortion statutes. Nevertheless, she does not use some of the best available evidence of the legislature's intent in Louisiana. She examines public opinion polls in which 79 percent of Louisiana's residents reported they were opposed to abortion "when childbirth might interrupt the woman's career" but reported they favored the choice of abortion in the case of rape or incest, when the child is likely to have serious birth defects, when childbirth might endanger a woman's health, or when childbirth might endanger a woman's mental health.[61] She uses this evidence to argue that "opposition to abortion reflected a judgment about women's pursuit of career opportunities in conflict with the maternal role."[62]

Those public opinion polls, however, did not reflect the actions taken by the Louisiana legislature. The legislature rejected a physical or mental health exception, an HIV exception, an amendment that would have conditioned passage on expanding Medicaid eligibility to 185 percent of the federal poverty income guidelines, and an amendment that would have removed the imposition of capital punishment for the commission of any criminal offense.[63] It never even seriously considered any other "good cause" exceptions such as interference with a woman's career. I believe that these rejected amendments are the best available evidence of the legislature's intent; they wanted to restrict abortion in the way that would impose the maximum harm on the lives of poor women. Accordingly, they rejected all amendments that would have mitigated the impact of their restrictions. Most likely, the legislature did want middle-class women to undergo compulsory childbirth but probably wanted poor women to forego sexual activity or become sterilized (which the state would fund under Medicaid) rather than bear more children. Thus, the state did nothing to lessen the financial impact on poor women of bearing additional children while also refusing to fund abortions for them. An anti-essentialist perspective reveals the different effect that this statute would have on women depending on their economic class. Outside the context of the Louisiana statute, Siegel recognized the importance of such evidence, although she did not describe it in class-based terms. Examining Utah's failure to assist pregnant women and mothers, Siegel commented: "Here the state's choice of sex-based, coercive means suggests that it is interested in controlling and/or punishing women who resist motherhood: It will promote the welfare of the unborn only when it can use women's bodies and lives to realize the potential of unborn life—and not when the community as a whole would have to bear the costs of its moral preferences."[64] Ditto Louisiana.

A more substantial problem with Siegel's argument is that it is not likely to be useful in fighting the abortion statutes of the 1990s. In light of the *Casey* decision, which I discussed in chapter 4, statutes criminalizing nearly all abortions are not likely to be the battleground of the nineties. Instead, states are more likely to impose waiting period rules, testing requirements, hospitalization requirements, and "informed consent" requirements. Each of these requirements will raise the cost of abortion and, in some cases, increase the risk of loss of confidentiality. In many cases, the states may justify these requirements by saying that they are for the benefit of the pregnant woman as well as the fetus by improving her deliberation process or by increasing the safety of the procedure. These are very different justifications than the ones considered by Siegel, but justifications that we must respond to if we are to defeat modern state restrictions on abortion. By focusing so heavily on the nineteenth century, Siegel has lost sight of our challenges in the twentieth century.

2. SYLVIA LAW

In contrast to the commentators previously discussed, Professor Law squarely confronts the role of reproductive biology in perpetuating women's subordination in society. She criticizes the presumption that sex-based differences are always insignificant.[65] Nevertheless, she also cautions that we need to be careful about creating a legal order that recognizes sex differences between men and women, because that legal order may perpetuate stereotypes about the differences between men and women rather than rely on the real differences.[66] She argues that feminists should hold a vision of equality that considers "the appropriate function of the law . . . not to enforce a general vision of what men and women are really like, but rather to respect each person's authority to define herself or himself, free from sex-defined legal constraints."[67]

Law provides a strong indictment of *Geduldig*, noting that even its principal proponent believes the Court was wrong to conclude that the challenged distinction was not sex based. She argues that

> [i]t is not easy to reconcile the ideal of sex-based equality with the reality of categorical biological difference, but the difficulty is not overcome by denying that laws governing reproductive biology are sex based. Further, because . . . it is easy for the Court to confuse real categorical biological

differences with sex-based differences that are culturally imposed, an equality doctrine that exempts laws based on real physical differences from its concern is likely to be a weak one. Finally, and most importantly, in a society constitutionally committed to equality, the reality of biological difference in relation to reproduction should not be permitted to justify state action exaggerating the consequences of those differences. This is what happens when those actions escape scrutiny by courts.[68]

The elegance of Law's argument is that she squarely confronts *Geduldig* by recognizing the sincere difficulty faced by the Court—trying to figure out how to incorporate the real physical differences between men and women into equality doctrine—and provides a creative answer. Law suggests that the courts articulate a new equality standard to deal with cases arguably involving biological differences between men and women. She argues that laws governing reproductive biology should be scrutinized by the courts to ensure that

(1) the law has no significant impact in perpetuating either the oppression of women or culturally imposed sex-role constraints on individual freedom or (2) if the law has this impact, it is justified as the best means of serving a compelling state purpose. Given how central state regulation of biology has been to the subjugation of women, the normal presumption of constitutionality is inappropriate and the state should bear the burden of justifying its rule in relation to either proposition.[69]

Law's suggestion is an ambitious one and, if adopted by the courts, would undoubtedly improve our constitutional case law in the area of reproductive rights. The problem, however, is that Law is asking the courts to turn the current jurisprudence on its head. Rather than exempt cases involving real physical differences between men and women from gender-based scrutiny, Law is asking the courts to impose the strictest possible scrutiny on such cases.

Even if Law could persuade the courts to accept her framework, it is not clear that the framework would work very well. Law's framework assumes that the courts will be able to distinguish between cases involving biological and nonbiological bases of discrimination. But, as Law herself acknowledges and I discussed in chapter 6, the courts do not have a very good record of knowing the difference between nature and nurture.

The most fundamental problem with Law's proposal is that she does not adequately explain why she distinguishes between biological and nonbiological sources of discrimination. The test that she posits for biological classifications would seem to work equally well for nonbiological classifications. In addition, by offering a framework that distinguishes between biological and nonbiological classifications, she is offering a bipolar model that is not consistent with reality. Many forms of discrimination, like those described in chapter 6, are really mixed categories involving both a biological and a nonbiological classification.

Despite my misgivings about Law's framework, I do believe that she has identified a core problem—that of what to do about cases involving biological differences between men and women—and has offered an important insight about those cases—that we cannot categorically assume that recognizing biological differences is good or bad. We always need to ask the further question of whether the use of such categories furthers the subordination of women in society. In chapter 6, I showed how the courts can ignore or exaggerate the biological differences between men and women to further women's subordination in society. Law is one of the few theorists to recognize the complex ways in which the courts have used biological categories to perpetuate as well as to alleviate women's subordination in society. Her framework can offer guidance to resolving the kinds of difficult cases that I have discussed.

3. JUSTICE RUTH BADER GINSBURG

Ruth Bader Ginsburg, writing on this subject before joining the Supreme Court, did not purport to offer a novel perspective on developing equality doctrine in the area of reproductive freedom. Nevertheless, she did offer some interesting insights on the benefits of developing such a perspective. Drawing on the work of Kenneth Karst, Justice Ginsburg said:

> It is not a sufficient answer to charge it all to women's anatomy—a natural, not man-made, phenomenon. Society, not anatomy, "places a greater stigma on unmarried women who become pregnant than on the men who father their children." Society expects, but nature does not command, that "women take the major responsibility . . . for child care" and that they will stay with their children, bearing nurture and support burdens alone, when fathers deny paternity or otherwise refuse to provide care or financial support for unwanted offspring.
>
> I do not pretend that, if the Court had added a distinct sex discrimination theme to its medically oriented opinion, the storm Roe generated would have been less furious. I appreciate the intense divisions of opinion on the moral question and recognize that abortion today cannot fairly be described as nothing more than birth control delayed. The conflict, however, is not simply one between a fetus' interests and a woman's interests, narrowly conceived, nor is the overriding issue state versus private control of a woman's body for a span of nine months. Also in the balance is a woman's autonomous charge of her full life's course—as Professor Karst put it, her ability to stand in relation to man, society, and the state as an independent, self-sustaining, equal citizen.[70]

Although Justice Ginsburg's analysis is not as sustained as Law's, she also emphasizes the importance of distinguishing between women's intrinsic biology and society's regulation of that biology. Justice Ginsburg, however, makes the additional suggestion that equal protection doctrine would do a better job in preventing society from stigmatizing women due to their reproductive capacity than would privacy doctrine. In particular, she argues that the hostile reaction to *Roe* has largely affected the poor woman "who lacks resources to finance privately implementation of her personal choice to terminate her pregnancy."[71] "If the Court had acknowledged a woman's equality aspect, not simply a patient-physician autonomy constitutional dimension to the abortion issue, a majority perhaps might have seen the public assistance cases as instances in which, borrowing a phrase from Justice Stevens, the sovereign had violated its 'duty to govern impartially.' "[72] Justice Ginsburg is one of the few commentators to focus on abortion restrictions as other than a total ban on abortion through her discussion of the funding cases. Moreover, she is one of the few commentators to apply an anti-essentialist perspective and see the disproportionate impact on poor women. Ginsburg's comments from the mid-1980s may have been brief; however, they ring as true in the mid-1990s as they did a decade earlier. And we can hope they will ring even louder as she speaks as a Justice of the United States Supreme Court.

D. Conclusion

The theoretical work on equality doctrine in the reproductive freedom context is not very practical, because it does not give us the tools to argue that *Geduldig* was wrongly decided. It is only through the kind of counterfactual examples I used in chapter 6 that we can begin to persuade the courts that pregnant women are treated far worse than men would be treated if they could get pregnant. As Justice Ginsburg has argued, it is crucial that we find ways to use equality doctrine in the reproductive health context in order to protect the lives of the most disadvantaged women in our society. With Justice Ginsburg's assistance, we will, I hope, soon be moving in that direction.

IV. A New Direction?

[I]t is necessary to consider whether pregnancy-based discrimination is discrimination on the basis of sex. I venture to think that the response to that question by a non-legal person would be immediate and affirmative. In retrospect, one can only ask—how could pregnancy discrimination be anything other than sex discrimination? (Chief Justice Dickson, Canadian Supreme Court, in *Brooks v. Canada Safeway Ltd.*)[73]

Despite the weakness of the theoretical work on equality doctrine in the reproductive freedom context, I believe that we can successfully use equality doctrine in a way that is sensitive to the anti-essentialist critique. In Canada, for example, women's groups recently persuaded the Canadian Supreme Court to conclude that pregnancy-based discrimination was per se gender-based discrimination in *Brooks v. Canada Safeway Ltd.* In order to reach that result, the Court had to overturn a ten-year-old precedent similar to the *Geduldig* decision. As the opening quotation from that case demonstrates, the Court finally adopted the commonsense understanding that pregnancy-based discrimination cannot possibly be anything other than gender-based discrimination. Inspired by our Canadian sisters and the appointment of Justice Ginsburg to the Supreme Court, we should continue to strive to make the courts see that pregnancy-based discrimination is gender based.

My practice of law has taught me that three criteria are necessary for an effective implementation of equality doctrine. First, I believe it is crucial that we focus our evidence on the "poorest of the poor" to show the courts graphically how restrictions on abortion have a devastating impact on disadvantaged women in society. Experiential and statistical evidence can provide that proof. (An example of such an attempt can be found in my Mississippi brief.) Such proof was strongly introduced in the *Brooks* case with the Court assessing it sympathetically under the perspective that anti-discrimination legislation should remove "the unfair disadvantages which have been imposed on individuals or groups in society."[74] Second, I believe that we do need to look more closely at contemporary society to show how men who are equivalently situated in comparison with women in the reproductive health context are treated far better than women. Moreover, we need to be quick to point out what kinds of comparisons are *not* appropriate, since the courts are as likely to exaggerate differences as to exaggerate similarities to suit their purpose. This evidence can supplement the historical record to demonstrate the continuing disrespect for women's reproductive capacity. In *Brooks*, the Court powerfully examined how pregnancy-based distinctions undermine women's equality in society and refused to compare pregnancy to nonanalogous aspects of men's lives. In the Court's words:

I cannot find any useful analogy between a company rule denying men the right to wear beards and an accident and sickness insurance plan which discriminates against female employees who become pregnant. The attempt to draw an analogy at best trivializes the procreative and socially vital function of women and seeks to elevate the growing of facial hair to a constitutional right.[75]

The Canadian Supreme Court has therefore met the challenge identified in chapter 6; it has identified appropriate gender-based comparisons while dismissing inappropriate ones to further women's equality in society.

The United States federal courts have not yet moved in that direction. Nevertheless, examples of such an approach can be found in state court cases. In these cases, plaintiffs have challenged the failure of states to fund therapeutic abortions under Medicaid. Because federal constitutional law under *Roe* was found not to require states to provide such funding in *Harris v. McRae*,[76] plaintiffs in these cases have sought remedies under state constitutional law.

Doe v. Maher[77] is the most successful case using equality theory to gain women greater reproductive freedom. The plaintiffs, a woman and her doctor, brought this action to challenge a state regulation restricting the funding of abortions under Medicaid to those abortions necessary because the life of the pregnant woman would be endangered if the fetus were carried to term. Plaintiffs sought to have the state fund abortions necessary to ameliorate a condition that is deleterious to a woman's physical and/or psychological health (therapeutic abortions); they did not challenge the state's failure to pay for nontherapeutic abortions.[78]

Plaintiff Rosie Doe was a thirty-five-year-old woman who already had five children and was eligible for the state's Medicaid program. An abortion was medically necessary so that her cervix could be biopsied in order to determine whether she had cervical cancer. Her pregnancy also endangered the life of the fetus, because she was on methadone; her last two children had been born suffering from methadone withdrawal and had to be hospitalized. In addition, the methadone itself could cause severe health problems to her during her pregnancy. Finally, her age posed some health risks. Nevertheless, she did not qualify for a state-funded abortion.

Doe was certified as representing a class of poor women who needed therapeutic abortions. The court described these women as "the poorest of the poor."[79] Their income was 66 percent of the federal poverty level. After examining the extreme poverty in these women's lives, the court concluded that "there is absolutely no fat in the AFDC grant that would enable a woman to skim enough from her budget for a medically necessary abortion."[80] The court also found that their poverty caused these women to have more medical problems during pregnancy than the general population, causing their pregnancies to be more dangerous.[81]

The plaintiffs successfully challenged the state's Medicaid abortion regulation on both statutory and constitutional grounds. First, the court concluded that the regulation exceeded the commissioner's statutory authority and was therefore invalid as a matter of law. Second, in a rather unusual step, the court also found that the regulation violated the due process and equal protection components of the state constitution. This second step was unusual, because a court ordinarily does not reach a constitutional issue if a statutory issue can dispose of the case.

The court found that the regulation violated the state's equal protection clause and Equal Rights Amendment (ERA) in three ways: (1) by paying all the medical expenses necessary to restore a male but not a female to health, (2) by paying all the male's but not all the female's medical expenses associated with their reproductive health, and (3) by perpetuating women's historical subordination through regulation of pregnancy. The court relied on the debates concerning the ERA to ascertain that it was the intention of the ratifiers to have pregnancy discrimination come within the purview of the sex discrimination prohibited by the ERA. Thus, applying strict scrutiny, the court found that the state could not justify the pregnancy-based discrimination against women.

The *Doe v. Maher* decision is remarkable, because of the depth of the court's understanding of the impact of the regulation on the lives of women. For example, in one section, the court summarized what it described as "the poor woman's dilemma."

> Under the Connecticut medicaid program, except for abortion, all necessary medical expenses for eligible recipients are paid for by the state. . . . On the other hand, the state pays for all incidents necessary for childbirth. . . . So if the pregnant poor woman finds herself requiring an abortion to preserve her health, she has no place to turn. The state has placed her in a trap. The cash welfare allowance (AFDC) the state grants is barely sufficient to maintain an adequate level of living for her and her family. Her benefits from the state are substantially under the poverty levels, and the cash allotment is hardly enough to cover food, shelter and clothing. Through an intricate network of statutes, she is not allowed to receive funds from other sources without those funds being deducted from her welfare cash allowance the following month. Thus, even a loan from a friend or family member would not help her, the obligations of repayment notwithstanding. And if she should fail to report the receipt of other income and assets, she could become disqualified for future benefits and subject to criminal charges. Because payments are made directly to the provider and no cash allowance is given for medical assistance, she is not even given the choice of being able to forego other medical necessities in favor of the abortion. In short, the state has boxed her into accepting the pregnancy and carrying the fetus to term, notwithstanding the sometimes substantial impairment to her health.

Faced with this dilemma, some women have resorted to desperate and dangerous acts of self-abortion, criminal activity and illegal abortions in order to exercise their constitutional rights. The only legal relief available is to allow the indigent woman's medical condition to worsen to a point where her life is endangered—only then, will the state come to her aid and fund the abortion. By then, however, it may be too late, for even if the medical condition does not kill her, the abortion procedure at an advanced stage of pregnancy may.[82]

Quite simply, the Connecticut court "got it." It understood the lack of real choices in the lives of poor women and how discrimination against those women constituted gender-based discrimination.

I would describe the court's approach as anti-essentialist, because the court focused on the impact on the most disadvantaged women and considered that impact to be gender based without considering whether all women were impacted in the same way. Moreover, the court did not needlessly require that a perfect male comparator be available to conclude that the impact was gender based. The court saw that poor pregnant women bore similarities with poor men who desired reproductive health services but did not require that such similarities be perfect in order to conclude that gender-based discrimination had occurred. Finally, the court understood that abortion regulations can discriminate against women without totally banning abortion. Less restrictive requirements, like failing to fund abortions under Medicaid, were found to have a similar effect to a total ban. Such insights are only possible by examining the impact of the statute on the most disadvantaged women in society.

Unfortunately, not all state courts have reached the same conclusion when presented with similar facts. A Pennsylvania court reached the opposite result in *Fischer v. Department Of Public Welfare.*[83] As in the previous case, plaintiffs challenged a state statute that prohibited the payment of state Medicaid funds for abortions except when the pregnant woman's life was threatened by the pregnancy or she was a victim of rape or incest.

Despite the fact that Pennsylvania has an ERA, the court concluded that no sex-based discrimination had taken place. In the court's words:

> The mere fact that only women are affected by this statute does not necessarily mean that women are being discriminated against on the basis of sex. In this world there are certain immutable facts of life which no amount of legislation may change. As a consequence there are certain laws which necessarily will only affect one sex. . . . [T]he E. R. A. "does not prohibit differential treatment among the sexes when, as here, that treatment

is reasonably and genuinely based on physical characteristics unique to one sex."[84]

In reaching this decision, the court had to distinguish *Cerra v. East Stroudsburg Area School District*,[85] in which the court had previously ruled in favor of a woman who had been forced to resign from her teaching job when she was five months pregnant. Ms. Cerra, the court found, was the victim of a presumption of disability, because men who were temporarily disabled were not treated so harshly. The *Cerra* case, however, was not found to be analogous to the abortion-funding context, because, according to the court, "the decision whether or not to carry a fetus to term is so unique as to have no concomitance in the male of the species."[86]

Fischer is a good contrast to *Doe v. Maher*, because it shows how courts can find a male comparator when it suits their purpose. When Ms. Cerra, a middle-class school teacher, was pregnant, she was considered to belong to the broader category of "temporarily disabled" people. The court could readily see that she was being treated more harshly than other temporarily disabled people. But when women on welfare were pregnant and needed an abortion for medical reasons, the *Fischer* court did not believe that they belonged to the broader category of "poor people in need of medical treatment." Instead, they became unique women with no male comparator. The *Doe* court, by contrast, could see the obvious analogy. The *Fischer* case therefore provides insight into how difficult it is to get the courts to genuinely compare women and men in the reproductive health context.

The state court cases show us the range of responses that are possible when plaintiffs bring reproductive rights cases under equality doctrine. Two funding cases were brought under equality doctrine, and two different results were achieved. The promising feature of these cases, however, is that equality doctrine has the *potential* as shown by the Connecticut court to reach the lives of the most disadvantaged women in society. One reason that the Connecticut court appeared to understand the importance of using equality doctrine to reach those women's lives was that the trial record was filled with compelling stories and statistics about the lives and lack of choices for those poor women. For equality doctrine to be successful and for *all* women to be represented by the courts' opinions, it therefore seems essential to put the lives of the poorest of the poor before the court—the group that has received the least protection under privacy doctrine.

Ironically, then, this chapter of the book that focuses on theory ends with lessons from practical state court cases. Our practice may have found ways to incorporate equality doctrine and anti-essentialism before our theory could explain that union. It is therefore crucial that we continue to struggle to learn from our practice so that our theory can ultimately reflect our practice.

Notes

1. Elizabeth V. Spelman, Inessential Woman: Problems of Exclusion in Feminist Thought 187 (1988).

2. *See, e.g.* Angela P. Harris, *Race and Essentialism in Feminist Legal Theory,* 42 Stan. L. Rev. 581 (1990).

3. *See* Harris, *supra* note 2.

4. *See* Catharine A. MacKinnon, *From Practice to Theory, or What Is a White Woman Anyway?,* 4 Yale J. L. & Feminism 13 (1991).

5. Harris, *supra* note 2.

6. *Id.* at 588.

7. *Id.* at 588 (quoting Spelman, at 165).

8. e. christi cunningham, *Unmaddening,* 4 Yale J.L. & Feminism 155, 158 (quoting Spelman, at 165) (1991).

9. Spelman, *supra* note 1, at 165.

10. *Id.* (my emphasis).

11. *Id.*

12. Harris, *supra* note 2, at 586; Spelman, *supra* note 1, at 14, 151, 176.

13. *See, e.g.,* Brief of Amici Curiae National Black Women's Health Project et al., Barnes v. Moore, No. 91–1953 (filed February 19, 1992) (arguing that the Mississippi restrictions on abortion violated the gender-based equality component of the Fourteenth Amendment).

14. *See, e.g.,* Ruth Bader Ginsburg, *Some Thoughts on Autonomy and Equality in Relation to Roe v. Wade,* 63 N.C. L. Rev. 375 (1985); Kenneth Karst, *Forward: Equal Citizenship under the Fourteenth Amendment,* 91 Harv. L. Rev. 1 (1977); Sylvia Law, *Rethinking Sex and the Constitution,* 132 U. Pa. L. Rev. 955 (1984).

15. *See generally,* Ruth Colker, *Rank-Order Physical Abilities Selection Devices for Traditionally Male Occupations as Sex-Based Employment Discrimination,* 19 U.C.D. L. Rev. 761 (1986).

16. Harris, *supra* note 2, at 586.

17. Spelman, *supra* note 1, at 186.

18. I have tried to engage in such a discussion in my previous book. *See* Ruth Colker, Abortion and Dialogue: Pro-Choice, Pro-Life, and American Law 58–80 (1992).

19. Carol Gilligan, In a Different Voice: Psychological Theory and Women's Development (1982).

20. Robin West, *Jurisprudence and Gender,* 55 U. Chi. L. Rev. 1, 3 (1988).

21. bell hooks, *Reflections of a "Good" Daughter,* in Double Stitch: Black Women Write about Mothers & Daughters 149 (Patricia Bell-Scott, Beverly Guy-Sheftall, Jacquelyn Jones Royster, Janet Sims-Wood, Miriam DeCosta-Willis, and Lucie Fultz eds., 1991).

22. Linda H. Hollies, *A Daughter Survives Incest: A Retrospective Analysis,* in Double Stitch at 160.

23. Interestingly, Catharine MacKinnon's feminist theory does not rest on or heavily dis-

cuss woman's role as mother. She talks a lot about *sex* but not the product that may result from sex and its implications on women's lives. Nevertheless, one still might ask if sexuality would be the linchpin of women's oppression (according to MacKinnon) if women did not have the biological capacity to reproduce. Is heterosexuality a centerpiece of society because of the presumed need to reproduce? Is that why it is so threatening to society when lesbians *desire* to reproduce and retain custody of their children?

24. The recently published book, Double Stitch: Black Women Write about Mothers & Daughters (Patricia Bell-Scott, Beverly Guy-Sheftall, Jacqueline Jones Royster, Janet Sims-Wood, Miriam DeCosta-Willis, and Lucie Fultz eds.) (1991) would seem to support West's thesis as applied to black women.

25. MacKinnon, *supra* note 4, at 17.

26. Catharine MacKinnon, Feminism Unmodified: Discourses on Life and Law 219 (1987).

27. *See, e.g.,* MacKinnon, *supra* note 4.

28. *See generally* Ruth Colker, *Pregnant Men*, Colum. J. of Gender & Law (1993).

29. Doe v. Maher, 40 Conn. Supp. 394, 434 n.43; 515 A.2d 134 (1986).

30. 120 L. Ed.2d 674, 748–49 (1992).

31. 417 U.S. 484 (1974).

32. Cass R. Sunstein, *Neutrality in Constitutional Law (With Special Reference to Pornography, Abortion, and Surrogacy)*, 92 Colum. L. Rev. 1, 31–44 (1992).

33. Laurence Tribe, American Constitutional Law §15–10, 1353–59 (2d ed. 1988).

34. Jeb Rubenfeld, *The Right of Privacy*, 102 Harv. L. Rev. 737 (1989).

35. Reva Siegel, *Reasoning from the Body: A Historical Perspective on Abortion Regulation and Questions of Equal Protection*, 44 Stan. L. Rev. 261, 350–80 (1992).

36. Sylvia Law, *Rethinking Sex and the Constitution*, U. Pa. L. Rev. 955 (1984).

37. Ruth Bader Ginsburg, *Some Thoughts on Autonomy and Equality in Relation to* Roe v. Wade, 63 N.C. L. Rev. 375 (1985).

38. Sunstein, *supra* note 32.

39. *Id.* at 35 n.129.

40. Tribe, *supra* note 33, at 1353.

41. *Id.* at 1354.

42. Laurence H. Tribe, Abortion: The Clash of Absolutes (1990).

43. *Id.* at 197–228.

44. *Id.* at 213–23.

45. Tribe, *supra* note 33, at 1354.

46. *Id.* at 1355.

47. *Id.* at 1355 (quoting Jenness v. Fortson, 403 U.S. 431, 442 (1971)).

48. *Id.* at 1355.

49. *Id.*

50. *Id.*

51. *Id.* at 1357.

52. *Id.* at 1358.

53. Siegel, *supra* note 35, at 367 n.419.

54. *Id.* at 371–80.

55. *Id.* at 354.

56. *Id.* at 354 n.373.

57. *Id.*

58. *Id.*

59. *Id.* at 357.

60. *Id.*

61. *Id.* at 360–61.

62. *Id.* at 361.

63. *See* Brief for Black Women for Choice et al. as Amicus Curiae Supporting Appellees, Sojourner T. v. Buddy Roemer, No. 91–3677 (filed October 18, 1991).

64. Siegel, *supra* note 35, at 366.

65. Law, *supra* note 36, at 966.

66. *Id.* at 968.

67. *Id.* at 969.

68. *Id.* at 1003.

69. *Id.* at 1008–1009.

70. Ginsburg, *supra* note 37, at 375, 382–83.

71. *Id.* at 383.

72. *Id.* at 385.

73. Brooks v. Canada Safeway Ltd., 59 D.L.R. 321 (4th) (1989).

74. *Id.* at 335.

75. *Id.* at 344.

76. 448 U.S. 297 (1980).

77. 40 Conn. Supp. 394, 515 A.2d 134 (1986).

78. *Id.* at 396 n.4.

79. *Id.* at 407.

80. *Id.* at 408.

81. *Id.*

82. *Id.* at 433–34.

83. 509 Pa. 293, 502 A.2d 114 (1985).

84. *Id.* at 314.

85. 450 Pa. 207, 299 A.2d 277 (1973).

86. *Id.* at 315.

Epilogue

I BEGAN THIS BOOK very concerned about the impact that waiting period rules will have on the most disadvantaged women in our society who seek abortions. I end this book very concerned about the impact that proposed health insurance rules will have on the availability of abortion services. This new problem is beginning to emerge on both the state and national level.

Pennsylvania, my current home state, is presently considering a Health Security Act[1] that would guarantee basic health coverage to all residents of the state of Pennsylvania. Although financing is not specifically enumerated in the proposed statute, it appears that a system of employer contributions, employee contributions, copayments, and government assistance is contemplated under the statute. In section 703 of this proposed statute, there is a list of twelve medical services that would be covered under the plan. The list is quite exhaustive, including both preventive and inpatient care. In addition to the eleven enumerated services, the statute includes broad language that provides that "other medical treatments, procedures, and services that are determined by the board to be medically effective and medically appropriate for a particular group of patients or set of clinical circumstances" would also be covered.

Both the House and Senate versions of this state health insurance law also contain the following language regarding exceptions to that general rule:

Section 704 exclusions.
(a) Recommendation of board relating to certain items.—Any other provision of this chapter notwithstanding, the board may, as part of the plan, recommend excluding items in section 703(3) through (11), if upon a scientific and clinical basis the board determines that same should be excluded.
(b) Certain exclusions enumerated.—The guaranteed benefits package shall not include any of the following:
(1) Surgery for cosmetic purposes other than for reconstructive surgery.
(2) Nursing home services.
(3) Medical examinations conducted and medical reports prepared for the purpose of purchasing or renewing life insurance or participating in a civil action for the recovery or settlement of damages.
(4) Abortion services except under the conditions and circumstances for

which public funding may be used under the enforceable laws of the Commonwealth.

In other words, it would be unlawful for abortion services to be covered under the state's health insurance plan unless the pregnant woman's life was threatened by the pregnancy or she was a victim of rape or incest. This program would put all women in the position of poor women under Medicaid, which rarely covers abortions. The challenge now is to convince the state legislature to include coverage of abortions or, if this statute is passed without such coverage, to challenge this exclusion in court.

One possible legal argument would be an equality argument under the state's Equal Rights Amendment (ERA). Under the ERA, one would argue that the statute discriminates against women on the basis of gender, because men, but not women, are covered with respect to all of their reproductive health care needs. Unfortunately, however, this argument suffers from the "pregnant men" problem, since pregnant men, like pregnant women, have no coverage for abortion services.

Although I am not optimistic that we could use the Pennsylvania ERA to challenge this statute, I believe that it is crucial for us to argue in both the legislature and the courts that this proposed legislation would be very detrimental to all women in the state. If approved, it would mean that physicians would receive direct reimbursement from the state's health care system for nearly all medical services except abortion. They would have to go to the trouble of direct billing for abortion services but not for any other service. Many women in the state would be in the position of having worse health insurance coverage under the new plan than under their existing plan. For example, abortions are routinely covered under most health insurance plans. Women currently covered under their health insurance would lose coverage for abortion services under the new plan, and they would have no opportunity to pay for a health care plan that covered abortion services.

The result of such a system (as I am sure its proponents are aware) is that access to abortion services would be severely limited. Physicians who currently find it minimally profitable and quite inconvenient (due to harassment) to offer abortion services would have yet another excuse not to provide such services. Because of the unique direct billing that would be required for abortion services, it also may be more difficult for women who seek these services to maintain their confidentiality. Moreover, the cost of abortion services would rise (due to these new burdens), thereby making the services even more unavailable for the working poor. Finally, as abortion services become less available, the travel time to obtain these services would increase, thereby adding to the cost and to the possibility of breach of confidentiality. Since Pennsylvania already has a waiting period rule, women would have to twice bear the costs of travel, rather than once, to obtain these medical services.

With Medicaid funding for abortion, the argument is often made that taxpayers should not be forced to fund abortions when they morally object to such procedures. Although I do not agree with that argument in the Medicaid context, I believe we can see its absurdity more clearly in the present context. Working women will pay taxes and whatever premiums are required under the proposed legislation, but they will not be able to pay for a package that suits their health care needs. Groups of women will not be able to band together to form an insurance network that covers abortion services and complies with the state's requirements. Women themselves will not be able to use their own financial resources in a way that best suits their reproductive health needs. The additional women harmed by this statute are not women whose abortions would be funded by the state.

Pennsylvania and other states realize that the Supreme Court will not permit them to outlaw abortion altogether. Their strategy then is to impose onerous requirements that will limit access to such a degree that abortion becomes unavailable for all but the rich. Waiting period requirements combined with the harassment of Operation Rescue have already taken a major step in that direction. A prohibition of coverage under *any* health insurance plan would be yet another major step.

Thus, it is crucial that we learn how to talk about "pregnant men" to reveal this deliberate attempt to harm women's but not men's reproductive freedom. A successful attempt on the federal level is unlikely due to the *Geduldig* decision. State law challenges may be our best hope, especially in states that have an Equal Rights Amendment. Unfortunately, as I discussed in chapter 7, the Pennsylvania Supreme Court has already ruled that the state ERA cannot be used to challenge the ban on Medicaid-funded abortions. If this bill passes, we will have to find ways to convince the legislature or, alternatively, state or federal courts that denying women access to abortion services constitutes unconstitutional gender discrimination. It is crucial that we find a way to make our theory work in practice. We need to find practical ways to demonstrate that pregnant men would never be denied access to a service so fundamental to their reproductive freedom.

Pennsylvania will certainly not be the only battleground requiring these kinds of arguments under proposed health insurance plans. As I write this Epilogue, Congress has yet to consider President Clinton's proposed Health Security Act. The version of the Act that has been introduced into Congress at this time does not take a position on abortion services.[2] Instead, it mysteriously reserves Subtitle H and I of Title I for discussion of abortion services. Although it is much too early to know what those provisions will contain, it is certainly likely that some abortion "compromise" will be reached that will make abortion services unavailable under health insurance to many working women who already receive such coverage. Several possible compromises have been suggested to me: a "conscience" clause that will give hospitals the option of not providing abortion services; delegation to the states to resolve this issue on a state by state basis; or a complete exclusion of abortion services under national health insurance for all women. Each of these options affords choices to people other than individual pregnant women to determine what type of health care coverage will be readily available to them. If any of these "compromises" are put forward, we will again have to learn to make political and legal arguments for the unacceptability of women not having available the full range of reproductive health services when a full range of reproductive health services is available to men. President Clinton promised the American people that the new Health Security Act would provide each American with coverage at least as good as what he or she currently enjoys under private health insurance. Many people will be watching to see if that is an agreement that Congress and the President keep with American women.

Notes

1. *See* PA H.B. 1958 (1993) (referred to House Committee on Health and Welfare, June 28, 1993); PA S.B. 1202 (1993) (referred to Senate Committee on Public Health and Welfare, June 8, 1993).
2. *See* 139 Cong. Rec. E2571 (daily ed. Oct. 28, 1993) (proposed Health Security Act).

Appendix

United States Court of Appeals
For The Fifth Circuit

Helen B. Barnes, M.D.; Joseph Mitchell, M.D.;
Joseph Booker, M.D., on behalf of themselves, their
patients, and all others similarly situated; New Woman
Medical Center, Inc.; Mississippi Women's Medical Clinic

Plaintiffs-Appellees

—versus—

Mike Moore, as Attorney General of the State of
Mississippi and his employees, agents, and successors

Defendants-Appellants,

No. 91-1953

On Appeal From The United States District Court
For The Southern District of Mississippi

*BRIEF OF AMICI CURIAE NATIONAL BLACK WOMEN'S HEALTH PROJ-
ECT, CENTER FOR CONSTITUTIONAL RIGHTS, MISSISSIPPI VOTING RIGHTS
PROJECT, MISSISSIPPI NATIONAL ORGANIZATION FOR WOMEN, NATIONAL OR-
GANIZATION FOR WOMEN, CENTRAL MISSISSIPPI CHAPTER, MISSISSIPPI HU-
MAN SERVICES AGENDA, WOMEN'S PROJECT, AND CERTAIN MISSISSIPPI CLERGY
IN SUPPORT OF APPELLEES*

Ruth Colker
Tulane Law School
6801 Freret St.
New Orleans, LA 70118
504-865-5968

INTEREST OF AMICI CURIAE

The National Black Women's Health Project (NBWHP) is a self-help, health education and advocacy organization which works to improve the health status and quality of life for African American women and their families. It consists of 150 developing and established chapters in 31 states serving a broad constituency of approximately 2,000 members. The NBWHP is deeply concerned about barriers that impede or prevent access to quality health services, including abortion. Because too many single family households in the United States are headed by Black women living in poverty, possessing few educational and job training opportunities, enduring inadequate, often non-existing child care services, subject to substandard housing conditions, and lacking access to appropriate health services of any kind; because more than half of all Black children are poor, born of mothers receiving inferior, if any, prenatal care, suffering the highest rate of infant mortality and neonatal deaths in the Western world; and because of the lack of fail-safe birth control methods, lack of adequate human sexuality education, and because Black females suffer also the highest rate of teenage pregnancy in the Western world, the NBWHP joins this brief to voice its opposition to any action which restricts or limits access to abortion information and services and which prevents African American women from exercising their right to abortion.

The Center for Constitutional Rights (CCR), a litigation/education organization headquartered in New York City, was founded in 1966. Born of the civil rights movement and the struggles of Black people in the United States for true equality, CCR has litigated for voting rights, civil rights, and the fundamental and necessary right of each woman to obtain access to safe and legal abortion. CCR decries the disproportionate and potentially devastating effect that the limitation or loss of the right to abortion will have on women of color and low-income and working women, and we urge this Court to protect the right to accessible, safe and legal abortion in their names.

The Mississippi Voting Rights Project (VRP) is based in Greenville, Mississippi. Its primary goal is to challenge those discriminatory voting practices which make it impossible for Black and poor people to win elections. Toward this end, the Mississippi Voting Rights Project utilizes an innovative strategy of community-based litigation and education, which enhances community leadership and builds and strengthens local participation in the democratic process. The VRP operates from an essential premise: that those people who are most severely affected by poverty and oppression must be key decision-makers in the formulation of strategies for their own cases. The VRP deplores the unequal and potentially deadly effects the loss of the right to an abortion would create among women of color and low income communities, and therefore VRP urges this Court to protect the right to safe and legal abortion for these people.

Mississippi National Organization for Women (Mississippi NOW) is a state-wide Mississippi grassroots membership organization dedicated to the advancement of women's rights, with members in both urban and rural parts of Mississippi. As the organization is dedicated to reproductive rights, racial equality, and economic equality for women, it abhors any attempts to impede women's access to health care including abortion.

National Organization for Women, Central Mississippi Chapter (Central Mississippi NOW), located in Jackson, Mississippi and the surrounding areas, is a grass-roots membership organization dedicated to equality and full rights for women. It opposes the Act because it limits the individual rights of women to reproductive choice.

Mississippi Human Services Agenda is a poverty research and advocacy organization that provides assistance to numerous community groups that represent low-income persons across the state, as well as individuals whose rights to services or judicial equity have been denied due to race, gender, age, or condition. It has been active in generating pressure for changes in public policy that have resulted in an expansion of accessible health care, a system of shelters for battered women, reforms in the treatment available for child victims of abuse and other public programs that impact on the lives of the poor.

The Women's Project works both in Arkansas and in neighboring states, including Mississippi, on issues of access for low income women, women of color, and other women traditionally under-represented in our society. It is particularly concerned about the needs of rural, poor women, and believes that it would be these women who would be hit hardest by the Act at issue in the instant case.

Individual Clergy in the State of Mississippi join as *amici* in this brief as follows:

Reverend Carol Burnett is a United Methodist minister ordained in the Mississippi Conference who, like the United Methodist Church, supports women's right to choose an abortion. Rev. Burnett works with Mississippi women as director of the Moore Community House, Biloxi, MS, and knows that many of them cannot afford the increased costs imposed by the Act's waiting period. Reverend Burnett also works with women victims of domestic violence whose lives would be endangered by the waiting period. Furthermore, she has learned from her personal experience counseling women that they do not approach the decision to have an abortion without serious reflection and that the hardships imposed by the waiting period will unduly burden poor, rural women.

Reverend Kathy J. Penrose is a United Methodist minister whose experience helping women and families in Mississippi leads her to believe the Act would further jeopardize the health and medical support needs of the nation's poorest and most vulnerable women.

SUMMARY OF ARGUMENT

Reproductive freedom is essential to women's equality in society. Coerced childbirth can dramatically affect women's educational opportunities, position in the workplace, and access to health care. By imposing reproductive burdens on women that are not imposed on men, the Act violates the equal protection clause of the Fourteenth Amendment and the right to privacy. This brief focuses on the denial of equal protection and on the harm the Act will inflict on disadvantaged women in Mississippi.

ARGUMENT

I. THE ACT DISCRIMINATES AGAINST WOMEN[1]

A. Introduction

Amici fully support the right to privacy as guaranteed by *Roe v. Wade*, 410 U.S. 113 (1973), and would have this Court affirm the district court's order enjoining enforcement of the Act on that ground. However, in the event that the Supreme Court overrules *Roe* and develops a new privacy standard, this Court should remand the case to the district court with instructions to apply the newly defined privacy standard to the facts regarding the burdens facing Mississippi women and to consider plaintiffs' equal protection argument.[2] *Amici* assert that under any conceivable constitutional standard, the Act places onerous and punitive burdens on women and thereby violates the Constitution.

The Act represents *per se* gender discrimination and, therefore, must bear a substantial relationship to an important governmental objective. *Craig v. Boren*, 429 U.S. 190, 197 (1976). Under any level of scrutiny, however, the State has failed to justify its disparate treatment of women and the Act must be invalidated. The Act does not advance the State's purported objective of improving women's abortion deliberation process and, in fact, will impair that process. It will particularly harm those women who are least well represented in the political process: poor women, adolescent females, women with handicaps, and battered women. Further demonstrating the total illogic of the Act is that it will aggravate the existing health care crisis in the State.

B. The Act Constitutes Gender-Based Discrimination

Reproductive freedom is basic to women's equality in society. Compulsory childbirth can preclude women from continuing their education, staying in the workforce, or obtaining adequate medical benefits. *See* Ginsberg, *Some Thoughts on Autonomy and Equality in Relation to Roe v. Wade*, 63 N.C. L. Rev. 375 (1985); Law, *Rethinking Sex and the Constitution*, 132 U. Pa. L. Rev. 955 (1984); Karst, *Foreword: Equal Citizenship Under the Fourteenth Amendment*, 91 Harv. L. Rev. 1, 53–59 (1977). Thus, a precondition of women's equality in society is that pregnancy be a *chosen* rather than a *coerced* experience. Congress recognized the centrality to women's equality of nondiscrimination in the provision of pregnancy-related services when it amended Title VII of the Civil Rights Act of 1964, 42 U.S.C. § 2000e to state that pregnancy discrimination is *per se* sex discrimination. *Id.* at § 2000e(k) (1991).[3]

---

[1]*Amici* use the same citation conventions as appellees.

[2]In the complaint filed in this case, plaintiffs alleged that the Act discriminates against them as women in violation of the equal protection clause. They explained that the Act "imposes burdens upon women's reproductive choices that are not imposed upon the reproductive choices of men." Complaint ¶ 143.

[3]This Court should defer to Congress' conclusion regarding the significance of pregnancy-related burdens on women's lives, because § 5 of the fourteenth amendment explicitly gives Congress the power to interpret and enforce the fourteenth amendment.

The Mississippi legislature has imposed a waiting period requirement[4] on women that, as we will show below, will dramatically affect their reproductive freedom and equality in society. By contrast, the legislature has declined to impose a waiting period requirement on any of the serious, complex, and irreversible medical decisions made by men that affect their future life and well-being. The legislature has therefore created a *per se* gender-based classification that directly undermines women's equality in society.

Geduldig v. Aiello, 417 U.S. 484 (1974), is not to the contrary. In that case, the Court held that the exclusion of disability associated with a normal pregnancy from a state-sponsored disability insurance system did not represent *per se* gender discrimination so as to trigger heightened judicial scrutiny under the equal protection clause. Viewed in the context of the statute as a whole, the Court found that the exclusion of coverage for pregnancy-related disabilities, along with other disabilities, was not an invidious gender-based restriction. Women were not singled out for exclusion from coverage. *Id.* at 495. In the instant case, however, the challenged restrictions relate solely to pregnancy, and therefore solely to women.[5] In addition, the restrictions in the present case interfere with women's equality in society, in that the Act, unlike the insurance system in *Geduldig*, would coerce women to experience childbirth, with its attendant lifelong consequences.

Thus, appellees have established a *prima facie* case of gender-based discrimination and the State must "carry the burden of showing an 'exceedingly persuasive justification.'" *Mississippi University for Women v. Hogan*, 458 U.S. 718, 724 (1982) (quoting *Kirchberg v. Feenstra*, 450 U.S. 455, 461 (1981)).[6]

II. THE ACT IS NOT RELATED TO ITS PURPORTED OBJECTIVE OF IMPROVING THE ABORTION DELIBERATION PROCESS

Whatever level of scrutiny the Court finds appropriate, the Act fails to pass constitutional muster. The means chosen by the State are in no way related to the purported objective of improving women's abortion deliberation process. They both *un-*

---

[4]While agreeing with the plaintiffs that other requirements of the Act (*i.e.*, the compelled speech, physician disclosure requirements, state-produced materials, and overly restrictive medical emergency definition) also substantially burden women's reproductive choices, this brief will focus on the waiting period requirement.

[5]Just as a statute that singled out African-American children for discriminatory treatment would not be acceptable simply because it did not affect *all* African-Americans, a waiting period imposed upon pregnant women cannot be justified based on the fact that it does not directly affect all women. *Cf. Hernandez v. New York*, 500 U.S. _____ , 111 S. Ct. 1859, 1868, 114 L.Ed.2d 395, 413 (1991) (noting that exclusion on the basis of language proficiency may constitute racial discrimination).

[6]Even if this Court were to conclude that the Act does not represent a *per se* gender-based classification, it must consider whether the "classification drawn by the statute is rationally related to a legitimate state interest." *City of Cleburne v. Cleburne Living Center*, 473 U.S. 432, 440 (1985). As Justice Stevens has noted, "[t]he term 'rational,' of course, includes a requirement that an impartial lawmaker could logically believe that the classification would serve a legitimate public purpose that transcends the harm to the members of the disadvantaged class." *Id.* at 452 (Stevens, J., concurring). The Act fails even this test.

dermine women's deliberation process and *cause substantial harm* to the women and children of the State.[7]

A. The Act Is Not Aimed at Improving the Abortion Deliberation Process; Its Aim Is to Stop Abortions

The State claims that the Act was created to enhance women's decision-making ability and to promote "choice." A.G. Br. at 11, 18–21. However, the Act as a whole— the forced information regarding specific, highly unlikely medical risks, and medical assistance and child support payments that in reality are unavailable or inadequate; a state-produced description of fetal development and list of prenatal care agencies and anti-choice groups; and the highly confusing, restrictive emergency exception—hardly reveals an intention to ensure the provision of neutral, non-directive, accurate information. Rather, these are all transparent attempts to persuade women not to choose abortion.

Furthermore, to justify imposing a coercive mandatory delay solely on abortion, the State has proffered a goal of ameliorating a problem that does not exist; there is no evidence that the abortion deliberation process is defective in any way in Mississippi. The State has neither performed a study nor cited to a study to document the existence or extent of the purported problem. In fact, the only such study of which *amici* are aware has found that there is no problem with women's abortion deliberation process.[8] None of the State's witnesses had expertise with respect to performing abortion services. *See, e.g.,* Tr. at 194–95 (Bush). Rather, they acknowledged that they are ideologically opposed to abortion. *See, e.g.,* Tr. at 212–14 (Bush) (App. 20–21). The Attorney General's sole support for his claim that a problem existed was vague and speculative testimony of nonexpert witnesses. A.G. Br. at 11.

Given the fact that there was no evidence before the legislature that women were rashly and improperly choosing abortions and that, in fact, any woman who chose to carry to term in reliance upon state-provided benefits for prenatal care and other health benefits could be sorely disappointed and medically neglected,[9] the Act reveals the actual goal of coercing childbirth over abortion.

B. The Means Chosen Will Impair Rather Than Effectuate Women's Abortion Deliberation Process

Even assuming that a state-wide problem existed regarding women's decision-making on abortion, the Act is neither substantially nor rationally related to solving such a problem. Rather, the Act will greatly complicate the process and make abor-

---

[7]Moreover, to the extent that the true objective underlying the Act is to make abortion unavailable to some or all women in Mississippi, this clearly is not a legitimate state objective.

[8]*See* Gold, Abortion and Women's Health: A Turning Point for America? 45 (1990) (hereinafter, "Abortion and Women's Health") (reporting that when Tennessee had a 48-hour waiting period in effect, 93% of the women who were subjected to that requirement stated that they were unable to name a single benefit they had experienced by being required to wait to have their abortions).

[9]See *infra* note 17; *see generally,* Carr et al., Report on Minority Health in Mississippi (1990) (hereinafter, "Minority Health"); Report to the Governor, Recommendations of the Infant Mortality Task Force (March 1991) (hereinafter, "Infant Mortality Task Force").

tion absolutely unavailable to many women, thereby impairing or eliminating the deliberation process.

Although the Act describes the waiting period requirement as a "twenty-four" hour requirement, it will often result in a far longer delay. Clinics do not perform abortions every day of the week.[10] Thus, the waiting period requirement can easily result in a four or five day delay; for a woman who can only visit a clinic on a Saturday, the delay will be a week or more.

The Attorney General does not deny that these delays will occur (although he continues to characterize the waiting period as "short"); instead, he amazingly tries to blame the providers of abortion services for these delays, rather than the State. A.G. Br. at 44 n.13. Any state regulation must be fashioned within the context of existing clinic practices, and Mississippi cannot exonerate itself from responsibility for the real effects that those regulations will have on pregnant women.

As discussed below, the waiting period requirement will increase the health risks of an abortion, raise its costs, and impose transportation, housing, and child care difficulties on women. Such burdens will make it nearly impossible for many women to effectuate their reproductive choices. Being unable to effectuate their real choices will *undermine* rather than enhance women's abortion deliberation process. These burdens will be most directly imposed on women who are least represented in the political process and most in need of improved access to health care—poor women, adolescent females, women in abusive relationships, and women with handicaps.[11]

1. Poor Women

Mississippi is the poorest state in the United States. *Twenty-five percent* of the persons in the state live below the poverty line—more than twice the national average and the highest percentage in the United States.[12] The median household income in Mississippi is the lowest in the United States.[13] Welfare payments are also very low in Mississippi. For example, the maximum monthly AFDC benefit for a family of three in 1989 was $120 per month—the second lowest in the United States. *See* Children's Defense Fund, The Health of America's Southern Children (Table 3.1) (1989).

---

[10]Plaintiff Mississippi Women's Medical Clinic has a physician in attendance only on Wednesdays and Saturdays. (Brown ¶ 2.) Plaintiff New Woman Medical Center has a physician in attendance only on Thursdays, Fridays, and Saturdays. (Booker ¶ 9.) Gulf Coast Women's Clinic has a physician in attendance only on Mondays, Tuesdays, and Wednesdays. (Booker ¶ 9.)

[11]Mississippi's voting process has been the subject of repeated litigation because of the way that it disempowers poor African-American communities. *See Mississippi State Chapter, Operation Push v. Mabus*, 932 F.2d 400 (5th Cir. 1991) (noting Mississippi's long history of impeding black citizens' participation in the political process). This historical disenfranchisement is, in part, responsible for the Mississippi legislature being able to impose a waiting period requirement on women seeking abortions without confronting the enormous burdens that such a statute would pose on disadvantaged women.

[12]U.S. Dept. of Commerce, *Median Income of Households and Percent of Persons in Poverty by State, Based on Three Year Average (1988–90)*.

[13]Mississippi's median household income is $20,414. The next lowest is Alabama's, at $22,610. *Ibid.*

Among the poor of Mississippi, women—particularly young women and African American women—are the poorest. Overall, 21.5% of the households in the State are headed by females; these households are disproportionately poor.[14] In fiscal year 1991, for example, females constituted nearly 75% of all of the people in the state on Medicaid. In addition, children under the age of 20 constitute 55% of the Medicaid recipients. Seventy percent of Medicaid recipients are African-American.[15]

Unfortunately, extreme poverty combined with a shortage of affordable and accessible health care providers places Mississippi at or near the bottom of all states in accessibility of both abortion services[16] and prenatal care.[17]

The mandatory delay in the Act will increase both the medical risks and the cost of abortions. Because of work, school, or family responsibilities, many poor women can only come to a clinic on Saturdays; the waiting period requirement, therefore, will delay their abortions by at least one week. (Mitchell ¶ 34, Rogers ¶ 12.) There is a 30% increase in rates of morbidity with each week of delay beyond the eighth week of pregnancy. (Henshaw ¶ 17.)

Delays of one week can raise the cost of an abortion by $50 to $200 dollars[18] which, especially for a poor woman, can be prohibitive. As established in the district court below, many women pay for their abortions in rolls of dimes, nickels, and pennies. (Brown ¶ 6 (App. 32).) Poor women already unduly delay their abortions as they scrape together the money to pay for them.[19] (Booker ¶¶ 7–8; Brown ¶ 6; Hill ¶¶ 9,11,14; Jenkins ¶¶ 16–19; Mitchell ¶ 38; Tucker ¶¶ 7–10.) The additional complications and delay of the Act, therefore, will hit poor women particularly hard, be-

[14]U.S. Dept. of Commerce, 1990 Census of Population and Housing: Mississippi, (Table 6) (1990).

[15]Mississippi Medicaid Management Information System, *Statistical Report on Medical Care: Eligibles, Recipients, Payments, and Services,* Section D(2)(1991).

[16]Medicaid does not cover the cost of an abortion for a poor woman. Women in Mississippi carry to term quite frequently and have few abortions. Mississippi ranks 49th in its abortion occurrence rate. Abortion Services in the United States, Each State & Metropolitan Area, 1984–1985 17 (ed. Henshaw 1988) and ranks 45th in the number of adolescents who obtain abortions. Cobb, Selected Facts About Teenage Pregnancy, Mississippi 12 1989 (1991).

[17]Mississippi has 12.5 doctors per 10,000 people; the lowest in the United States. *See* U.S. Dept. of Health and Human Services, Health United States: 1990 (Table 87). Mississippi ranked 36th in the United States in its provision of prenatal care from 1984–86. Singh et al., Prenatal Care in the United States: A State and Local Inventory 20 (1989). Mississippi has the dubious distinction of having the highest percentage of low birthweight babies; 8.7 percent of all babies in Mississippi were born at low birthweights in 1986. Minority Health at 19. Mississippi's 1989 infant mortality rate was 11.6 infant deaths per 1,000 live births; the national rate for infant mortality was 9.7. *Id.* at 19.

[18]Plaintiff New Woman Medical Center charges $200 for an abortion up to 12 weeks gestation, $300 at 13 and 14 weeks gestation, and $400 at 15 to 16 weeks gestation. (Rogers ¶ 5.) At Plaintiff Mississippi Women's Medical Center, the cost of an abortion increases $205 between the eleventh and twelfth week of pregnancy, an additional $50 at week fifteen, and an additional $100 beyond week sixteen. (Brown ¶ 5.)

[19]In one study, sixty percent of women having abortions after 15 weeks attributed the delay to their needing "time to raise money" for the abortion. Torres and Forrest, *Why Do Women Have Abortions?,* 20 Fam. Plan. Persp. 169, 174 (1988).

cause the increase in cost per week is steeper in the second trimester than in the first trimester.

Mississippi's serious transportation problems exacerbate the burdens of the mandatory delay in three ways. First, the difficulty of procuring transportation adds to the delay. This, in turn, increases the cost of the abortion. In addition, making two trips instead of one to the abortion provider will at least double the cost of transportation itself.

Most abortion providers are located in Jackson. Of the 82 counties in Mississippi, 79 have no known abortion providers, although nearly 3,000 women from these counties obtained abortions in 1989. (Henshaw ¶ 8 (App. 34).) Nearly half of all abortion patients travel 100 miles or more for abortion-related services. *Id.*[20] Poor women living in remote rural areas of the State must often travel 200 miles to obtain an abortion in Jackson. Families living in poverty are likely to be female-headed households in remote rural areas of the State. Six of the seven counties in the State in which more than 30% of the families live below the poverty line are located in the northwest corner of the State. *See* Stone, Handbook of Selected Data: Mississippi 71 (1989).

Poor women seeking abortions are dependent upon a very inadequate public transportation system. Tr. at 44 (Barnes) (App. 6–7).[21] Virtually no women on welfare own an automobile and exceedingly few have access to a reliable one. (Hill ¶ 12; Jenkins ¶ 19.)[22] Travel expenses to a clinic average $40 to $50; for a woman who has to make two trips, these expenses will be $80 to $100. (Barber ¶ 6.)

The waiting period requirement will often necessitate an overnight stay in Jackson. Poor women, however, will find it very burdensome to bear the extra expenses of an overnight stay,[23] along with the expenses of an unpaid absence from work and the increased childcare costs attendant to an absence from their home. Some women

---

[20] For example, Lisa Brown stated in her Declaration:

> The average patient travels approximately 2 hours to obtain an abortion at the Clinic. Over 650 of our patients in 1990 traveled over 100 miles total to obtain abortion services.
> (Brown ¶ 7 [App. 32])

[21] For example, at trial, Dr. Morrison testified:

> One case recently had to come from Clarksdale, and you might think that's not a far journey, but if you have to take the Trailways bus you have to go to Memphis. Then you have—to catch the bus you have to leave at 4:00 o'clock in the morning, get the bus to Memphis, then come to Jackson, get here at 12:00. Then that woman would have to go back the same route, get in at midnight, turn around and come back the next morning. And I think that puts a burden on that woman and on me as a physician that would be ridiculous and onerous and certainly is true of no other medical condition.
> Tr. at 108 (Morrison) (App. 15).

[22] Only 3.6% of the families on welfare in Mississippi in 1989 owned a car. *See* U.S. Department of Health and Human Services, *Characteristics and Financial Circumstances of AFDC Recipients, FY 1989*, P. Ex. 29.

[23] The cost of lodging near the various clinics ranges from $22.50 to $43.00 per night. (Barber ¶¶ 8–9.)

will have no alternative but to spend the night on the street in order to comply with the waiting period requirement.[24]

Many women will be forced to choose illegal abortions, because they will not be able to afford either the increased costs or health risks caused by the Act. While few abortion-related deaths presently occur, the higher incidence of illegal abortions can be expected to increase abortion-related mortality—particularly for the poor and disadvantaged. Mishandled criminal abortions were the principal cause of maternal deaths in the 1960s, when most abortions were performed illegally.[25] Women of color, who are disproportionately poor, suffered the most from the lack of safe, legal abortions; they accounted for 64% of the deaths associated with illegal abortions in this country in 1972.[26] The mortality rates for African-American women were nine times higher than for white women.[27] Thus, we can expect this Act to cause poor women, who are disproportionately African-American, to find it difficult to choose a lawful abortion and to face increased rates of death from mishandled illegal abortions.

2. Adolescent Females

The Act would make it nearly impossible for adolescents to choose an abortion and would therefore exacerbate the dramatic health and socio-economic consequences that accompany high adolescent birthrates. Mississippi already has the highest adolescent birth rate of any state in the United States. (Henshaw ¶ 6.) In a report issued in February, 1991, the Mississippi State Department of Health summarized the problems of the high birth rate for adolescents: it leads to a high infant mortality rate, disproportionately high adverse health consequences for the pregnant adolescent, and perpetuation of the cycle of poverty.[28]

Because adolescents are frequently unable to travel to a clinic during the week, they must visit a clinic only on Saturdays, with at least a week delay between visits. In addition, if the temporary injunction against the Mississippi juvenile bypass statute were to be lifted,[29] some adolescents would have to schedule two clinic visits after obtaining court approval for their abortion decision. *See* Miss. Code Ann. §§ 41-41-51 to 41-41-55 (juvenile bypass statute). Delays of several weeks could easily occur while adolescents try to schedule clinic visits and court appearances at times when they are not in school and can be away from home. Even the Attorney General ac-

---

[24]For example, Dr. Hill stated in his Declaration:

> If my patients are required to stay overnight in Jackson they will most likely sleep in the car, if they get the other person [who gave them the ride] to stay overnight, or outside the clinic in the street. None of my patients have ever stayed in a hotel that I know of, and I don't believe they could afford to do so.
>
> (Hill ¶ 14.)

[25]Niswander, *Medical Abortion Practices in the United States*, in Abortion and the Law 53 (Smith ed. 1967).
[26]Cates & Rochat, *Illegal Abortions in the United States: 1972–1974*, 8 Fam. Plan. Persp. 86, 87 (1976).
[27]Gold, *Therapeutic Abortions in New York: A 20 Year Review*, 55 Am. J. Pub. Health 964–65 (1965).
[28]Cobb, Selected Facts About Teenage Pregnancy, Mississippi 1989 10 (1991).
[29]*See Barnes v. State of Mississippi*, No. J86-0458(W) (S.D. Miss. July 2, 1986) (granting plaintiff's request for a temporary restraining order enjoining juvenile bypass statute).

knowledges that such lengthy delays may have negative health consequences. A.G. Br. at 12.

Additionally, to require a waiting period after an adolescent obtains court or parental approval serves no conceivable purpose. The parental or judicial process should have already ascertained that the adolescent has made a thoughtful, mature decision.

Even without the additional juvenile bypass statute, the Act's waiting period delays will frequently cause an abortion to occur late in adolescents' pregnancies, because, unfortunately, adolescents disproportionately delay seeking abortions until the second trimester of pregnancy. (Henshaw ¶ 18. (App. 35).) As discussed above, such delays raise the cost of abortion and the health risks. In addition, such delays threaten the adolescent's confidentiality as the physical manifestations of her pregnancy may become more apparent during this delay.

3. Women In Abusive Relationships

Domestic violence has recently been described by the United States Surgeon General as "the largest hidden public health problem facing women." Novello & Soto-Torres, *Women and Hidden Epidemics: HIV/AIDS and Domestic Violence*, 17 The Female Patient 17, 22 (January 1992) (hereinafter "Domestic Violence"). Domestic violence affects at least 25% of all American families. *Id.* It is the single largest cause of injury to women in the United States. Indeed, as many as 35% of women who visit hospital emergency rooms do so for symptoms related to ongoing abuse. *Id.* at 23.

Many pregnant women live in abusive relationships in which they cannot inform their partner of their pregnancy and desire to obtain an abortion. Studies indicate that there is a correlation between pregnancy and battering; for example, some men *only* beat their wives when they know that their wives are pregnant. *See* Pagelow, Family Violence 314–15 (1984). For such women, even one unexplained visit to a doctor may be quite dangerous.[30] Requiring such women to visit a doctor twice, and possibly incur an overnight stay away from home, may make the "choice" of an abortion impossible. Although these women's lives or health may be threatened if their partner discovers that they are seeking an abortion, the medical emergency exception does not apply to their situation. The Act serves no legitimate purpose in their reproductive lives; instead, it threatens their lives.

4. Women With Handicaps

The medical emergency exception does not respond to the enormous difficulties that exist for women with handicaps or high-risk pregnancies in traveling to a physician's office to exercise their reproductive choices. As discussed above, public transportation is generally inadequate in Mississippi, and rarely handicapped-accessible. Each additional visit to the clinic will therefore be an enormous burden on

---

[30]For example, Lisa Brown stated in her Declaration:

> I fear for the health of battered women who need abortions. Battered women seeking abortions already have to reschedule several times because it is difficult for them to get away from their batterers. The Act would only further thwart their attempts to obtain high quality health care.
> (Brown ¶ 10 [App. 32])

many handicapped women, as will the costs and difficulties of staying away from home for several days.

Pregnancy itself can be a handicapping condition for many women. The complications associated with pregnancy include nausea, varicose veins, placental abruptio, preeclampsia, eclampsia, liver failure, and blood clots to the lungs or brain. (Morrison ¶¶ 24–28 (App. 28–29); Mitchell ¶ 42.) These conditions will not satisfy the Act's definition of a medical emergency, but they will make it very difficult for a woman to travel twice to a clinic and stay away from home for many days. These women, who are experiencing risks of pregnancy or are quite ill, may have to spend the waiting period being cared for as patients in a hospital—at an exorbitant expense. (Morrison ¶ 35.)

Women with HIV infection will be particularly harmed by the Act. Unfortunately, this group of women cuts across all of the categories previously mentioned— they are disproportionately poor, members of minority groups, and living in abusive situations. Domestic Violence at 22. An abortion may often be medically indicated for them, but they have extremely poor access to health care. Creating one more barrier may make it nearly impossible for HIV positive women to choose abortions and will thereby threaten their lives.

C. *In Addition To Being Ineffectual For Its Stated Purpose, The Act Will Exacerbate A Real And Severe Health Care Crisis In Mississippi*

The Act will clearly exacerbate Mississippi's current crisis in the provision of reproductive services. Numerous State-commissioned reports have urged the State to improve access for the poor to pregnancy-related health care.[31]

Despite recommendations from its own health care agency that access to pregnancy-related health care should be improved and that cost barriers should be eliminated, the legislature did exactly the opposite. It imposed a waiting period requirement on a reproductive health service and thereby decreased access to health care. Such actions serve no rational relation to any legitimate state purpose and violate the equal protection clause.

CONCLUSION

For the foregoing reasons, *amici* supporting appellees urge this Court to affirm the district court. Alternatively, this Court should instruct the district court, in the event of a remand, that the Act violates the equal protection clause of the Fourteenth Amendment.

---

[31]Accordingly, a report by the Mississippi Department of Health recommended that the State "provide easy access to information *at no additional direct or indirect (transportation, child care) cost.*" Minority Health at 25 (emphasis added). Similarly the Infant Mortality Task Force (March 1991) highlighted the importance of the State tackling its infant mortality problem through cooperative health care efforts targeted at disadvantaged communities. Moreover, increasing the availability of abortion has been associated with a reduction in the proportion of infants born at low birthweight and a decrease in the neonatal mortality rate. *See* Abortion and Women's Health at 36.

Respectfully submitted,

RUTH COLKER
Tulane Law School
6801 Freret Street
New Orleans, LA 70118
(504) 865-5968

Attorney for Amicus Curiae
Supporting Appellees

The assistance of seven students in the Tulane Law School Community Service Program is gratefully acknowledged.

Index